By the same author

Fiction

NO EASY ANSWER

Michael Llewellyn Smith

The Great Island

A Study of Crete

ALLEN LANE

To my Mother and Father

Copyright © Michael Llewellyn Smith 1961, 1965

First published in 1965
Reissued in 1973

Allen Lane
A Division of Penguin Books Ltd
21 John Street, London, WC1
ISBN 0 7139 0510 7

Printed in Great Britain by
Lowe & Brydone (Printers) Ltd, Thetford, Norfolk

Contents

	Foreword	ix
1	Introduction	1
2	Roman, Byzantine and Arab Crete	12
3	Venetian Crete	24
4	Art under the Venetians	34
5	The Cretan Renaissance	50
6	The Fall of Candia	63
7	Turkish Crete	74
8	The Revolt of Daskaloyiannis	81
9	The Nineteenth Century	89
10	The Death of Pan	103
11	The Song	113
12	Sphakia – Impressions	126
13	Sphakia – the Vampires	142
14	Return to Asi Gonia	157
	Epilogue	169
	References	176
	Select Bibliography	178
	Index	180

Plates

Arkadi Monastery View of Sphakia *–both Julie du Boulay*	*facing page* 20
The church of St Fanourios at Valsamonero *–Julie du Boulay*	21
Looking towards Heraklion from Agia Pelagia at sunrise The Morosini fountain in Heraklion *–Julie du Boulay*	36
Fresco of the Abbot Zosimas from the Panagia Kera at Kritsa Fresco from Skaloti	37
Canea from a 17th century print by Boschini	148
Western Cretan wedding The latouto (lute)	149
George Psychoundakis and family Pavlos Gyparakis	164
The author with Aleko above the gorge of Samaria Goat-skinning at Anopolis *–both Julie du Boulay*	165

Illustrations by the author except those credited above

Foreword

This book contains plenty of history, and a fair amount of 'travel'. It is intended to be an introduction to Crete. It is one man's view of the island and its culture and its place in Greek history. In the attempt to see Crete whole I have to move from the general (objective history) to the particular (the impact of Crete on us now). The form therefore – I am aware of the dangers of falling between two stools – is deliberately chosen. Caution: the book is not concerned with Minoan civilization and archaeology.

Anyone well read in Cretan studies will recognize my debts, especially in the chapter on art, a subject about which I am ignorant. This chapter could not have been written without the expert work of M. Hadzidakis and K. Kalokyris to consult. Authors whose works I have found useful are mentioned in the references and bibliography. But I must make a general acknowledgement to the periodical Κρητικὰ Χρόνικα (*Cretica Chronica*), whose pages are essential to anyone who studies Crete.

I must also thank Anthony Bryer, for my initiation into the mysteries of Byzantine art; George Psychoundakis, for valuable information about the folklore of his own village, Asi Gonia; Pavlos Gyparakis, for permission to quote from his unpublished diary. I am indebted to Galaxias Editions, Athens, for permission to quote from Pandelis Prevelakis's *The Chronicle of a City* and George Sepheris's Introduction to *Erotokritos*. The Editor of *The Listener* has allowed me to reproduce an article of mine originally entitled 'The White Mountains of Crete' (12 January 1961) in the Introduction.

Finally, especially warm thanks to Julie du Boulay, who accompanied me on an exhilarating trek through the White Mountains, supplied the better of the photographs, and sent useful and hard-won material from Athens while I was writing the book in England.

M. J. Ll. S.

I
Introduction

I first saw Crete, which the Greeks call simply the Great Island, on 13 August 1957, in the course of a month's holiday in Greece. I did not know what to expect, and so was hardly disappointed with the little that we were able to see. One of my friends had studied Pendlebury's handbook to the excavations at Knossos and was able to conduct us round them efficiently. We slept the night in the ancient Caravanserai, bathed at the Florida beach next day and left for Athens after only thirty-six hours on the island. I had read a book called *Freedom and Death* by the Cretan, Nikos Kazantzakis, and had in my mind a vague image of wild mountains, savage, heroic mountaineers, poor but indomitable villages. It was probably because we had seen none of these mountains at close quarters that I decided to come back some day. At any rate, I knew then that thirty-six hours had not been enough.

On the ship *Kanares*, as we steamed back across the Cretan sea after that first short visit, I was woken by a bottle which someone had thrust into my mouth. A middle-aged Greek was jogging my elbow and inviting me to drink. The taste was unfamiliar and unpleasant. I now know it was *ouzo*. All around us on the deck lay sleeping bodies.

'Where you from?' he said in broken English.
'From England,' I answered in broken Greek.
'Speak English, no speak Greek. No speak Greek.'
'From England.'
'Ah, I know England. I go Liverpool, London, Chull' – the *ch* guttural as in loch. 'You know Chull?'
'No.'
'Here, drink. *Ouzo*. Good.'
'No, thanks. I want to go to sleep now.'
'You beautiful. I know you English. I have darling boy in Chull. You all the same.'
'Go away now, please.' His hand was groping somewhere around the entrance to my sleeping-bag.
'Where you going now?'

1

The Great Island

'The Peloponnese. Now go away!'

'Ah, Pelo*pón*nesos. You come stay in Piraeus. I pay hotel, you stay, eh?'

I pointed to the head of my school's classics department who lay peacefully sleeping about three yards away. 'Shut up. You'll wake the whole ship up. Now get out and go away!' I made a manic gesture sufficiently violent to get him to leave. This was my first experience of an offer of the hospitality for which Greeks are famous. I kept a diary on that trip; it reads for the next day: 'I wouldn't have missed that odd experience. Rest of night uneventful, but deck rather hard on the hip.'

It was, I suppose, the desire to know the Cretans at least as well as this Cretan knew the English – and to know them in a rather different way, I must add – that led me back to Crete.

Three years later I was back, with a friend, Brian Saperia, who wished to join me in recording Cretan folk music. There was something arbitrary about the whole enterprise. We might just as well, I feel now, have found ourselves in Epirus doing social work, or in Africa measuring skulls, as in Crete recording music. We were bored and dissatisfied with the university, and wanted to *do* something. Whether you travel to distant parts, as in the old days, because you have been jilted, or as nowadays, because the materialism and mechanism of our civilization become oppressive, the effective motive is likely to be frustration. And whether he knows it or not, the traveller is often searching for a kind of power, a charm derived from foreign lands, which will send him home changed, invested with an authority which sets him apart from the nine-to-fivers. When I came back from Crete in 1960 and read the remarks of the French anthropologist Claude Lévi-Strauss on the subject of travellers, I had the astonishing feeling that he was analysing me.

Lévi-Strauss compares foreign travel with the initiation ordeals of certain primitive tribes. In adolescence the youth will separate himself from the tribe, plunge himself into a way of life where the rules and values of the tribe count for nothing. He will isolate himself on a raft, or in the mountains, going for weeks without cooked food, attempting to sever contact with his environment by physical privations such as freezing baths, or torment such as the cutting off of the finger-tips. In the state of weakness and delirium which these hardships produce, the youth hopes to see, in a vision, the spirit who is from now on to be his guardian, and to discover the power, derived from that spirit, which will define his rank and privileges when he returns to the tribe. The strange thing about the initiation ordeal is that it is imposed by society. Society itself sends out the young men beyond its well-defined borders, to snatch power from the unknown territory, to free themselves for a

Introduction

time from the tyranny of the group. In the same way our society sends out travellers who return to feed the public with vicarious, and often falsified, sensations.

'Any young man who isolates himself for a few weeks or months from the group and exposes himself to an extreme situation of any sort may count on being invested, on his return, with a kind of magic power. . . . In our world the power comes out in newspaper articles, best-selling books, and lectures with not an empty seat in the hall.'[1] Its magic character is evident in the process of auto-mystification of the group and by the group which is, in every case, 'the basis of the phenomenon'.

If this explanation is correct – and I think it is, even though Lévi-Strauss exaggerates – then embarking on a travel book must be a hazardous undertaking. But there is always the consolation that what one says may be true or interesting, that one may try to avoid the subtle and insidious magic of exaggeration, of making places sound better or stranger than they are. Lévi-Strauss himself was writing a travel book when he made these observations. And this is not, for the most part, a 'travel book'.

It might seem from all this that Crete is remote and primitive. It is in fact a civilized island, easily accessible from Athens, and discomfort is tempered by the generosity of the Cretans. Brian and I had no need to fear discomfort anyway, since we had been lent a car. We crossed to Crete on 4 August, testing our battery tape-recorder on the boat, and broaching the second of the enormous tins of biscuits which we had been given by Huntley and Palmer's in deference to our adopted name – 'Oxford Cretan Expedition 1960'.

The panegyric which I wrote then records the immediate impact of Crete better than I could recall it now. Perhaps the emphasis is sometimes wrong; failure of the grape harvest, for instance, means difficulty, not starvation; but the general impression still seems to me to be correct. I wrote:

Western Crete: home of the fabulous plant dittany, whose healing powers have been admired since Homer's day: home of the unique *agrimi*, the Cretan ibex: home of the Sphakians, who kept alive the spark of independence in the darkest times of Turkish domination: a harsh, bare country, which moulds its people in its own image: a poor country where pleasures are few and the failure of the grape harvest can mean starvation: a country where disillusioned dons can go to find the noble savage, and where I found a society in a state of suspended

[1] References to superior figures are given on pp. 175-6.

animation. The mountain songs still uphold the traditional heroic ideal of *levendia*, the gallant attitude to life. But the successive oppressors of the Cretans have gone and the songs now exist in a vacuum. For the first time in hundreds of years there is no enemy. The Cretan mountaineer is living in the past, but the twentieth century is beginning to catch up with him.

Brian Saperia and I were in the White Mountains recording folk music, the traditional dances played on the lute and the three-stringed Cretan lyre, and the *rizitika*, songs from the roots of the mountains which express in heroic terms the Cretans' independence and longing for liberty under Venetians, Turks and Germans. We arrived one evening in Asi Gonia, a tiny village which emerges from a sea of olives, surrounded by precipitous mountains on every side. Here we were greeted by George Psychoundakis, who was runner to Professor Dunbabin in the resistance after the German invasion of 1941. And within half an hour we were recording.

I shall not forget that night. In the village café a large tin of Californian squid was turned out on to a communal plate, and glasses were filled with the sharp, red Cretan wine which is so much more pleasant than the resinated variety drunk on the mainland. The Californian squid was incongruous: native Greek squid is delicious as I discovered in Piraeus. We had arrived in the middle of the fast which precedes the Feast of the Assumption. How squid was excepted from the list of forbidden foods I do not know. Perhaps the villagers shared vicariously in our status as *bona fide* travellers.

We ate and drank. And then, quite suddenly, the singing began. Immediately, the room was filled with people, children intent on us and our equipment, old men in traditional costume who had come to see this strange phenomenon. We were tired and we had not had time to check our recording apparatus. But this was an audience which could admit of no exceptions. We were caught up in the atmosphere.

Two men were sitting at the table with us, Pavlos Gyparakis and the shepherd Andreas Petrakis, both veterans of the last war. Pavlos threw his great head back and began to sing, while Andreas put an arm round his shoulders as if to bind the two of them together in one performance. Their absorption was complete. The lamplight flickered on their faces as they sang:

> The Lord made the earth, the Lord built the heavens,
> But three things in this world the Lord did not provide;
> A bridge over the sea, a return from Hades
> And a ladder up to heaven.

Introduction

And then they were drinking again while Brian played back the tape through our inadequate loudspeaker. There was not room for everyone in the café. Those who were excluded craned in through the window to hear the playback.

They sing again:

> Hitler, be not so eager to trample on Crete.
> Unarmed you found her – her children in distant lands,
> Fighting far away, up in Albania. . . .

And with the same voice which has spoken for Crete throughout her turbulent history, sings the young man, wounded perhaps by the Turks:

> Mother, should my friends come, should my brothers come,
> Do not tell them I am dead, for they will weep.
> But spread the table, give them food and wine.
> Spread the table, let my brothers sing,
> And in the morning, when the sun comes up,
> Tell them I died.

So the words poured out, until we were almost too tired to stand up, and George took us to his home to sleep on the terrace, while the moon softened the harsh outlines of the mountains.

Our best opportunity for recording came at the wedding of Pavlos Gyparakis's son. A Cretan wedding starts the day before the church service, with a plundering expedition conducted by the groom's relations, who march down to the bride's house and carry off to the new home anything they can find. This is performed in the best of spirits: at every opportunity there is a pause for food and drink. I was forced to eat sheep's entrails, piping hot, while others were swallowing whole eyes with relish. The next day, shortly before the service, the groom's relations set out again for the bride's house. On this occasion Andreas Petrakis led the way, his arms round two friends; and the three of them led the singing:

> My bride, tree without stars, moon without stars,
> Bride of my house, where you will go to blossom and bear fruit,
> My bride, respect my friends and they will love you.

The procession waited while the final touches were added to the bride's trousseau. Then she appeared, dazzling in white, with a touch of make-up for the first and last time in her life. On we wound down to the church. Inside, the heat was stifling. Children played and laughed round the walls while the rest of the congregation crowded round the altar to see the couple made man and wife by the symbolic crowning with garlands. Soon it was done. The guests processed round the altar, dropped a present into a large basket, received a sugared almond and left the church. Outside, the procession formed up again, to go back to the groom's house for the feast. This time we walked along with them, recording as unobtrusively as possible.

> Come outside, mother of the bridegroom, mother of the bride,
> To see your precious son and golden bride.

Later in the evening we slipped out of the feast, where the guests were happily singing the *mantinades,* or rhymed couplets, of which every Cretan has an apparently inexhaustible repertoire. We went to the café of Stelios the mayor, where two instrumentalists from Rethymnon had come to play. Twenty yards away we stopped and listened. They were dancing the Syrtos, most ancient and graceful of Greek dances. As I stood in a pool of darkness I could see the dancers silhouetted, clapping their hands and crying out. The reedy tones of the lyre pierced the stillness. Far away a dog barked. Quietly Brian laid the tape-recorder on a stone wall and switched it on. The atmosphere of this tape is indescribable. Whenever I hear it I shall see those Cretans, their legs gliding and growing from the ground in the side-lit semicircle of the dance; see Stelios, too, as he tried later to dance on a wine bottle for our benefit and gashed his thumb on the shattered wreck.

One night we gave a dinner party up in our camp where the village spring emerges from under the olives and holm-oaks. George Psychoundakis, Pavlos the singer, and Stelios, our young interpreter, were the guests. With us were two girls from Cambridge who had spent a domestic week learning to spin and bake with the women of the village. Out of slender resources (meat and fish, eggs, milk and cheese were still not allowed) they produced a wonderful meal. Munching an olive, Pavlos jokes with George. Occasionally Stelios translates. 'The girls are looking even more beautiful than when they arrived.' Brian says it is the sun, food and friendliness of Asi Gonia. The conversation warms up, the laughter increases. The bottle of wine is exhausted and we go on to *retsina.* Pavlos roars with delight and keeps putting out his glass for more. He circles his finger in a typical Greek gesture, throws back his head, and cries, '*Po-po-po,* only a little', then drains the glass and asks again. He does his imitation of Xan Fielding, his favourite among the English who fought here during the war. Fielding used to chain-smoke. 'Ninety a day,' says Pavlos, sucking in breath through his cigarette holder, throwing away an imaginary stub, and immediately lighting

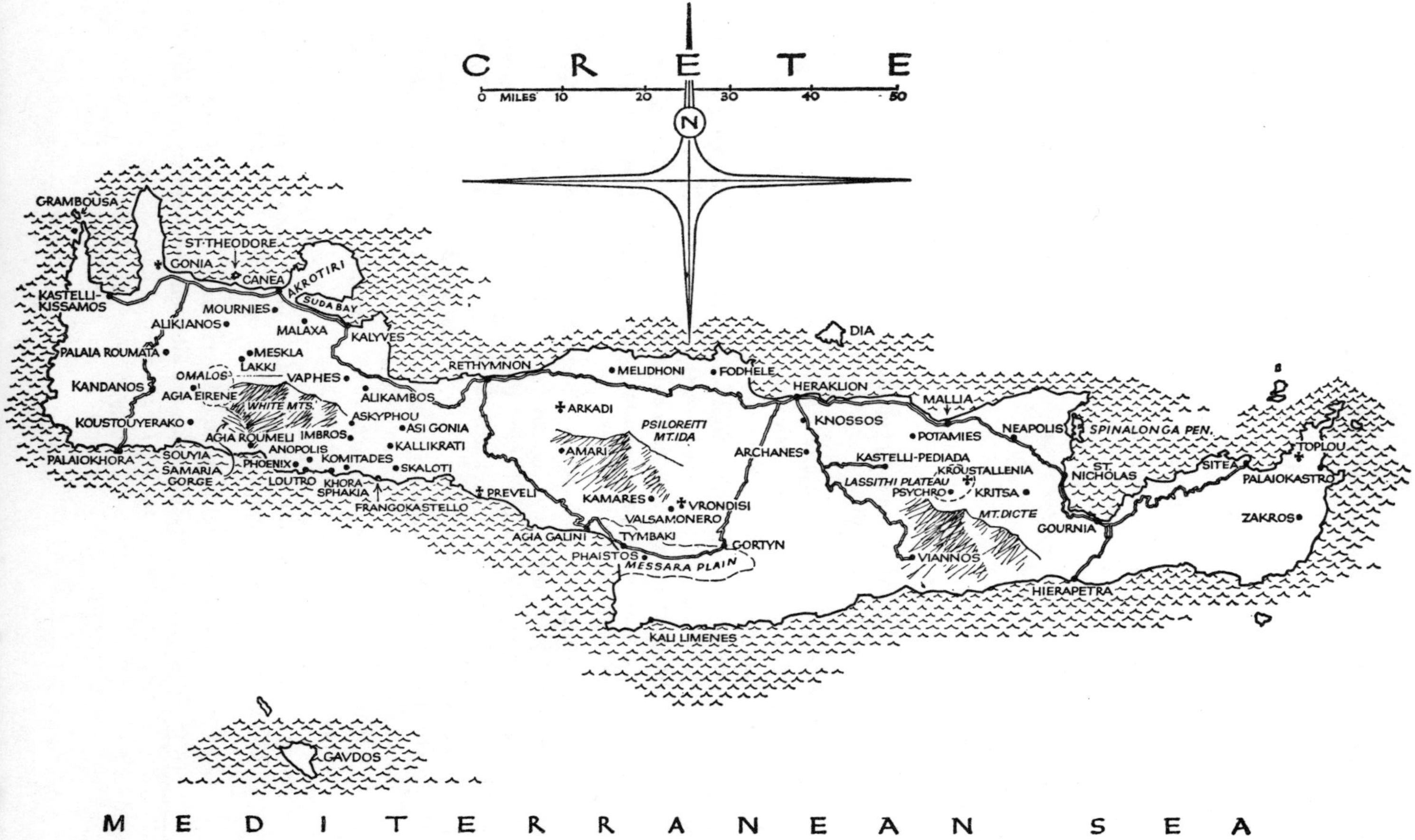
CRETE
0 MILES 10 20 30 40 50
N
GRAMBOUSA
KASTELLI-KISSAMOS
ST. THEODORE
GONIA
CANEA
AKROTIRI
SUDA BAY
MOURNIES
ALIKIANOS
MALAXA
KALYVES
PALAIA ROUMATA
MESKLA
LAKKI
OMALOS
VAPHES
KANDANOS
AGIA EIRENE
WHITE MTS.
ALIKAMBOS
ASKYPHOU
ASI GONIA
KOUSTOUYERAKO
AGIA ROUMELI
IMBROS
KALLIKRATI
PALAIOKHORA
SOUYIA
SAMARIA GORGE
ANOPOLIS
PHOENIX
KOMITADES
SKALOTI
LOUTRO
KHORA SPHAKIA
FRANGOKASTELLO
RETHYMNON
MELIDHONI
FODHELE
DIA
HERAKLION
ARKADI
PSILOREITI MT. IDA
AMARI
PREVELI
KAMARES
VRONDISI
VALSAMONERO
AGIA GALINI
TYMBAKI
GORTYN
PHAISTOS
MESSARA PLAIN
KALI LIMENES
KNOSSOS
ARCHANES
MALLIA
POTAMIES
KASTELLI-PEDIADA
LASSITHI PLATEAU
KROUSTALLENIA
PSYCHRO
KRITSA
MT. DICTE
VIANNOS
NEAPOLIS
SPINALONGA PEN.
ST. NICHOLAS
GOURNIA
HIERAPETRA
SITEA
TOPLOU
PALAIOKASTRO
ZAKROS
GAVDOS
MEDITERRANEAN SEA

another. He is like a big baby. Then as the *retsina* mellows him he begins to philosophize. 'He is a philosopher,' says Stelios. 'He says he will never forget this, never. He says that you will be great men because you "psychologize" him. You understand him and he understands you. For the girls he wishes a good marriage. He has daughters of his own and is often considering this matter.'

What can one reply? There is no need, for George is conducting an absurd mime, rolling on his back on a sleeping-bag, peering into his mug, tapping it on the bottom. We have mercy and fill it up. 'Only a little,' he says automatically, and then 'Bottoms up!', one of the odd selection of phrases he learnt in the war. Smoke from the wood-fire drifts overhead. Stelios does his trick of lighting a cigarette from the paraffin lamp. In the half-light faces are happy, friendly. We ask Pavlos for a *mantinada*. He sings, *mezza voce*, his throat moulding the words with loving care:

> Friendship is the most beautiful thing in the world.
> My heart is full: my heart knows how to repay.

Our last night in Asi Gonia was a Sunday, and most of the villagers had gathered in the café of Stelios the mayor. The gramophone was playing. Some of the young men started to dance the Syrtos, a semi-circle linked by handkerchiefs so that the rhythm and pulse of the dance is passed down the line from the leader. The circle gradually snakes round. At one end the leader sets the pace, graceful, tied to the ground. It is a strange dance, popular but not quite satisfactory. There is an air of indifference which disappears entirely when they dance the wild Pendozali, warrior dance of Crete. With hands on each other's shoulders they move round the tiny space under the plane tree. The leader leaps, slaps his boots behind his back, turns a convulsive circle in the air and falls back to pick up the measure again. The sweat stands out round his headband. Eventually he falls out exhausted and the next man takes his place; and so it goes on until each has had his turn. The Pendozali speaks for Crete as clearly as any of her songs.

Meanwhile, the party has warmed up. There is a glazed look in the mayor's eye as he starts singing:

> Round the high mountains, round the peaks swirls the air,
> But earth and heroism are not found every day.

On the back of a cigarette packet I scribble a couplet of my own. Stelios (the English-speaker) takes it, alters it, polishes it, and then typically hands it round, saying I have written it:

Introduction

> My Crete, lovely island, I long to come back to you,
> And to repay this whole company of friends.

Back comes the reply at once:

> The hand that wrote those words I shall fill with gold,
> Apples from Paradise I shall cut down to give you.

Someone reminds me that we must be off early next day. So arm in arm we wind up the hill to our camp, Greeks and English together, singing as we go:

> Long live Crete and her mountains, long live London,
> Long live our Venizelos, the flower of the Greeks.

Back in camp the mayor settles down on a groundsheet and is ready to continue far into the night. But he is tactfully removed, and they are gone, George, Stelios and the rest, their voices fading away into the night.

Next day we left Asi Gonia: her simple message rang in my ears as we came down to Canea and civilization:

> The courage of man is great wealth;
> Eat, drink and enjoy this deceitful world.'

We went, of course, to many places besides Asi Gonia, and there were many other recording sessions. We had the luck to discover the only woman in Crete who plays the Cretan bagpipe; but this instrument, the *askomandoura*, is intolerable to the ear, unrelieved by even a drone. In Kritsa, a large shambling village of eastern Crete, we found a slow, graceful wedding song which escaped the conventions of Cretan folk music and was easy on the westerner's ear:

> My bride, angels wove your wreath,
> Crowned you with eagle's wings and deathless flowers.
> Golden birds sing at your windows,
> Call down good omens on your marriage garlands.

But the most hilarious session occurred in a small village called Palaia Roumata, near Canea. We had a letter of introduction to Idomeneus Papagregorakis, the editor of a folk-lore magazine. We called on him at a bad time – during the afternoon – and he came to the door in pyjamas. I like to think it was the effects of siesta hour, rather than my imperfect command of Greek, which made communication so difficult. Papagregorakis heard some of our recordings, expressed his satisfaction, showed us his own book of Cretan folk-songs with proper pride, and agreed to come with us next day to help. I think that when he found himself in the front seat of the car he regretted this decision. Perpetual muttering on the hairpin bends.

We waited all day in Palaia Roumata while Papagregorakis talked to villagers and watched me from time to time to see if I was studying his book. By seven in the evening he had collected a team of singers and we settled down in the village school to record. I transcribe from my work notes, bowdlerizing in places:

Tape 20: THE GARDEN. (Fantastic amount of noise – talking, walking about, a meal being brought in.)

THE KING'S DESIRE. (One semi-chorus packed up – forgot words? – about half-way through, so we re-recorded.)

Tape 21: MANTINADES. (Old man reaches across with his stick to stop the leader tapping his foot. Cigarette lighted.)

Tape 22: THE HEROES AND THE CAPTURE OF THE FORTRESS. (One chorus talks while the other sings. Not word-perfect. They know their own words, but Papagregorakis insists on coaching them from his own text, which makes them so damn self-conscious. Chain-smoking.)

Tape 23: CHARON'S REPENTANCE. (Nervous strain – will they get through a song without someone talking and spoiling it? During this excellent song there was a perpetual undertone. They will keep rattling their worry beads.)

All songs introduced by 'One, two, three . . .' instead of the usual wave, because tonight's leader is blind.

Anyone who has made recordings in the field will have encountered similar difficulties. It was due entirely to Brian (constructing plugs out of pieces of wire, hissing at turbulent children, whisking the microphone out of harm's way when some Cretan hero was about to slam down a wine-glass next to it) that the final tapes were any good at all. And even at that, one of the best tapes was obtained as it were by accident. George Psychoundakis was reminiscing. Brian asked him if he had ever driven a car.

'Once. I was very drunk. I drove a jeep to Canea. Almost to Canea. I saw many trees in the road, they were in the road. Oopah! We hit the trees. One passenger loses an ear. I get a hole in the stomach. I never drive again.'

And for some reason he started singing English songs. 'Old Macdougal had a farm.' Out came the tape-recorder. And after Macdougal, without a gap –

> Hitler had only got one ball,
> Goering had two but very small.
> Himmler was somewhat similar,
> But poor old Goebbels had no balls at all –

Introduction

in perfect tune. I seem to remember that George was forced to translate for the benefit of his friends. A variant reading was noted by Xan Fielding in his book *The Stronghold*; broadly speaking the same but with superior transliteration ('mpall' for 'ball').

Since that second trip to Crete I have been back five times and visited most parts of the island. It never ceases to attract. But these pages are not a day-to-day record of those trips. English readers, or most of them, are by now familiar with the taste, or at least the description of the taste, of *ouzo*, *retsina*, *moussaka* and even *raki*. Rather, here is some of the information, the stories, legends, songs and history which I should have liked to know when I first went to Crete, and which may be of some interest to other travellers and Philhellenes.

2

Roman, Byzantine and Arab Crete

*Nel mezzo 'l mar siede un paese guasto
Diss' egli allora, che s'appella Creta.*
                                            Dante

The island of Crete was cut off from Asia Minor in the Pleistocene period when the Aegean basin began to assume its present form. Crete was left in her lonely position commanding the sea route from Europe to Africa. But her connections are with Europe, through the islands which can be seen northwards from the summit of a Cretan mountain on a clear day. Another chain of islands, Kasos, Karpathos and Rhodes, links Crete to Asia Minor. Crete even faces north; her fertile coastal strip, her harbours, lie open to the north-easterly *meltemi* which in summer drives down over the Aegean; while to the two-hundred-mile expanse of Libyan sea to the south Crete presents a wall of barren mountains, rarely broken, hospitable only to corsairs. Crete is the sixth continent, equidistant from three others. If you looked at a map of the world and knew no history, you could guess from her position that foreigners would covet this lovely island, and indeed they have. From the time when the Romans annexed Crete until these last fifty years, successive waves of barbarians and colonialists have passed through, cheating, exploiting and murdering. They treated the Cretans to a greater or less degree as an ignorant, brutal and licentious peasantry; the strange fact is that even after hundreds of years of such oppression the Cretans were better than that.

On two things every traveller and historian is agreed: the bravery of the people and the beauty of the land. The Cretans know that these are their two resources. They sing of the one:

> This Cretan earth of ours, wherever you dig it,
> You will find blood of heroes, you will turn up their bones.
>
> I shall cut laurel and myrtle on Psiloreiti,
> Garlands for the dead who have honoured Crete.

And of the other:

Roman, Byzantine and Arab Crete

My Crete, lovely island, flower-planted garden,
There is none like you in all the peopled world.

Other folk cultures, our own for instance, are not so insistent on the beauty of their own country. It is something they can take for granted. For the Cretan it has been one of his only solaces. Consciousness of the blood that nourishes the flowers has never been far from his mind. It is the foreigner who looks at the island without having to remember her people, and praises the clean line of the mountains or the comfortable orchards of lemon, orange, fig, almond and pomegranate – in Belon's words, '*moult beaux jardinages et vergers d'excellente beauté et en grande quantité, qui leur sont de grand revenu, dont les uns sont en pays si plaisant qu'un homme ne s'ennuirait à les contempler*'. Crete has not changed much. In the evenings you can feel a great stillness, which is the best comfort, and is harder to find in England. Even in a town, say Athens, the noises of pneumatic drills, children playing, tyres screaming on the corners, and the fishman shouting 'Fine Seafood', make a disjointed counterpoint; but you have to impose the form on them. In the country, sounds arise as it were naturally, point against point, from the earth. In the evening Scop's owl calls (that odd noise: pok . . . pok . . . pok . . .) against the stream; and then the frogs croak; and then it is still night, with maybe a dog barking, and if you are lucky a nightingale, but often silence. In this silence, for one hour each night, the water sleeps in the springs and streams, and flows gently. Whoever wishes to drink at this hour must not be rough, but must disturb the water tenderly with his hand to awaken it, for otherwise it may steal away his brains.

I want to turn over the Cretan earth and uncover some of those bones; to stab a knife into the vein of Cretan history at certain selected points and let the blood flow again. But where to start? Not with the Minoans, who are to be found in the books of archaeologists. Their great sites, Knossos, Phaistos, Gournia, Zakros and the rest, do not touch the life of Cretans today except indirectly by attracting tourists and offering a new field for defying the law, in the smuggling and sale of antiquities. The assiduous hunter of survivals can point to strange facts. In Minoan religion the emphasis was on female goddesses – the huntress goddess with her beasts, the snake goddess, those whom Sir Arthur Evans provisionally regarded as 'the same great Nature Goddess under various aspects', or the Mother. Later, we find in Plato and others that the Cretans were unique in calling their country *Mitris*, the motherland, instead of the usual *Patris*, the fatherland. And the image of the land as mother has persisted through folk poetry and speech into the novels of Kazantzakis, where Crete is seen as a hard and demanding

The Great Island

mother, sometimes requiring the blood of her sons as the price of their eventual liberty.

You could relate, too, the somnolent water which steals your wits, and the Nereid fairies who swim in the streams at night, to the Nereids of classical times and the goddesses who must have presided over sacred Minoan springs. And it was from Minoan religion that the worship of mountain-tops was transmitted through the classical era to Christian Crete, so that the peaks are crowned with chapels sacred to Christ, the True Cross or the prophet Elias, where once perhaps there was a shrine of Zeus.

But these survivals do not bring the Minoans any closer to us. They remain, despite the humanism of their art, a secretive and alien people, for ever separated from the Crete which was moulded by the impact of barbarians on Greeks and the impact of Christianity on paganism. Since it is the purpose of this book to deal with this dual impact, we shall be more concerned with the last seven hundred years, which are comparatively well documented. But first two invaders, the Romans and the Arabs, must be dealt with shortly.

Crete fell to Rome in 67 B.C. Quintus Caecilius Metellus, one of that family of Metelli which was pre-eminent in Roman dynastic politics at the time, crushed the resistance of the pirate-ridden island in three years' hard campaigning and took the *cognomen* 'Creticus' for so doing. The long period of petty feuds among the city states, when Crete was distinguished only for her legal systems, her mercenary slingers and archers, and finally her pirates, came to an end. Peace was imposed; and because Crete could contribute to the solution of a perennial Roman problem – that of feeding the populace – she entered on a period of prosperous government. Crete, Cyrenaica (which together with Crete constituted a province) and Egypt were Rome's granaries. To ensure the corn supply the Romans built roads and aqueducts, turned Gortyn into a worthy capital, and irrigated the highland plain of Lassithi in the east. Little remains from these times: a few statues in the museums, the ruins of fountains, amphitheatre, temples and other public works at Gortyn, a few scraps of mosaic, and some columns and capitals which have been taken from earlier temples and worked into the older of the Christian churches.

The important event was St Paul's arrival in about A.D. 47. The apostle sailed past the island of Gavdos after sheltering for a time at Kali Limenes, the Fair Havens, on the south coast of central Crete. He was on his way from Jerusalem to Rome. Local tradition has it that he landed near Loutro, a few miles west of Sphakia, and there is a chapel on the shore where Paul is said to have baptized his first Cretan converts. Xan Fielding, following this tradition, writes that St Paul landed at Phoenix 'after barely escaping shipwreck on one of his many propaganda tours. And when he did land he barely escaped with his life, for he was looked on as a busybody and promptly beaten up. That, at least, is what they say in Loutro today: and I can well believe it. The preaching of the apostle could hardly have endeared him to such happy-go-lucky pagans.'

Acts xxv:11, however, tells a totally different story. Paul's ship was stuck in the Fair Havens, which is a long way down the coast from Phoenix, 'which is an haven of Crete', and lies near the modern Loutro. The sailing season was just about over. So Paul recommended wintering where they were, in the Fair Havens. 'Sirs, I perceive that this voyage will be with hurt and much damage, not only of the lading and ship, but also of lives.' The ship's captain and owner, however, were anxious to push on, especially as they knew that Phoenix, the haven down the coast to westward, was more commodious for wintering. They took advantage of a favourable wind and embarked, immediately falling victim to a tempestuous wind called Euryclydon – the north-easter – which sprang up and pursued them all the way to Malta, where Paul was bitten by a snake. It was while they were being driven by this storm that they sailed past Clauda, the modern island of Gavdos; but they never reached Phoenix. So Paul, as so often, was able to say, 'I told you so.'

The tradition that Paul landed at Phoenix, then, and preached at the modern Loutro, certainly arises from a misunderstanding of the Acts. And the tradition that he was beaten up as a busybody probably stems from his remarks in the epistle to Titus, whom he appointed first bishop of Crete. In this letter Paul points out that there are all too many, especially among Jewish converts, who talk wildly and lead the unwary astray, all for the sake of filthy lucre. He adds, 'One of themselves, even a prophet of their own, said, The Cretians are alway liars, evil beasts, slow bellies. This witness is true. Wherefore rebuke them sharply, that they may be sound in the faith.' Since these were Paul's opinions, it is safe to say that if he *had* landed near Loutro they *would* have beaten him up. The prophet of their own was the Cretan poet Epimenides, who thus has the distinction of having initiated the saying that the Cretans are liars, and indirectly the famous logical paradox of the liar.

A number of legends grew up around the apostle. One of these is that he banished poisonous snakes and noxious creatures from the island. In antiquity Hercules was credited with this feat. Others say that bishop Titus did it. Whoever it was, he did not entirely succeed, for although those snakes that are found are harmless, there remains a snake-like creature called the *liakoni*, whose bite is dangerous.

Pococke, in the middle of the eighteenth century, was sceptical about this beast: 'They have an animal like a lizard called Jäkoniè, which the people apprehend to be exccedingly venomous in its bite, and some say by a sting in its tail; but having some of them caught, I saw they were the very same as the sinco or stink marin of Aegypt, which are harmless there, and are sent dried to Europe from Aegypt, without dismembering them, and go into the composition of the Theriaca.' But even he recognized the danger of the only other really unpleasant animal on Crete – 'a sort of spider called Phalangium, which is very venomous, especially in hot weather, and it is said that music and dancing helps towards the cure, as in the bite of the tarantula'.

An apologist for St Paul could argue that the *liakoni* and the phalangium, not being snakes, were exempt from the ban. For the legend clearly arose from the lack of poisonous snakes, and was attached to St Paul on the grounds that he was bitten by a snake on Crete and suffered no harm, from which time the Cretan snakes lost their venom. In fact he was bitten on Malta. This part of the story again was picked up from Acts xxv:11 and manhandled to fit Crete.

In any case, the importance of St Paul to Crete lies not in his clearing the place of a snake, like Hercules the Deliverer, but in his instructions to Titus for organizing the Church, and thus establishing once and for all the Christian religion, which survived without much difficulty the defections to Islam under the Arab régime.

St Paul returned to Crete four years ago with BBC Television, which was making a film of his life and chose Crete for those parts of it, such as the shipwreck, which had to be shot on location. The great western gate in the Venetian walls of Heraklion was turned into the gates of Jerusalem, Cretan extras donned biblical robes, and a local caique was converted into a Roman ship. According to Evan Christou, who acted as a kind of liaison officer to the British team, the shipwreck itself was disappointingly tame, because down at St Nicholas in the east, where it was shot, there were no waves. I like to imagine the photographers throwing themselves up and down and from side to side in an attempt to make the caique wobble. There were other hazards. When the shots were sent back to the studio in England for processing, they were returned slashed through as it were with a red pencil. As it cruised its majestic, slave-driven way across calm waters the ship could be seen to bob up and down as if animated by an unseen hand – or a petrol engine. Which it was; only, unless Evan was exaggerating, the engine was not even totally unseen. A new batch of film was again rejected; above the sweating, labouring bodies of the oarsmen, diesel fumes were curling into the unpolluted Cretan air. The film, when finally achieved, was a great success.

It was not Paul but Titus who became patron saint of Crete – the obscure bishop whom one life calls the son of noble Cretan parents of the race of Minos, and another the nephew of the Roman proconsul who sent him to Judaea to report on the Galilean. As patron saint of the island Titus established himself so firmly that even the Venetians were prepared to recognize him, rather than St Mark, as protector of the Duke of Candia; their prayer for the Doge of Venice was '*Sancte Marce, tu nos adiuva*': for the Duke of Candia, '*Sancte Tite, tu nos adiuva*'. But in the country districts he never supplanted the more popular saints, such as St George, in the love of the people.

Christianity having reached Crete, not only through Paul and Titus but also doubtless through the Cretan Jews who were in Jerusalem at Pentecost, the Church flourished, new sees sprang up subject to the Metropolitan see of Gortyn, and martyrs gave their lives for the faith. The most famous of these, the *Agii Deka*, ten saints who were martyred at Gortyn, are for modern Cretans the supreme patriots and heroes of the first thousand years of the Christian era. It was in the mid-third century, when Decius was emperor, and another Decius proconsul of Crete. The late encomia of these martyr saints show how Cretans saw their virtue as being not only the love of God – also patriotism. Very early in Greek history these two virtues came to be connected, and even by some people identified with each other. Gerasimus Palladas, a Cretan priest, told the story thus in his sermon:

When the ten heard the news they went boldly to the place of judgement. The tyrant [Decius] saw how they stood without fear and filled with courage, and said to them, 'Who are you, what sort of men are you to come before me with such impudence?'

Theodoulos answered, being the eldest, 'We are foreigners, sir.'

He says to them, 'How can you be foreigners, you're from this place! Look, these officers here know you. Officers, don't you know these men?'

The officers answered, 'We know them, your Highness, they are our men all right.'

And the ten said with one voice, 'Sir, these bodies are from this place; of this earth, which your Magnificence and the Roman emperor Decius rule. But the souls are not from here, but from the kingdom of the Lord . . .'

At once the tyrant became angry. 'All right, you've consented to your own suffering. Since your bodies are of this earth, I rule them, that's what you said. So now see what your bodies are going to suffer . . .'

Decius handed them over to the mob, who dragged them through the mud, beat them and tortured them for thirty days, which Theodore Palladas, the father of Gerasimus, calls 'a token of those thirty years of life which Christ lived in the world'. All this had no effect. Decius threatened worse, and they replied in a long speech that he was wasting his time. Which is real, a piece of wood shaped into an idol of Zeus or Apollo, or a God who laid down his life? In Palladas senior's account: 'Get it into your head that you are dealing with ten witnesses, with ten *Cretan men*, with ten who are ready to let their blood flow for the love of the Saviour Christ the Lord.'

So Decius decided to behead them. In their last moments they joined hands and formed a ring as of a dance, and sang with shining faces and cheerful voices, 'Mountains and peaks, plains and ravines, let fall drops of sweetness, because today ten Cretan men were united to bear witness with their blood to the blood of Christ.'

Their heads were chopped off on a block of stone. 'Oh, stone, more richly adorned than the expanse of heaven, for that is adorned with seven planets, and you with ten strong heads!'

It does not matter that the true details of the martyrdom may be lost. These encomia show us how later Cretans regarded them. Their festival is celebrated every year on 23 December; and the Catholic Church continued to recognize them after the Schism. The hollows in a marble slab in their church at Ambelouzou were reputed to be the prints of their knees, made while they waited for execution. The faces of two of them, Theodoulos and Zotikos, stare from the walls of the church of the Virgin at Kritsa. Without much doubt the others, Euporos, Gelasios, Agathopoulos, Euarestos, Satorninos, Eunikianos, Basilides and Pompios accompanied them, but their pictures are now destroyed.

This martyrdom, and others like it, is on one side of the coin. On the other is the adaptation of Christianity to suit the Cretans. The old gods merged into the new saints, all over the Greek world. In mountainous Thrace, for instance, through which Dionysus came from the east to Greece, elements of Dionysiac ritual survived. Some of these elements fused with Christianity, some failed to be absorbed. An example of the second sort is found in the Mummers' Plays which

Roman, Byzantine and Arab Crete

Professor Dawkins saw in Thrace in the early years of this century.[1] In one of these, the men of the village parade in goat skins. One of them goes through a marriage ceremony, after which he is killed, mourned by his wife, and finally resurrected. In another, a masked man dressed in sheep- or goat-skins is called king and escorted in a cart led by boys in girls' clothing. His page distributes wine. The king scatters seed and finally he is thrown into the river. The connections of these crude vegetation ceremonies with Dionysus are obvious; they are part of the submerged nine-tenths of the iceberg of belief and ritual which has survived right through the Christian era.

Christianity did not try to assimilate these Mummers' Plays. Other primitive rituals, however, turned Christian. There is a festival – Thracian in origin, but since the exchange of populations in 1923 it takes place in Macedonia – called the Anastenaria, where villagers dance on red-hot coals in a state of semi-hysteria. They are attempting to escape from normality, to enter a mystical communion with god, like Euripides's Bacchants. But they commune nowadays not with Dionysus, the pagan god of the sap, but with SS. Constantine and Elene; and they claim that Elene goes before them, pouring cool water on to the coals.

In this sort of way, all over Greece, Christianity did not so much destroy as incorporate paganism. The same thing happened in Crete, though not so much with Dionysus and the gods of the east, for they were never so powerful in Crete. Crete's biggest stake was in the old pre-Hellenic deities, and in Zeus, who was a local. His fortunes make an interesting story. The Greek mythologers tell of the birth of Zeus; luckily we know from other sources that he died as well.

Cronus the Titan, castrating his father Uranus and throwing his genitals into the sea, usurped the power. But fearing that, according to the prophecy, he in his turn would be dethroned by one of his children, he swallowed each of them immediately after birth. His wife Rhea in her despair hit on a resourceful trick. She bore Zeus secretly at dead of night and gave the baby to her mother, Mother Earth, to be spirited away. Then, wrapping a stone in swaddling clothes, she offered it to Cronus, who swallowed it, suspecting nothing. Mother Earth took her grandson and left him in a cave on Goat Mountain – probably the cave of Psychro on Mt Dicte, the highest peak of the Lassithi massif in eastern Crete.

In this cave the baby Zeus was cared for by two nymphs, daughters of Melisseus, king of Crete. Around his golden cradle stood the Curetes, dancing a leaping dance – and the leaping *Pediktos* of eastern Crete is still renowned – and clashing their spears on their shields so that Cronus, wherever he should be, might not hear the crying of the infant god. For food there was honey and the milk of the goat Amaltheia. Zeus grew to manhood on the wooded slopes of Cretan Ida, among the shepherds and their flocks, preparing to take his vengeance on father Cronus. Thus grew the president of the Olympians.

All this is part of orthodox Greek mythology; but the Cretans went further and claimed that Zeus was not only born on the island, but died there as well, and they showed his tomb to prove it. Epimenides, the Cretan poet whom St Paul quoted, early castigated them for this heresy, and he was followed by the Alexandrian Callimachus in his hymn to Zeus:

> The Cretans are always liars;
> They even built your tomb, O king,
> But you died not, you are for ever.

The explanation of this curious belief in the mortality of the Thunderer can only be that the dying Zeus was not the Olympian god at all, but a primitive pre-Hellenic Minoan god; very likely a vegetation god who *did* die every year, only to rise again.

Invaders from the north swept through Greece in the second millennium B.C., bringing with them new gods and gradually destroying the old matrilineal structure of society. Herodotus describes how the indigenous Pelasgians originally offered sacrifices and prayed to the gods without making any distinctions of name and title – this is, of course, an extreme simplification – so that later when the names of new gods reached Greece, they were forced to enquire of the oracle at Dodona whether it was proper for them to adopt these foreign names. The oracle gave permission. But it was Homer and Hesiod who composed the first theogonies and attributed to the various gods their appropriate offices and powers. It seems then that in the period of religious confusion between the Achaean and Dorian invasions of the second millennium and the enlightened standardization performed by Homer, the old Cretan Zeus was identified with the new Zeus, the Sky Father, who in the end surrendered his holy places and attributes to Christ and St Elias.

Zeus's tomb is now a heap of stones on the top of Mt Iouktas, the isolated peak near Heraklion whose very shape is that of the god's head, so that it is claimed that here, for ever petrified, he sleeps his perpetual sleep. It was mentioned by Cicero, Lucian, Origen, Diodorus and others – proof of the legend's vitality. Half a century after Constantine

Arkadi Monastery

View of Sphakia

The church of St. Fanourios at Valsamonero

Looking towards Heraklion from Agia Pelagia at sunrise

Roman, Byzantine and Arab Crete

adopted Christianity as the religion of the Roman empire, Julius Firmicus proclaimed that the tomb of the dead Jupiter was still worshipped by the unreliable Cretans. The hallowed spot induced near-ecstasy in the sober Robert Pashley: 'I now stand on the spot, in which Zeus was supposed to be at rest from all celestial and terrestrial cares, and which was so celebrated during many ages! The testimony of a long series of ancient and ecclesiastical authors proves fully and distinctly that the tomb remained an object of curiosity to strangers, and of veneration to the Cretans, from an early period till after the reign of Constantine.'*

But the Spanish emperor Theodosius's persecutions wiped out many such overt pagan superstitions throughout the Empire. After the fourth century we hear no more of the tomb until foreign travellers began to investigate the classical history of Crete many centuries later. The Cretans were forced to preserve their old polytheism by less blatant means.

Over the uncharted centuries from A.D. 395, when Crete was assigned to the Eastern Empire, to the Venetian conquest, we must pass quickly. It was natural that the island fell within the domain of the eastern emperor, just as it was natural that it should come under the aegis of the patriarchy of Constantinople in 731 and thus go with the Eastern Orthodox Church in the great Schism. By the eighth century, however, it looked as if Crete might be torn away from the Byzantine Empire, for the relentless aggression of the Arabs brought Crete within their range; and not only Crete – Byzantium itself was besieged in 674.

---

* Robert Pashley deserves an introductory note, since he will be mentioned or quoted in the following pages more than any other writer. He was an Oxford don, a classicist, who visited Crete in 1834, when the countryside was still suffering from the effects of the 1827 uprising against the Turks. A large part of his book is wasted in speculation about the topography of ancient Cretan cities: a fashionable game at the time, but exceedingly boring for the reader today. Skip the topography, for the rest is pure gold. Pashley was patient, very inquisitive, fluent in Greek (and soon in Cretan dialect as well), and well read, in the Venetian sources as well as the classics. The pity is that he never wrote his projected history of Crete.

My favourite Pashley story is that of the Archbishop and the dancing girls. The Metropolitan of Crete had recently given a party attended by distinguished Cretans, foreign consuls and the Turkish pasha himself. In deference to the Turk, the good Archbishop had the dancing girls brought in. Pashley's cool footnote is a couplet from the Acharnians of Aristophanes. And he comments, 'I suppose that, at the present day, such an exhibition of the free and easy motions of such females, cannot be of ordinary occurrence in the palaces of Christian prelates, either in the Oriental or in any other church.'

The Great Island

Since the Prophet's death some fifty years before, neither the might of Persia nor Byzantium had been able to halt the inexorable expansion of his devotees, who soon occupied Egypt, Palestine, Syria, Persia and much of the West. Bands of marauding Muslim horsemen, driven out in all directions by the social conditions of their homeland, and driven on by the dynamic force of a new faith which was prepared for a perpetual state of religious war with the infidel, found European dynasts and the Sassanids of Persia equally rotten. Byzantium herself repelled the blockaders in 678, and was saved. Crete, despite passing assaults in the seventh and eighth centuries, was spared until 827, when she fell to the Saracens of Spain.

These conquerors had been exiled from Cordova. They settled temporarily in Alexandria, but being driven out of that city too they mounted an expedition round the Aegean islands, and under their commander, Abu Hafs Omar, sailed into Suda bay with forty ships – which Abu then burnt to discourage thoughts of retreat. Crete was taken without difficulty. It was now that the future Heraklion was fortified. The Arabs surrounded the site with a moat and made it their base, naming it Al Khandak, 'The Ditch'. 'Candia', the Venetian name for the town, and by extension for the whole island, is merely a corruption of Khandak.*

To the Arabs, Crete was a temporary base from which to progress in their victorious course, advancing the faith. To the rest of the world it seemed as if Crete had turned once again into a nest of pirates. The Arabs were not particularly interested in the island for its own sake. They were few. They came without women and remained near the sea; men of war, unready to exploit the country as those adroit colonialists, the Romans and the Venetians, exploited it. Hence it is probable that stories of mass conversions to Islam are exaggerated. There were conversions; no doubt in precisely those coastal areas near the larger settlements which were always most receptive to foreign influences, whether artistic or religious. After Phocas recovered Crete in 961, Nicon the Armentian was canonized for 'extirpating the false doctrines of Mohammedanism from the island'. Nevertheless, in the countryside the social life, and the life of the Orthodox Church, must have continued much as before.

Michael the Stammerer, in whose reign Crete was lost, sent two expeditions to recover it. Both failed, the second apparently because of the laxity of the commander Craterus, who at one time looked to be

---

* Under the Turks the name used was Megalokastron (the great fort), or simply *to kastro*, the fort. Heraklion is an archaism.

successful. '*Mais s'étant un peu trop abandonné au plaisir et à la débauche,*' wrote Dapper, '*aussi bien que ses soldats, s'imaginant que les Sarazins étoient abatus, et ces derniers aiant un jour été avertis que lui et toutes ses troupes étoient ensevelis dans le sommeil et dans le vin, . . . ils vinrent fondre sur eux avec tant d'impétuosité et de furie, qu'ils les taillèrent en pièces.*' Thereafter the Saracens terrorized the Aegean. It was not until 961 that Byzantium, forced by the Saracen pirates to reorganize her fleet, recovered Crete. Nicephorus Phocas subdued the enemy after a ten-month siege, during which he catapulted the heads of Muslim prisoners over the walls of Khandak as a grim warning to the defenders. He erected a fortress, which the Venetians later took over and named Castel Temene, on the route from Khandak to the Messara plain. And he reduced the Arabs to serfs who worked the lands of Cretan masters unless they could redeem themselves. Then Phocas left, to become emperor two years later. His campaign marked the beginning of the resurgence of Byzantine naval power, for Cyprus followed Crete back into the fold, and Phocas was able to boast to the Italians that he alone disposed of a really strong fleet. His successors, the warrior Tzimisces and Basil the Bulgar-slayer, were no less militant.

For Crete, the second period of Byzantine rule was comparatively uneventful, and so poorly documented that it is impossible to say whether the establishment of foreign settlements, claimed by some scholars on the strength of Slavic and Armenian place-names such as *Armenochori* and *Sklaverochori*, ever took place. The second could mean 'Village of Slaves' as well as 'Village of Slavs'. One group of colonists, however, certainly was sent to stiffen the morale and to undertake the government of this turbulent island. The Emperor Alexius Comnenus I sent certain families of Byzantine nobles, endowed with special privileges, to settle in Crete and constitute an aristocratic ruling class. Tradition, and late documentary evidence (designed to prove descent from this *élite* and therefore suspect of forgery), would have it that these families were twelve. Not even this is certain. These nobles were called the *archontopouli*: chieftains. Their descendants, under many different names assumed as the families ramified and mingled with the indigenous Cretans, crop up again and again in the bloody history of the Cretan revolts.

3

Venetian Crete

> In the City and in Venice I never saw a plant
> Which bears fruit first, and only then sprouts leaves.
>
> *Cretan* mantinada, *referring to the wild squill, which flowers in late summer and sprouts leaves after the winter rains.*

The City is Constantinople, New Rome; and the couplet shows how the Cretans' conception of the world remained one in which Constantinople was the centre. The Arabs passed through and were forgotten. The Venetians, masters of Crete for over four hundred years, were enabled through the austerity of their administration and the magnificence of their building to impress themselves more firmly on the memory of the people. But the City remained as a dream. One day the interrupted mass would be completed in Agia Sophia. A Constantine built the City, a Constantine would take it back. A Cretan singer during the Cyprus troubles could still warn the Turks:

> Turks, listen to this, men and women, all of you,
> The Christians will complete the mass in the City!

And it is partly because the Turks captured the City and made it the capital of their empire that they were and are regarded as enemies far more obnoxious than the Venetians, who were, if the occasion demanded, no less brutal and far more intolerant of religious differences.

Nevertheless, it was under the Venetians that Crete saw an artistic and literary renaissance that was unique in the Greek world; a literature which culminated in the epic-romantic poem, the *Erotokritos*; and an art which threw up Domenicos Theotokopoulos, El Greco, who signed himself 'The Cretan' long after he left for western Europe. When Crete fell to the Turks the artistic life of the island was snuffed out immediately. It was of incalculable importance to the Greek nation that Crete was held so long by the west.

The distribution of Greek territories after the Fourth Crusade consolidated Venice's mastery of Levantine trade. The Serene Republic had been invited by Alexius Comnenus I to assist the Byzantine Empire against the Norman Robert Guiscard when he appeared off Corfu in 1081; as the price she demanded trading concessions throughout the Empire. Thus when the world was carved up by the crusaders in 1204, well over one hundred years of commercial activity in the east had shown Venice where her interests lay and which parts she needed. The crusaders had wished to proceed to the recovery of the Holy Land by means of the conquest of Egypt. Reliant, however, on Venetian naval power for their transport, they were easily diverted by the Venetians, who were interested neither specifically in the submission of Egypt, from which they received commercial privileges, nor generally in the overthrow of the Muslim. The crusade turned on Constantinople. The Emperor Alexius III fled. Count Baldwin of Flanders assumed the throne. Crete was assigned to Prince Boniface of Montferrat, leader of the crusaders; but preferring a compact territory on the mainland, he sold the island to the Serene Republic of Venice for 1,000 silver marks, and established himself as lord of Salonika. But 'sold' is perhaps the wrong word; the sum is so suspiciously small that Boniface clearly regarded it as a token; the real price of Crete was the diplomatic support of Venice for his other claims.

Thus Venice acquired the key ports and markets in the Near East; for through Crete, the Cyclades, Gallipoli and other strategic points, she commanded the sea routes to Egypt and the Crimea. She did not take over Crete painlessly, however. The Genoese, Venice's rivals for mastery in the Aegean, forestalled her and got a foothold in Crete before Venice could send a force strong enough to claim possession. Venice had made only tentative incursions when the arch-pirate Enrico Pescatore, the Genoese count of Malta, landed and quickly took control of the island in 1206. He embarked on an energetic building programme, strengthening the Cretan defences with fortresses which the Venetians took over and used to hold down the islanders and to repel the assaults of corsairs and Turks. The Cretans on this occasion, and again in the future, showed themselves inclined to support Genoa against Venice. A stronger force, of thirty galleys, was sent to drive out Pescatore, and from 1212 Venice controlled Crete. But this was not the end of the pirate Genoese ambitions; they took Canea in 1263, profiting from the support of the Paleologue dynasty at Byzantium, and succeeded in remaining in the west of Crete for twenty-three years.

Once established, the Venetians set up in Crete a microcosm of their own Republic. A year by year narrative of their occupation would be unprofitable, for the mind wearies of repeated examples of oppression and extortion. Venice was prepared to invest both money and men in Crete; but the incessant revolts meant that she never got a full return for her investment, and the rivalry first of Genoa and then of the expanding Ottoman Empire ensured that her energies were diverted to strengthening the island's defences and manning her warships rather than increasing the productivity. In the end, as her influence declined throughout the Greek world, with her expulsion from the Morea and the successive fall of her islands to the Turks, ending with the loss of Cyprus in 1571, Crete became a liability, to be retained only at excessive cost in arms and blood. But she was a symbol. With her loss would go not only the wines, silks and oils of the island itself, not only the valuable spices of Alexandria, but also the hope of a Hellenic-Latin culture in the Aegean – the last outpost of art and learning and literature set amid the encroaching barbarism of the Ottoman Turks. Europe knew this. It was not only Venetians who fought in defence of Candia in 1669.

Anyone who reads the descriptions of Crete by travellers in the last two centuries of Venetian domination must wonder that Crete, given such natural resources, was not a better place to live in. Belon describes not only those gardens and orchards in country so beautiful that one would not tire of contemplating it; also pastures which nourish great flocks of sheep and goats which bring them much revenue in cheeses and wools. Jean Struys, in 1668, only a year before the fall of Candia, admired whole forests of apricot, oranges, lemons, figs, almonds, olives, apples and pears. *'où il n'y a ni blé ni vignes ce n'est que thym, que marjolaine, que serpolet, que romarin et autres herbes de bonne odeur.'* Those herbs which elsewhere are odourless, he says, are perfumed in Candia. This was the paradise which might have been for the Cretans; the paradise for which they sometimes fought. The land was fertile. The slopes had on them more life-giving trees than today.

And yet between 1204 and the end of the sixteenth century the population decreased, according to Pashley's expert calculations, by 300,000 – from about 500,000 to 200,000. The reason was not only the pressure of Genoese and Turks, who took Cretans away to service in the galleys, and the epidemics which ravaged Crete in the sixteenth century; also there was the exploitation which caused bloody revolts, and this exploitation was a part of the feudal system imposed by Venice.

When Venice took Crete she divided the island into nearly two hundred fiefs, to be held in perpetuity by Venetian colonists, who had military obligations to the Republic. Crete was governed by a Duke, sent out from Venice every two or three years. The central government of the island was at Candia, where the Council met. In practice the great Cretan families, the *archontopouli* and *archontes*, had to be loyal if peace was to reign in Crete. But buying their loyalty was a risky business – it meant playing off one family against another; hence rivalry, envy and revolt. And apart from this, the system of government, with its tight controls exercised from Venice itself, tended to alienate not only the Cretans but also the colonists. The revolts began at once.

1212. Tiepolo, the first Duke, asks help from Duke Marco I of Naxos in quelling the Cretans.

1268. Some Venetian colonists revolt and demand separation from Venice.

1283-99. A series of revolts in which the noble Cretan Alexios Kallergis razed the whole island. In the end he made terms, was created a Venetian knight, and urged his sons to be loyal to Venice.

1333. In this revolt one Kallergis fights for Venice, one against.

1341. The revolutionary Leon Kallergis negotiates with the Turks. The Venetian governor invites him to parley, sews him up in a sack and throws him into the sea. This dastardly action provokes long resistance.

1362-3. The newly appointed Duke Dandolo demands money from the Venetian knights for the repair of Candia harbour. His excessive demands – the knights were farmers not merchants – provoke the worst revolt of all. The knights rose under Tito Venier and Tito Gradenigo, and proclaimed Marco Gradenigo Duke. The insurgents trampled down St Mark's banner in Candia, and announced their acceptance of Orthodoxy. The Greek *archontes* therefore joined in the revolt.

It took reinforcements from Italy, Naxos and Euboea to crush this movement, and its seriousness can be judged by the panic caused at Venice. Western leaders such as the Pope and the Emperor Charles IV had boycotted Cretan trade in sympathy. Venice celebrated victory with three days' thanksgiving, and the anniversary of the rebels' capitulation was declared a public holiday in Candia. The leaders were cruelly put to death.

Very soon the Kallergis family were embroiled in yet another revolt, this time in Lassithi in the east. After its suppression cultivation and pasturing on the Lassithi plain were forbidden, and the plateau lay fallow for nearly a century; a more spiteful and lunatic prohibition one could hardly imagine.

This bare summary (which ignores the more trivial uprisings) shows how the Venetians failed to cope with the hostility of the Cretans. In

The Great Island

the fifteenth century things were better, but even then external threats (the City fell in 1453) kept Crete in a state of continual tension. Meanwhile the colonists became more and more Hellenized.

The last great revolt, and the most mysterious, caught the imagination of the Greek writer Zambeliou to such an extent that he wrote a historical novel, *Cretan Marriages*, which surrounded it in still greater mystery. It is Kandanoleon's revolt. For most of the incidents the only authority is the notary Antonios Trivan, who was in Crete until the fall of Candia in 1669. This is his story:

Exasperated by the compulsory services – work in the galleys or on the coastal defences – which Venice demanded of them, the Cretans of the eparchies, Selino, Sphakia and Kydonia – that is, a large part of western Crete – rose in revolt in 1502. (The date is in dispute, but for the moment I shall stick to Trivan's version right or wrong.) They refused to acknowledge the authority of the Republic or to pay taxes, and they appointed their own private administration, electing as governor – *rettore* – George Kandanoleon of Koustoyerako, a tiny village above Souyia. Kandanaleon set up his headquarters in the village of Meskla in the roots of the White Mountains, together with supporters from some of the great families of Crete: Pateri and Mousouri for instance, who claimed descent from the Byzantine *archontopouli*. He appointed officers to command other strong-points in the insurgent area. Taxes were paid to the revolutionary chest. Thus there existed, side by side, two independent powers in Crete. And although the leaders of several revolts have proclaimed Crete independent, this was the only time when the proclamation had any substance, for the rebels were able for a time to live, and govern their people, under their own administration.

Perhaps Kandanoleon, having achieved this extraordinary feat, tired of his powers and responsibility. Perhaps, seeing that in the end the enterprise must fail, he resolved on the desperate expedient of reconciling the Cretan and Venetian nobilities by the dynastic marriage he proposed. For he went down to the country house of the Venetian noble Francesco Molino at Alikianos, and asked the hand of the baron's daughter in marriage for his son Petros – 'the finest and bravest of my sons'. If the marriage took place, he would resign his offices in favour of his son.

It is not a love story, as the novelist Zambeliou makes it. From all we are told by Trivan, it could be that the boy had never seen the girl. And if he was in love, there was no need for this approach. He could have abducted her in the time-honoured fashion of western Crete. No wonder the Venetians were staggered at his father's proposal.

Molino, however, proved a master of dissimulation. His shocked expression might have been due to gratified amazement. After consulting with his wife, he accepted the proposition, and the betrothal took place at once. Kandanoleon gave his son a gold ring. The boy kissed the girl and placed the ring on her finger. The wedding was arranged for the Sunday after the next. Molino would send for a notary and three or four gentlemen from Canea, while Kandanoleon was to bring not more than 500 of his friends and relations. He departed suspecting nothing.

Next day Molino went down to Canea. He bought the customary presents for the groom and sent them up to Meskla. He sent dressmakers to his house at Alikianos to prepare the bride's trousseau. And he paid a call on the Venetian rector of Canea.

The day before the wedding Molino returned to his house with about fifty friends, to prepare for the festivities. They slaughtered and roasted a hundred sheep and oxen. On the Sunday morning Kandanoleon and his son Petros arrived, with some three hundred and fifty friends and one hundred women. The merrymaking began as soon as the marriage contract was signed. Molino's servants had orders to let the wine flow. The guests ate and drank, danced and sang. The Venetians appeared to be keeping pace. By sunset not one Cretan was left on his feet. All lay where they had fallen in swinish stupor, and their hosts too were scattered around the courtyard in what looked like a profound sleep.

It was feigned. 'When night fell, the rector came out of the city [Canea] with the army and the nobles and two hundred who had disembarked from the galleys silently and in good order.' For Molino in Canea had begged the rector not to miss this opportunity of avenging a personal insult to his dignity as a Venetian noble and a Catholic, and of chastising the unruly and rebellious Orthodox. He had demanded a punishment such as would serve as an example to posterity. The rector, sending for reinforcements from Candia and Rethymnon, had marshalled 1,700 foot and adequate horse.

'The signal was given with two rockets, and they answered from the tower [Molino's house] in the same way, and the forces from the city proceeded to the tower and succeeded in arresting all the Cretans as they slept so deeply, and bound them hand and foot with ropes brought for the purpose. And they were bound as they slept, without realizing it, like sheep!'

The Great Island

In the morning, Kandanoleon was led before the Venetian rector, with his chief supporters, and questioned. Why had he rebelled? He replied that he had been chosen by the people. He was exercising his prerogative as his forefathers had done; for he was a descendant of those noble Byzantine *archontes* who had come to Crete before the Venetians. He was hanged from a tree, together with his son Petros, the bridegroom, and another son. Of his friends, three were shot at once, and some thirty hanged, of the distinguished families of Mousouros and Kontos. Others were sent to the galleys in chains.

The rest of the prisoners were divided into four groups. Some were hanged at the gates of Canea; some at Koustoyerako, birthplace of Kandanoleon – and the village was then razed to the ground; some at Apokoronas castle on the road from Canea to Candia; and the last group at Meskla, the rebels' mountainous headquarters, one of the loveliest and greenest villages in Crete. 'Thus were they annihilated, and men of faith who respected their God and their leaders were comforted and consoled.'

But this was not the end. The Senate of the Most Serene Republic sent out Marino de Cavalli with instructions to crush any remaining rebels – '*Per l'estirpazione degli huomini seditiosi*'. Cavalli went straight to the village of Photeiniako, near Mournies; organized mass arrests; burnt the village; hanged twelve of the prominent inhabitants; and for the greater terror of the people took four pregnant women, and had their bellies slit open with cutlasses and the embryos extracted. All the captives were taken down to Canea, where many were executed and the rest deported. Five or six out of the original four hundred escaped; and thus a prosperous village ceased to exist.

Cavalli continued his destructive march through Kydonia. He then summoned the Cretans of the rebel territories, Frangokastello, Selino, Apokoronas, Kissamos and Sphakia to appear before him and swear submission. Some obeyed, but the majority, which included the leaders, mistrusted his proposal and stayed in their mountainous retreats. Cavalli therefore proscribed them, pronouncing their property confiscated and offering them one terrible means of securing their lives by demonstrating their loyalty to the Republic. Any of the outlaws who appeared in Canea with the head of a proscribed relation (father, brother, cousin or nephew) might buy his pardon with it. A priest of the family Pateros-Zappa obeyed this monstrous command. He went with two sons and two brothers, each of them carrying the head of a close relative, which they threw at the feet of the Venetian.

It was only after this incident, which moved even the Latins, that

Venetian Crete

moderation prevailed. Cavalli sent out Greek and Latin priests to proclaim an amnesty. These mediators remained in Sphakia as hostages, while the Cretans came before Cavalli. In return for his promise of amnesty he won their loyalty. Thus the last traces of the independent state of western Crete disappeared. The Cretans had not since 67 B.C. so nearly tasted liberty; they were not to do so again until 1821, and then too it was delusive and short-lived.

So Trivan. The story at first seems plausible; it is not more fantastic than others which are well authenticated. And apart from those like Zambeliou who accepted it for its dramatic qualities, others as conscientious as Pashley have not questioned Trivan's account – partly, I think, because Trivan so clearly approved of Cavalli's conduct and gloated in the downfall of the hubristic Greeks, that he seems to have no reason for inventing it all. One could understand a patriotic Cretan chronicler's motives for embellishing some trivial brush with authority, to the honour of his dead relatives and compatriots. But Trivan has no reason to do this. If we look closely at his account, however, we cannot escape the implausibilities and puzzles which it presents. These concern the date of the rebellion and the motives of Kandanoleon.

Trivan places the affair in the early years of the sixteenth century. But there is no reference to it in the reports of Venetian officials of the time, nor in historians such as Cornaros, nor in the official list of the Dukes of Candia, which contains a précis of notable events in each Duke's tenure of office. Moreover, that Marino Cavalli who in Trivan's account suppressed the revolt was Proveditor General in 1570. This is an established fact. Cavalli marched on Sphakia and reduced the area to ruins, executing, imprisoning or banishing his captives. The campaign was in reprisal, for the Sphakians had been descending to the plains and carrying off the nobles' sheep. Since western Crete was in ferment at this time, and Cavalli was called on to restore order, most authorities have placed Kandanoleon's revolt in these years: 1570-1.

But it will not do. The total ignorance of the sources for 1570 onwards rules out this period too. Even though this is an argument from silence, it is conclusive; for the great merit of the reports submitted by Venetian Dukes and Proveditores is that they do not omit events of this importance. The Republic's controls were too tight for careless reporting to escape notice.

Did Kandanoleon then never exist? Was Trivan, too, a historical novelist? The possibility cannot be ruled out. Trivan had no access to the essential source materials in Venice, and hence was a prey to what local material he could find. And as those who have had to study the political history of the last war in Greece either on a local or a national scale testify, the evidence of partisans is always unreliable and often forged. Fielding describes how fictitious tales were circulated after the Civil War by those who wished to make heroes of themselves, often in the hope of material gain. And George Psychoundakis told me that he was driven to write *The Cretan Runner* by the lies which he heard repeated and saw in print. As to mainland Greece, C. M. Woodhouse, who wrote *The Apple of Discord* – by far the best account of the war in Greece – was so suspicious of forgery that he rejected entirely all documents which emanated from resistance groups.

Now in the rigidly classified society of Venetian Crete it could be important to prove one's membership of a certain family, if, say, it had been granted privileges by the Venetians. And there must always have been competition among the rival claimants of descent from the original twelve families of the *archontopouli*. But even if we grant that Trivan may have used suspect material, the ingredients of the Kandanoleon story do not look as if they would have helped anyone in his claims. It is likely, *a priori*, that there is some truth in the account. And this likelihood becomes a certainty when we observe that Filippo Pasqualigo, the Capitano Grande of Canea, referred to Kandanoleon in a speech dated 1594. There are also the Kandanoleons, he says; one of them at that time was so audacious as to become rector. And the context makes it clear that 'that time' was the time when certain rebellious families were suppressed by Hieronymus Corner in 1527.

Thus the rebellion of 1527 was Kandanoleon's rebellion. This solution was proposed by Zoudianos and seems to fit. It involves, however, identifying Kandanoleon with the Lissogeorges who is referred to by contemporary sources as the rebel leader, and assuming that Kandanoleon is a subsequent nickname. This is likely enough; the name means 'lion of Kandanos' – a most appropriate description. The 1527 revolt was serious, for the following year the Duke of Candia reported that all western Crete had risen and there was a danger of the infection spreading throughout the whole island. Corner succeeded in mopping up the insurgents by putting a price on their heads. Even Lissogeorges, 'without whose capture all our efforts would have been wasted', was betrayed. And the reprisals were savage, including the execution of some seven hundred, the banishment of others to Cyprus and Cythera, and the reduction of still more to slavery in the galleys.

It is a pity to chip away at a story which has become part of the Cretan mythology, and even, since Zambeliou's book, of the Greek consciousness. But the central and intriguing part of the original story, the marriage, has gone. It was, in any case, extraordinary. For any Cretan, schooled in the history of revolts and reprisals, to believe that a Venetian noble would accept the hand of his rebellious son without question, and to attend the wedding without taking precautions, shows an unusual trust. It was always evident that the marriage did not take place exactly as Trivan describes it. It now looks as if the marriage very probably never took place at all.

4

Art under the Venetians

What did the island look like, what did it feel like? It looked greener, more fertile, than today; but for the feel of it we have to go to sources other than overtly historical ones – to folk poetry, to the churches, which reveal a life untouched by this historical summary.

The Venetian occupation was the great time for the building of churches and monasteries. In the centuries before the occupation, church history is incomplete, relics are few. One of the few remembered figures is John the Stranger, a hermit saint of the early eleventh century, who founded several monasteries in the Akrotiri area. He slept nights in a cave, and his ascetic life gave rise to rumours after his death – how, being dressed in skins of wild beasts, feeding on wild green-stuffs and wild honey, he was one day mistaken for an animal by a solitary hunter, and shot. He, with the ten martyr saints, remains fresh in the Cretan memory, and villagers will tell you his story and point to his cave.

When the Venetians took Crete, the hostility between the Roman and the Orthodox faiths was too great to allow of reconciliation. Already one hundred and fifty years had passed since Humbert, the papal legate, laid the bull of excommunication on the altar of St Sophia, thus putting the Patriarch of Constantinople outside the Roman communion. The lamentable events of the Fourth Crusade, in which Latin Christians turned on the capital of Greek Christendom, confirmed the Greeks' mistrust. Wisely the conquering Venetians did not persist in attempts to reclaim Crete and all her people for Rome.

Their first move was to seize the churches, and expel the dignitaries of the church. All the bishoprics were filled with Latins. Latin monasteries were established. Orthodox clergy, who were ordained by bishops from outside Crete, were subject to the Latin bishops. The system sounds unworkable; in fact, it must have meant pockets of Roman Catholicism in the towns where the sees were situated, and more or less undisturbed Orthodoxy in the country. In any case, it was not long before the system was altered from inside itself. Originally the nobility was almost exclusively Venetian. The local Cretan nobility, the *archon-*

topouli, was a tiny minority. But as time passed the *archontopouli* and *archontes* multiplied. At the same time the Venetian nobility became gradually Hellenized, and there was intermarriage between the two races. Thus there emerged a class of Orthodox nobles, with property: houses in one of the three cities, fiefs in the country. These were the patrons and pillars of the Church.

They built their own little churches. They patronized the painters, sometimes from abroad, who made them beautiful. We can see their names recorded in the founders' inscriptions of chapels all over Crete. Especially in the last fifty years of occupation, when plague and revolts and Turkish attacks had exhausted the Venetians, and they were at least sometimes conciliatory, the builders were active. Arkadi, the jewel of Cretan monasteries, was built in 1587; Gonia in 1618. By about 1600 the two faiths were co-existing happily. Symbol of co-existence is the church built at Spinalonga by Luca Michiel, Proveditor from 1572 to 1574; it was divided into two parts, one for the Greek, and the other for the Latin rites.

Gerola in his great work listed more than eight hundred frescoed churches in Crete. Most of these are fourteenth- or fifteenth-century. The area of Crete is about 8,300 square kilometres. Thus for every ten square kilometres there is a painted church. When one considers the extent of barren mountains – though even here there are some chapels – this abundance of churches is the more striking. It is only in the last few years that we have been in a position to guess what the churches looked like in these centuries. For, if interest in Byzantine art is a fairly new phenomenon, the sub-class of Cretan art was more or less invented by Gerola. Previous scholars, such as Pashley, went over Crete with a fine toothcomb finding evidence of classical and even Venetian antiquities, but not a single wall-painting; the reasons being first that they did not recognize the existence of Byzantine art and therefore ignored what traces there were, and second that many of the frescoes had disappeared. Just as Minoan art had to be excavated from beneath layers of earth, so Byzantine paintings had to be uncovered from behind layers of plaster. The best examples of Cretan art have been cleaned and restored since the war, and thanks to scholars like Hadzidakis and Kalokyris they are now being published and discussed.

How to approach these eight hundred churches? 'The liveliness of the faces, the expressive movements of the bodies, the translucent colours make this a remarkable example of Paleologue *expressionismus*.' This sort of thing is intolerable except as the footnote to a comprehensive set of reproductions where the parallels and the colours can be observed. Art history is not my object. Rather, I wish to communicate some of the feelings you might have had in these churches. Hence a naïf approach will serve better, and I shall describe what you would have seen, and can still see in places.

Most of the eight hundred are in ruinous condition. Subsequent generations have covered many of the frescoes with plaster; painted new scenes; allowed the churches to go neglected, open to the disastrous effects of wind and weather. Sometimes marauding Turks would gouge out the eyes of saints, and sometimes the Christians would anticipate such desecration by removing the eyes themselves to safe keeping. Even the smoke of pious candles helped to spoil the colours. Nowadays the Cretans are conscious of their treasury of Byzantine art, and one might expect that the churches would now be safe. But their remote situation does not make preservation easy. Even now one finds windows open to admit the damp which will eat away the walls. At Valsamonero, for instance, one of the best churches. The difficulty lies in persuading the villagers to look after their local churches. Their indifference to monuments irritated Tournefort, who remarked that at Gortyn 'they plough, sow, feed sheep among the wrecks of a prodigious quantity of marble, jasper, granite-stone. . . . In the room of those great men who had caused such stately edifices to be erected, you see nothing but poor shepherds, who are so stupid as to let the hares run between their legs, without meddling with them; and partridges bask under their very noses, without offering to catch 'em.'* Their indifference to the hares and partridges is far more surprising than indifference to ancient ruins.

Do not expect to find, then, eight hundred perfect churches. Only a handful are as they were. But there are many more where the head of a saint, perhaps blinded, or a fold of rich, glowing drapery reamed by cracks in the plaster, offers merely a hint of former glory. Do not expect the grandeur of early Byzantine churches in the City, or of mosaics in Ravenna. There are no mosaics in Crete, except a few fragments of Roman work. Almost all surviving Cretan churches have only one nave, and those with more, at Kritsa and Valsamonero, are still small enough to have the privacy of chapels. Within these little churches

---

* The title of Tournefort's book is *A Voyage into the Levant performed by command of the Late French King*. His job was primarily to collect simples (he was a professional botanist); and secondarily to report anything of interest to the king. This he did excellently; see, for instance, his chapter on 'The Present State of the Greek Church'. His voyage took place at the turn of the eighteenth century. I have used and quoted throughout this book the English translation of his work, by John Ozell (1718).

The Morosini fountain in Heraklion

Fresco of the Abbot Zosimas from the Panagia Kera at Kritsa

Fresco from Skaloti

almost the whole interior is painted. Thus in the commonest scheme:

Apse: The Pantokrator, Christ in majesty, stares down from the cupola. Sometimes there is the Virgin with Christ at her breast (*Platytera*). In one rare case – the church of St George near Preveli monastery – there is the Trinity, being the Father with the Son on His chest and the Holy Ghost proceeding from His lips.

In the lower part of the apse, four hierarchs bearing scrolls with sacred inscriptions.

Nave: Around the lower part of the wall, the martial figures of saints: the women, Barbara, Eirene, Kyriaki, Paraskevi: and the warrior saints, Demetrius, George, the two Theodores, often on horseback. These fill the lower band.

In the larger churches, above this lower zone there is an intermediary band of saints, head and shoulders only, framed in circular medallions.

The upper part of the nave is filled with scenes from the gospels; scenes from the life of Christ and the Virgin. They cover the whole vault; each panel separated from the next by a reddish band after the style of the Paleologue period. At the south-east end of the nave is the first picture of the series, the Nativity. From there in order, the Purification, Baptism, the Raising of Lazarus, Palm Sunday, the Transfiguration, the Last Supper, the Crucifixion, the Women at the Tomb, the Descent into Hades. Interwoven with these are the scenes from the Virgin's life: the Visitation, the Nativity of the Virgin, the Presentation, and the Dormition. The cycle ends at the north-east of the nave. At the east end is the Ascension.

On the west wall is the Last Judgement – a grim warning to those leaving the church by the main door. Brief inscriptions, often crudely written and strangely spelt, indicate the sins of those who are being conducted into the flames of Hell. The usual criminals are there: the forger, the thief, the usurer, the false witness, the man who gives short measure; and also those who were regarded as peculiarly Cretan, the sheep rustler, the man who damages your land, the adulterer.

This bare schema cannot convey the richness and life of the Cretan church. One must just try every approach, the factual, the enthusiastic, the historical, in the hope that some of this richness will come over. Consider for a moment the painter. He is a reticent figure. He remains deliberately in obscurity. Usually he is anonymous, and when he signs his name it is tucked away in a corner; the glory belongs to the Lord, not to the painter.

In painting as in dogma Orthodoxy has prided itself on Tradition. The emphasis on tradition is both the strength and the weakness of

Orthodoxy; tradition has been a force for unity and strength, a source of authority which is lacking in the Protestant theology and which comes from some sort of consensus of opinion rather than from the top of the hierarchy as in the Roman Church. At the same time there is no more reason to believe that the Orthodox tradition must be infallible than that the Pope of Rome is. The appeal to tradition rather than to reason has been responsible for some very odd arguments by the Orthodox. In art the tradition was so strong that everyone understood the language; and thus humble villagers, without extensive training, were enabled to paint with power and authority. The tradition covered both the subject matter – the iconographic types – and the technique. But in art as in dogma the tradition could lead to a dead end. Orthodox churches are full of the melancholy examples of a tradition petrified and finally sentimentalized. When I was staying in the monastery of the Virgin Mary (Kroustallenia) on Lassithi plateau, two new icons arrived. The abbot was impressed by them, and obviously could not understand my reserve. They were terrible: the colouring like the garish decoration of a chocolate box, the treatment like the most degenerate and sentimental of English religious art in the Tarrant tradition. The faces of saints and elders had turned cherubic, rosy-cheeked, blue-eyed and cherry-lipped, like choir boys. But the icons being painted now, it is only fair to say, are no longer part of the Byzantine tradition at all. Thematically they cannot escape it; but in technique and colouring they have lost all relationship.

The artistic tradition was rich enough, anyway, and complex enough, to last for over a thousand years, altering within itself, enriching itself with new technique, undergoing renaissance, yet remaining always true to its original purpose. This purpose is undefined; if definition must be attempted, I should say this – Byzantine art is the representation or mimesis for the human flock of the divine order which holds together the created universe, and of God, man and angels in their true, divine relationship with each other.

The painter therefore is to reveal what lies behind the transient surface of the phenomenal world; and since he is uncovering the truth, rather than creating, he is reliant on the grace of God for clear seeing. The painter must be pure in heart. He is not the romantic victim of inspiration, he is the servant of God – *doulos tou Theou* – and so he will often sign himself. Prevelakis describes how a bishop of Rethymnon fasted for a fortnight before painting the Pantokrator in the church of St Barbara, as if in preparation for Holy Communion. The third week he took his paints and brushes and climbed up on the scaffolding and began to paint. The face of omnipotent Christ grew from his brush; the nostrils dwarfed the hand that was painting them. On the twelfth day, the face completed, the bishop climbed down, totally exhausted by the struggle to convey his vision. His legs gave way beneath him; the muscles of his neck were set stiff; the body succumbed to fever.

Another approach. Look for a moment at one church. Among those eight hundred the most rewarding are perhaps the Virgin at Kritsa, St Fanourios at Valsamonero, the monastery at Vrondisi, the Asomatos at Archanes, the Archangel Michael at Vathi on the west coast, the Dormition of the Virgin at Alikambos, and the Virgin at Potamies. Of all these none is richer than the church of the Virgin, Panagia Kera, at Kritsa.

Kritsa is the largest village in Crete. It lies in the hills north of St Nicholas; in the area which the film-makers frequent. The French film *Celui qui Doit Mourir*, from Kazantzakis's novel *Christ Recrucified*, was made here, and more recently Walt Disney has been filming an extravagant story set in Crete and entitled *The Moonspinners*, with Hayley Mills. The church of the Virgin – which is not the only painted church in Kritsa; do not miss St George Kavousiotis – lies below the village among groves of olive and orange trees. Cypresses, which are the signposts of holy ground, rise beside the church.

The Panagia Kera is one of the few Byzantine churches of Crete with more than one aisle; it has three, and is crowned with a dome. To stand in this church in the time of its perfection was to read a book full of the gospel stories.[1] The south aisle was devoted to St Anne, the Virgin's mother, and in the upper part her story was told in scenes from the Apocryphal Gospels, thus (from east to west):

The Announcing of the Good News to Joachim: The angel descends and tells the reflective Joachim the good news of his wife Anne's pregnancy.

Joachim's House: Joachim and Anne at table, probably celebrating the news.

Joachim meets Anne: Joachim returns from the desert where he had gone and fasted forty days and nights before the angel appeared to him. He embraces Anne.

Anne's prayer: She prays in a garden, among trees with birds' nests in their branches, her arms raised. The angel descends, to tell her: 'Anne, Anne, the Lord has heard your prayer, and you shall conceive and bring forth.'

The Priests Bless the Infant Mary.
The Birth of the Virgin Mary.
Joachim holds the Infant Mary.

The Proof by Water: A test of the Virgin's chastity. The priest Zacharias offers a pitcher of water to Mary and she prepares to drink. 'And the whole people was amazed that no sin was revealed in them.'

The Presentation of the Virgin: Almond-eyed maidens accompany her as she is led before Zacharias.

Joseph's Sadness over the Pregnant Virgin: As the gospel says, 'He was minded to put her away privily.' Mary sits on a chair, plainly pregnant. Joseph rests his head on his right hand as he grieves. An angel appears to reassure him. In the Apocryphal cycle: 'Joseph found her pregnant and struck her face and threw himself to the ground and wept bitterly ... and Mary wept bitterly saying that I am pure and know no man.' In subject matter this is the most interesting picture in the church, since it incorporates elements from commoner types (Joseph's dream etc.) to make a new design.

The Journey to Bethlehem: The pregnant Virgin on a donkey, followed by Joseph.

The Closed Gate: The Virgin and Child before the closed gate, a symbol of virginity derived from Ezekiel. This picture takes the place of the usual Nativity.

Below these panels are the saints and martyrs – a row of busts above a row of full-length figures.

The northern aisle lacks the intermediary row of busts. Above the upright saints and the founders of the church (a couple and child), is the Second Coming. Here is Paradise: the garden enclosed by a wall; trees in blossom, and birds; the Virgin with an angel, and the patriarchs Abraham, Isaac and Jacob. The gates of Paradise are set in the wall, and St Peter stands outside with the keys. The four rivers of Paradise, each designated by an initial letter (T for Tigris, E for Euphrates, etc.) are outside the wall.

There are the wise and the foolish virgins, the apostles, the Baptist, the woman with the beasts and the four winds of the Apocalypse. On the west wall there is the angel of the Lord who trumpets on earth and sea; the *Psychostasia* (an angel holds the scales while a soul is weighed); and a rough sketch of souls in torment, their naked limbs being devoured by snakes. Apart from these scenes, there survive only the sea rendering up its corpses, and the dance of the martyrs and saints entering Paradise. The rest of the panels, covering much of the north wall, are destroyed.

Thus in the two side aisles the worshipper could follow the preliminaries to the great drama of the incarnation and life of Christ, and the epilogue to that drama – the sounding of the last trumpet, the raising of the incorruptible dead, the gathering together of the great communion of saints, and the terrifying chastisement of the damned. The central section of the church was reserved for the central mystery of Christ's incarnation, life and death. There is the Massacre of the Innocents, with Herod on his throne, the mother weeping for her slaughtered children, and Elizabeth with the baby John the Baptist in the protection of the mountain. (According to the Apocryphal Gospels, when she heard of the Massacre, she went up to the mountain with John, and finding no hiding place, cried out, 'Mountain of God, receive a mother with her child'. The mountain at once split open and received her.) Also the Nativity; the Presentation of the Virgin; Paradise; the Descent to Hades; Herod's Banquet (Salome dressed as a dancing girl with the Baptist's head); and the Last Supper, one of the masterpieces of Cretan art. The table is spread with Venetian ware, delicate green jugs and plates of food. Christ is on the left, and the apostles, in two rows behind the table, stare towards him.

On the west wall, above, the Crucifixion, badly damaged. Below, the punishment of the sinners again. Men and women, naked, consumed by the flames. They have their tags: 'the harlot', 'the water thief' who diverts water from his neighbour's field, and 'the thief', who is portrayed in the utmost misery, his hands tied behind his back, with a spiky long-eared animal, which looks more like a white fox than a stolen sheep, around his neck.

I have already spent too long on the Panagia Kera, and still not mentioned much of the contents; the painting of the dome, for instance, and the calm austere faces of the saints. But it must be clear now what the church was for the Orthodox: a constant reminder of the gospel story; a representation of the central story of the Christian faith for a congregation most of whose members could not read; and more than this, a representative of the Christian communion, from the lower ranks (the founders), to the higher (saints and angels). For the Cretan church, small as it was, had the same function as the great cathedrals and churches like St Sophia. It was an imitation, in symbol, of the cosmos. In the cupola, which represents heaven, was Christ. In the sanctuary, as in the church of St Fanourios at Valsamonero, Christ and the angels celebrating the Divine Liturgy. Paradise and Hell are in the middle zone, and earth in the lower. And the Virgin Mary, the most favoured of God's creatures, mediates between heaven and earth from her place in the apse.

The Virgin is venerated above all other saints. Some Orthodox have believed in her Immaculate Conception, though this is not dogma.

The Great Island

Nor is the doctrine of her Assumption, though all Orthodox accept this; after her death her body was taken up to heaven and the tomb left empty – and this Assumption is celebrated on 15 August as the Feast of the Dormition. (The Greek word, *Koimesis*, means 'falling asleep'.)

There is an interesting passage on the veneration of the Virgin in Crete in Prevelakis's book, *The Chronicle of a City*:

Most of the churches and chapels around Rethymnon were dedicated to the Virgin. . . . You see, a country which has gone downhill, which cannot live off its own resources, needs someone to intercede for her. . . . It was to the Virgin that her faithful people had entrusted this mission with the Lord, and she never disappointed them. And the people in recognition of this filled the place with churches and chapels for her. . . . They painted numerous icons in her honour and gave to each icon a different name to distinguish them. . . . Each name was a song in itself. She was called the Immaculate; the Sweet-Caresser; Higher than the Heavens; Lady of the Angels; Child-carrying; the Nurse; the Joy of all; the Source of Life. . . . Also the Rose that withers not; the Hope of the Angels; the Queen of all; the Mistress of the Waves; the All-Glorified; the Protectress of God; the Gracious; the Exalted; the Warrior Lady; the Golden Lioness. . . . She was invoked as the Swift to Hear; the Saver of Souls; the Comforter; the Consoler; the Deliverer; the Healer . . . She was also given the more humble names of Lady Nightingale etc. . . . Each of these names was a hymn of praise, a salutation. . . .

A church, then, is a microcosm of the whole universe both create and uncreate. And thus the worship of the whole church can be realized in the Eucharist as it is celebrated in one small Cretan chapel. For those saints who stare at you from the walls, dressed in rich bejewelled robes, sometimes stern, sometimes remote and untroubled, are themselves present. There is in the Orthodox church no separation among the communion of saints. In St Symeon the New Theologian's words, 'The saints in each generation, joined to those who have gone before, and filled like them with light, become a golden chain, in which each saint is a separate link, united to the next by faith, works and love. So in the One God they form a single chain which cannot quickly be broken.'[2] The church is one and indivisible and is present in its entirety whenever the Eucharist is celebrated. In this mysterious sacrament Christ, and the saints departed, and those on earth, meet together. Thus in the church of the Virgin at Kritsa, the saints around the walls are more than mere pictures. The seven martyred children of Ephesus, the ten martyr saints of Gortyn, John the Eremite, Alexius the Man of God, the Abbot Zosimas, Simeon Stylites, Constantine, founder of New

Art under the Venetians

Rome, and the rest, are the representatives of a great multitude, examples of virtue to all those still on earth.

I have concentrated on this one church as an example. It is probably the best of them, and must be seen. But others may prefer other chapels: for instance, the superb little church of the Asomatos ('church of the fire-formed generalissimo of the upper powers, the Archangel Michael') at Archanes, with its vigorous Old Testament scenes including the capture of Jericho, in which the tiny Joshua is dwarfed by the Archangel with his naked sword. This church is notable, too, for a Crucifixion in which the Christ bends at the waist as if being torn apart by the weight of His own body, while the Virgin bends fainting, her hands falling limp; a painting moving and realistic in a new style which marks the last flowering of Byzantine fresco work in both Macedonia and Crete.

Others again may prefer the church of St Fanourios (Valsamonero), where the elongated figures in the fresco of John the Baptist in the desert put one in mind of El Greco. And others may simply wish to wander in search of little-known churches. For these last, good areas to explore are Amari, west of Mt Ida, and Selino, Kydonia, and Apokoronas in western Crete. But the whole western end of the island is studded with painted churches. I remember one morning visiting two near Sphakia. I noticed in the first (St George at Komitades) the face of a saint, only a boy, with long hair and large limpid eyes, a face astonishing in its grave beauty; and in the second (the half-ruined, roofless Prophet Elias at Skaloti) a Roman face, tough, realistic, authoritarian, blazing in the light of the midday sun. Sheer luck had shown me within an hour of each other these two representatives of the Byzantine genius, the withdrawn lover of God, and the worldly lover of good order and lawful government. But in an island of eight hundred churches one may expect luck.

In Crete herself the art of painting frescoes seems to be moribund by the sixteenth century; yet outside Crete it is Cretan artists who are decorating the great churches of the Meteora and the Holy Mountain. One of the reasons for this must be the fall of Constantinople in 1453; for that turned Crete into the cultural centre of the Greek world, either as a permanent home for refugees or as a resting place on the way to Venice and the west. So it is natural that Cretan artists are prominent in this last flowering of Greek wall painting. But why were they painting not in Crete but in the mainland monasteries?

I incline towards the simplest answer, which is economic. On the

The Great Island

mainland under Ottoman rule, the larger groups of monasteries tended to be isolated outposts of culture. Art found shelter in Athos and the Meteora, where there was enough money for patronage. But the sixteenth century in Crete was a nervous time, of resistance to corsairs and preparation for Turkish attacks. Neither time nor money was easily to be spared. Patronage does not flourish in such circumstances. Ambitious painters would eventually require something larger than the tiny chapels which stud Crete; something less awkward than the newer churches with their western influences and their mouldings which got in the way of the paintings.

And so they emigrated. The greatest of them, Theophanes the Cretan, painted the Catholikon of the Laura monastery on Athos in 1535, and the monastery of Stavroniketas in 1546; and worked also at St Nicholas in the Meteora. He was followed by other Cretan masterpainters: Anthony, Zorzis, Neophytus. Together they constitute their own miniature renaissance – painters confident in the orthodox tradition, yet beginning to admit the influence of Italy. Theophanes himself had an almost legendary reputation.

Meanwhile in Crete the icon replaced the fresco. (An icon is an image. For convenience, I shall in this chapter use 'icon' to mean 'portable icon' as opposed to a fresco or bust.) From about 1550 until the fall of Candia, scores of Cretan painters, most of them trained in or near Candia, left Crete for Venice. The demand for icons increased. Individual painters acquired reputations, and tended more and more to sign their own work. Cretan icons were to be found all over the Orthodox world, from Cyprus to Russia. And the painters usually followed the trade route; from Crete to the Ionian islands, from there to Venice. We can sometimes trace the movements of individuals: Andreas Ritsos, for instance, in Italy and Patmos, or Michael Damaskinos.

Damaskinos is the best. If you visit Heraklion, do not miss his superb paintings in the Cathedral church of St Menas. (An unfortunate setting for them. The icons were brought here from Vrondisi.) Damaskinos was in Venice from 1577 to 1582. In 1588 the Greek Brotherhood of Venice invited him to paint the Orthodox church of St George, but he did not go.* It must have been about this time that he was painting his

---

* M. Hadzidakis in his article on Cretan painting and Italian engraving (*Cretica Chronica*, 1947) quotes the terms under which the Greek Brotherhood finally commissioned John Kyprios for the job. Kyprios was to accept the supervision of the great Tintoretto; but was still to paint 'the rhythm, the clothes, the forms and the expressions Greekwise, as the authentic Greek art demands'.

Art under the Venetians

masterpieces which are now in the Cathedral, for the last of them, the icon of the Ecumenical Council of Nicaea, is dated 1591. If you look at these paintings in turn: *The Burning Bush*, the *Adoration of the Magi*, the *Noli me Tangere*, the *Last Supper*, the *Divine Liturgy* and the *Ecumenical Council*: you may feel some puzzlement. Here was a man who knew what was going on in the west, who had copied western paintings, whose technique was excellent. How was he not bowled over by Raphael and Tintoretto? How could he go home and paint these indubitably Byzantine pictures?

Because he had to remain in the orthodox tradition. In a way the surprising thing is that he absorbed so much that is western. Hadzidakis notes Damaskinos's debt to Tintoretto and to the engraver, Marcantonio Raimondi, whose copies of Raphael also influenced Theophanes the Cretan; and says of the *Last Supper* that it is perhaps the first post-Byzantine painting to attempt a solution of the problem of space on western lines. (For not only are the interior fittings and columns western; so is the use of perspective in the walls and paving slabs, and the feeling of three-dimensional space thus created. Even so, Damaskinos has not ceased to use also that other space where a figure's size and position in the picture may depend not on the laws of perspective but on his value and importance in the traditional hierarchy.)

Despite Damaskinos's virtues and reputation there is something wrong; for me at any rate. It is not easy to look at Byzantine art and see what we are meant to see. Perhaps it is sometimes impossible; but sometimes even the non-believer succeeds in making the imaginative jump and seeing right. It is partly a negative approach that is required, like the orthodox approach to God; i.e. it is a question of shutting out some of the usual assumptions about art, of forgetting part of our western tradition. Damaskinos, by referring to the western tradition, made this impossible for me. I do not see what else he could have done, for to have shut his eyes to the west would have been disastrous. His imitators, by seizing on his works as prototypes, showed how even the limited novelty supplied by Damaskinos was badly needed. Nevertheless, those western elements which he used are enough, for me, to shatter the illusion, or the reality – which it is depends on your belief – which is the basis of Byzantine art. When I see the *Last Supper* I find myself wanting a set of western qualities which are not there; as if, having started to tread this slippery path, Damaskinos should have gone further. But this is all subjective.

This excursus on Damaskinos is not as pointless as it might appear, for his career is conveniently contrasted with that of another, greater

Cretan painter, in whom the west has an interest. I mean Domenicos Theotokopoulos, El Greco.

Greco was born in the Candia area in 1541. The village which claims him – Fodhele – lies in low marshy ground a few miles below the main Heraklion to Canea road. It is a straggling, dirty, unfriendly, well-watered place, standing in orange groves. There is a plaque in honour of the master, set up by Spanish well-wishers, and the little church contains a book of Greco reproductions. One can make the pilgrimage easily from Heraklion. For some reason we chose to make it the most arduous, but exhilarating way, by bicycle; and so, since we took the coast road, did not miss the marvellous coves below Fodhele.

Research on Greco goes on continuously, of course, and his early life has recently been illuminated. It seems that he did not leave Crete until 1566. For the one-time Greek consul in Venice, Mr Mertzios, found quite recently in the Venetian archives a paper dated 1566, which comes from Heraklion and bears the signature: 'Maestro Menegas Theotokopoulos, painter. . . .' This means that Crete figures more largely in the painter's life than was thought; for it had been assumed that he left for Venice some years earlier. If Greco was at least 25 when he left, and called maestro at that, he must have learned the trade in Crete.

The fact is that Greco followed exactly the path which, as we have seen, so many other Cretan painters took; only he went further afield than most when he left Rome for Spain in 1576. He will have learnt at Candia to paint in the Byzantine tradition. As a younger contemporary of Damaskinos, he may have known him; may even have studied under him, as tradition has it, though there is no evidence. At the same time he could see the Italian paintings which decorated the nobles' houses in Candia, and doubtless he will have learnt to paint in the Italian style. For provincial Cretan painters at this time, like Ritsos and Pavias, could use both.

Till Venice then, the same course as Damaskinos. This is not mere speculation, for the two icons in the Benaki Museum of Athens which have the signature *Cheir. Domenikou* (hand of Domenikos) – an *Adoration of the Magi* and a *St Luke Painting the Virgin* – are almost certainly early Grecos, and very likely from his Cretan period. The *St Luke* is a post-Byzantine painting, and the *Adoration* shows that Greco already had Venetian technique. And so to Venice, where he stayed till 1570. Sometime in the three or four years he was there, he made the decision that Damaskinos did not make – to break away from the Byzantine tradition. The rest of the story is well known.

Art under the Venetians

It is not for me to enter the lists and fight on behalf of some label to pin on El Greco – 'the last of the Byzantine painters', 'the first of the Spanish Baroque', etc. Art historians can thrash out this sort of thing; and the reader will find the Byzantine case put with enthusiasm in *The Birth of Western Painting* by Robert Byron and D. Talbot Rice (long out of print, alas). This much, however, may be worth saying. Arguments that depend on individual stylistic traits are pretty easy to demolish. The famous elongation, for example, is not a feature of Greco and of Byzantine art only. But since Greco definitely rejected the Byzantine tradition in its major externals, we shall not find evidence *except* in traits like this. So we must be very careful to know what we mean when we say Greco was in some way Byzantine. We may mean just that we get the same sort of thrill from a painting of Greco as we get from a Byzantine work. Or we may mean that Greco would have been a quite different sort of painter – and not just in the trivial, tautological sense – if he had not been born in Crete, in the Byzantine tradition. And with this unprovable, indeed counter-factual proposition, I rest content.

Postscript for travellers.* On the bluff north coast of Crete, very near the north-eastern tip of the island, stands the monastery of Toplou, which contains the last treasure of Cretan art. Toplou is only a few miles from Sitea, twenty minutes' walk from the bus route. I visited it during the great Lenten fast, and thus tasted several foods which otherwise I might have missed. The snails were especially good, and the Abbot especially proficient at eating them. There was a pleasing irony about the first meal I had there. Oil was prohibited. The monks therefore ate enormous potatoes baked in their jackets, while I was given cold boiled potatoes swimming in deep oil.

There is an untrue (I hope) story about a party of Frenchmen at Sitea, who ate the local snails, expressed their pleasure and mentioned that another delicacy in their home country was frogs' legs. The next night their plates were heaped high with the legs of frogs which had been fished out of the local river and marshland. The Frenchmen ate unflinchingly to the last bite, and died during the course of the night.

* And a footnote for travellers. It is impossible to show the exact location of all the best Byzantine churches in a small map such as that on p. 7. There is an adequate map of western Crete published by the Tourist Office at Canea, and sold in any stationers. The best churches are marked on it. For information about central and eastern Crete, I should recommend a visit to the office of the National Tourist Organization, where there are maps. But really good maps are difficult to come by in Crete.

The Great Island

Toplou's pride is a large icon called *O Lord Thou Art Great*: 'the work of John Kornaros when he was 25 years of age . . . in 1770.' The picture is inspired by a prayer composed by Patriarch Sophroniou of Jerusalem, from which I quote:

O Lord, Thou art great and wondrous are Thy works and no word shall suffice to hymn Thy wonders. The sun hymns Thee, the moon glorifies Thee, the stars intercede with Thee, the light is subject to Thee, the abysses tremble before thee, the water-springs serve Thee. Thou hast stretched out the heavens, Thou hast founded the earth upon the waters, Thou hast fenced in the sea with sand, Thou hast poured forth the air in breezes. . . .

Angelic powers serve Thee, the choruses of Archangels reverence Thee . . .

Thou hast blessed the waters of Jordan sending down from heaven Thy All-Holy Spirit. . . .

Thou art our Lord who drowned our sin through the waters of the Flood in the time of Noah, who delivered Thy people through the sea from the slavery of Pharaoh, who burst open the rock in the desert, and waters gushed out and torrents flooded forth, who through water and the fire of the sun delivered Israel from the error of Baal.

The icon is a grand design in illustration of this prayer. Each of the sixty-one scenes is labelled with its own phrase – 'The moon glorifies Thee' next to the moon and so on – and there are other phrases too which represent the words spoken by the figures portrayed. The Holy Trinity is surrounded by the whole worshipping universe – sun, moon and stars, the heavenly bodies represented by the signs of the zodiac, angels and archangels. In between the scriptural scenes the artist has poured his talent into a host of details, marvellous or extravagant. There are monsters, snakes, a gryphon, a wild pig, a fox with long, rigid tail, a lion, a dwarf elephant the same size as the lion, birds, a long-necked beast like a dinosaur, a malignant ape. Sea monsters too, in Jordan water, with wicked, grinning faces. The ram which is about to appear to Abraham has a sweet expression, a generous bushy tail. The blood-red sun and moon contain angels curled up within them. At the bottom of the picture, on either side of Christ's descent into Hades, the Tigris and the Euphrates, two of the rivers of Paradise, wind down toward the sea. There are swans proudly swimming on the Tigris, and one is preening himself on the bank. The river flows under a three-arched bridge, part of a little Italian town of sun-warmed stone walls and red roof-tiles. Two peasants drive a yoke of oxen over the rich earth. Cypresses shoot up like needles. And best of all, between two fir trees where the river bends, two white animals are sitting on the bank, clearly each other's mates, with long curly graceful necks and rubbery jointless legs, basking in total innocence. All this in one small corner of the icon.

Art under the Venetians

Kornaros – what a name it is in Cretan history – was an artist of talent and rich imagination, which led him far away from the Byzantine tradition, to Italian landscapes and perhaps even mediaeval bestiaries. I know of no other work by him. This one remains as the most pleasing memorial of the Venetians in Crete: the more moving and pleasing in that it was painted in 1770, a hundred years after the fall of Candia and the departure of Venetian and Cretan artists from the island.

5

The Cretan Renaissance

Constantinople fell on 29 May 1453. There were Cretans involved in the defence, and Cretan ships arrived at Candia with the shattering news early in June. An anonymous poet described the horror:

> Groans, sobs, lamentation, sighs, grief,
> Sadness inconsolable have fallen on the Greeks.
> They have lost their home, their Holy City,
> Their courage, their pride, their hope.

How was the news brought? A ship sailed down from Tenedos:

> 'Where are you from, ship, where have you come from?'
> 'I come from the curse and the heavy dark
> From the storming hail and lightning, the dizzy wind;
> I come from the City burnt by the thunderbolt.'

He describes the pillage and murder, and the fate of the Emperor Constantine XI:

> He looked humbly to right and to left;
> The Cretans are fleeing, the Genoese,
> The Venetians are fleeing, and he remains.
> He cried humbly with his lost lips:
> 'You are fleeing, my children, you are slipping away,
> And where do you leave me, the unhappy-fated?
> You leave me to the dogs and the wild beast's mouth.
> Christians, Greeks, cut off my head,
> Take it, good Cretans, and carry it to Crete,
> For the Cretans to see it and be sad at heart.'

But in fact the emperor's body was lost. The poet ends:

> Angels and saints protect us no longer.

Thus the Cretans heard of the most important event in Greek history. The emperor's words signified that, Constantinople now lost, Crete was become the refuge of Hellenism.

1453 therefore marks conveniently the beginning of Crete's importance to the west. Refugees had fled to the great island before this; but

The Cretan Renaissance

in 1453 what had been a trickle became a stream. Cretan letters began to flourish. Cretan scholars began to move westward. A hundred years before El Greco made the journey, the route lay open from Constantinople to Crete, from Crete to Venice, and thence throughout the west. Crete was an essential link in the transmission of classical learning to Italy, and thus in the flowering of humanism.

This sounds abstract. In fact this renaissance was a personal movement, which a few teachers, copyists and scholars created by their energy. If I mention a few names, it will show what some of these individuals were doing.[1]

First a refugee from Byzantium: Michael Apostolis, an assiduous copyist of ancient manuscripts. When the Turks sacked Constantinople, priceless manuscripts had gone up in flames, including some of Euripides's plays which are lost to us. Still, much was preserved in the monasteries. Michael went back to Constantinople on collecting expeditions, and was active in searching out rarities throughout the east. On Crete he copied them, and trained others to do so. And from time to time he would go to Italy to visit his patron the great Cardinal Bessarion. When Bessarion died, he left the Venetians nearly five hundred Greek manuscripts, of which many were copied by Michael Apostolis.

Michael's last surviving manuscript is dated 1474. His frustrations were typical of the refugee and the client; it was not a happy life. He complained repeatedly to Bessarion that he needed more money; he was always going on about getting a job as a teacher in Italy; but worst of all, he came to hate Crete, and became very unpopular there because of his religious views. For he was a staunch supporter of the Union of the Greek and Roman churches proclaimed at the Council of Florence in 1439, and Union was never in the least acceptable to the Cretans. Michael became more and more Latinized. He wrote to Bessarion in 1467:

> From the time I expressed my opinion of the Latins and supported the adherents of the Roman church with words – and rejected the other [Greek] church – from that time, whenever I am in the city [Candia] they call out to me: 'Look, the devil got him, too. Look at the accursed one, behold the wretch!' And these men, who would have killed me long ago had they not feared the authorities, drew my students away from me. So now I live miserably by my pen....[2]

There must have been many refugees in similar difficulties. Apostolis is not a very attractive figure, with his whining; but he believed in what he was doing – he believed in the supremacy of Greek culture, which must be transmitted from the moribund east to the vigorous west. It was his misfortune to live half-way between the two worlds.

Candia was now a centre for the copying of manuscripts. Michael's son Arsenios continued his work, before leaving for Italy. But Cretans tended more and more to emigrate to the west, for the island could not contain them. Before 1453 the level of education in Crete was low, even among the clergy. The monastery of St Catherine in Candia taught the rudiments of ancient Greek, philosophy, theology, rhetoric and so forth. Elsewhere there was little learning. After 1453 the learned, like Michael Apostolis, had to set up their own schools. But it was no life for the ambitious. All that scholars could do in Crete was to copy for Venetian patrons or teach privately. There was no university; whereas in Italy the Greek language had begun to sweep through intellectual circles, revealing a whole new world. There were openings for teachers, for printers, for professors.

At the centre of this Italian movement was the Aldine Press. Aldus Manutius himself was not merely a publisher – he gathered round him eminent Hellenists, both Greek and Latin, in an Academy where only Greek was spoken. From 1495 on, the Aldine Press employed émigré Greeks, mostly Cretans, as compositors, editors and correctors. Aldus's chief editor, for instance, was the Cretan Markos Mousouros, the leading Hellenist of his time and indeed one of the great Hellenists of all times, who edited among others Sophocles, Euripides, Aristophanes and Plato. (His Plato was the first complete edition of the philosopher in Greek.) Mousouros was not only an editor. He also held the Greek chair at Padua for six years. Students of this exciting, rapidly expanding subject came from all over Europe to hear him lecture. Erasmus, who met him at Padua, was full of praise for his scholarship. In 1509 Mousouros moved back to Venice where he became professor shortly afterwards; and Aldus wrote that Venice was a second Athens because students of Greek congregated from everywhere to hear Mousouros, the most learned man of his age. Aldus died in 1515, Mousouros in 1517, and by that time most of the major authors of antiquity had been published in new editions in Venice.

Mousouros is a well-known Cretan name. So is Kallergis, a name which figures so prominently in fourteenth-century revolts. One of this noble family, Zacharias, set up the first exclusively Greek press in Venice; (for the Aldine Press published also Latin). The first publication was the enormous *Etymologicum Magnum*, a mediaeval Greek dictionary whose effect on Greek studies in Italy was profound.

The Cretan Renaissance

Mousouros wrote the preface to this work, and took the opportunity to pay tribute to the Cretans:

But why should one be amazed at the talents of the Cretans, since it is Athena herself who by order of her father taught them many arts? It is a Cretan who has fashioned the type. It is a Cretan who has joined together the copper letters, a Cretan who inserted the accents one by one. The man who poured the lead was also a Cretan. It was a Cretan ... who paid the expenses, and the one who closes this book with these [verses] is also a Cretan. May the Cretan Zeus be favourable to the Cretans.[3]

The nationalist Cretan may note with pleasure that the type used by Kallergis's Press is more beautiful than that of the Aldine Press. Kallergis later introduced Greek printing to Rome, which under Leo X became an intellectual centre unrivalled in Europe.

I have said enough to indicate Crete's contribution to the revival of Greek learning in the west. These three, the copyist Apostolis, the teacher and editor Mousouros, and the printer Kallergis, are representative in their skills; but they are the most brilliant examples. There were many others: Demetrios Doukas, for instance, who moved from Venice to become professor of Greek at Alcala university in Spain. When he arrived he found 'a great want of Greek books, or rather, so to say, a desert' – only fourteen Greek works in the chief Library, and these a motley bunch including bores like Aratus. Doukas started to publish. And with the encouragement of his patron Cardinal Ximenes, he collaborated with learned Spaniards in the great enterprise of printing a Polyglot Bible. The New Testament appeared in the original Greek and in Latin Vulgate, and the Old was printed in parallel columns of Greek, Latin and Hebrew. The Alcala Bible marked a new starting point in biblical studies.

There were also the Cretan Peter Philarges (Pope Alexander V); and the Orthodox Patriarch of Constantinople Cyril Loukaris, who worked for a reconciliation of Orthodox and Protestant, and was murdered in 1638 for this revolutionary design. But their importance lies in the work they did far away from Crete. It is time we returned to the island.

Not all the learned and the talented went to the west. Throughout the Venetian domination of Crete a native literature was growing up; a literature quite unlike anything else in Greek letters, for it was produced by a unique cross-fertilization. Venice met Byzantium on Cretan soil. The result was a miniature renaissance. The best works of this sixteenth- and seventeenth-century Cretan revival have always been popular with the people. By the scholars and the intellectual circles in Athens, however, they were comprehensively ignored for some time; one reason being the simple myth that Greek literature stopped in 1453 (or a thousand years earlier if one was a classical-Greek-nationalist rather than a Byzantinist), and started again with the poet Solomos and the war of independence.

'I confess it is not a tasty business,' wrote the revolutionary propagandist Koraes in 1805, 'for anyone to read the *Erotokritos* and other such abortions of wretched Greece, but whoever loves the loveliest mistress must not fail to flatter even the ugly handmaid if she can make the entrance to the mistress easier.' Recently this attitude has changed. Cretan literature now gets plenty of scholarly attention. It even enjoys at the moment, something of a vogue. Two plays, the bloodthirsty *Erophile* and a miracle play, *The Sacrifice of Abraham*, have been successfully produced in recent Athens Festivals. And Nikos Koundouros, the young director whose film *Young Aphrodites* won first prize in the Berlin Festival of 1963 is planning to film the epic *Erotokritos*; the result will be a great event for Greek culture.

The flowering of Cretan literature came in the seventeenth century. Before that time a number of poets, more or less in the Byzantine traditions, had prepared the ground. There was, in these early stages, a strong didactic, religious and moralist strain. The first of the Cretan poets, for instance, Linardos Dellaporta, composed his works as a justification and consolation for himself while he repined in prison – unjustly accused, he claimed, by a woman of fathering a natural child on her. It was a sad end to a distinguished career. He was born at Candia, where he learnt Italian. After serving the Republic as a soldier, he returned to Crete as a lawyer. Later he was sent on diplomatic missions to the Sultan of Tunisia, the Despot of the Morea, and the Porte itself as envoy of Venice – an important job. He was thrown into gaol in 1403.

One would not bother to read Dellaporta's work for fun; nor any other of the early Cretan poets except perhaps Sachlikis. One would merely note some interesting facts and then move on. The most interesting fact is that the subjects which are deepest embedded in Cretan folk poetry also fascinate these literary poets. There is an anonymous fifteenth-century poem on *xeniteia* (exile) which recalls the many folk poems on the same theme. And both folk poet and literary poet take a melancholy interest in Hades and Death. In the 'Rhymed Complaint on the Bitter and Insatiable Hades' by John Pitakoros of Rethymnon, the poet goes down to Hades in his thoughts and is conducted round by

The Cretan Renaissance

Charos himself, who not only demonstrates his kingdom but also teaches how it is original sin which caused human death.* Of course all this preaching is quite alien to folk poetry. Nevertheless there are popular elements in the poem, as there are also in the similar *Apokopos* of Bergadis, where the shades might be speaking in a folk poem:

> You come from the world, the country of the living.
> Tell us, does the sky hold up and does the world still stand?
> Does it lighten, tell us, and thunder, are there clouds and rain,
> Do the waters of the Jordan river still run down,
> Are there gardens and trees, and birds to sing,
> Do the mountains smell and the trees blossom,
> Are the meadows cool, the breezes sweet,
> Do the stars of heaven shine, and the Morning Star?

It is a bitter poem. The insistent question of the dead is 'Are we remembered?' and the poet offers little comfort. The young women whom you left behind widowed, plant their kisses on other lips, dress their new lovers in your old clothes, and if they speak of you at all, speak only ill. Only a few remember.

Most of these Cretan poets were worthy and uninteresting. The exception is Stephanos Sachlikis, whose racy satires enlivened Candia around 1500. One scholar remarked that he preached virtue by a complaisant description of his own immorality; but with Sachlikis as with some other satirists, there is the feeling that he was trying to convince himself, that even after his 'conversion' he was fascinated by vice. He was born at Candia. He loathed school and 'culture'; spent his youth and his substance on debauch, until a connection with a widowed whore named Koutayiotaina landed him in gaol. Like Dellaporta earlier, he was inspired by his imprisonment to write. Sachlikis's poems are scurrilous, bitter and autobiographical. He tells of his riotous youth, his imprisonment under tyrannical warders, his attempt to find peace in the country, and his return to town as a lawyer. Neither lawyer-colleagues nor whores escaped his lashing tongue. The whores are listed one by one, and Koutayiotaina, the origin of his misfortunes, comes in for especially vicious treatment.

Sachlikis's verses give a surprising picture of the life and manners of Candia under the Venetians. One tends to forget – through concentrating too much on the life in the countryside, which has changed little – that town society was quite different then. Time after time

---

* Charos (no longer Charon) in modern Greek folk-lore is not just that grim ferryman, but the black knight of death himself. He combines, in fact, the functions of the ancient Charon and Thanatos, and his kingdom is called Hades.

travellers and commentators and Venetians call the Cretans an adulterous, deceitful and immoral people. This is not only a prejudice derived from ancient testimony of Epimenides and St Paul. It is also a reflection of the bourgeois society at this time. Even the folk songs reflect it. For early Cretan folk song displays more sophistication over sex than is common in Greece and Asia Minor. (These Cretan girls in the songs tend to have lovers rather than mere admirers; and adultery is a common theme as well as fidelity.) Sachlikis, who castigated this society with the vigour and disgust of a Juvenal, had a right to do so, one feels, since he spoke from experience. But others who knew Crete less well undoubtedly went too far. Dapper, for instance: '*La plupart des Candiots ou habitants Grecs de cette île sont de grands mangeurs et de grands ivrognes, adonnez au vin, à la débauche, à la gourmandize et à la luxure, et surtout aux plaisirs sales et impurs de la chair. En un mot ils mènent une vie fainéante et paresseuse.*' Fair enough, if exaggerated. But he goes on unbelievably: '*Ils sont pourtant la plupart, et sur tout ceux qui vivent à la campagne, des gens tendres, effeminez, délicats, lents et paresseux, qui n'aiment pas le travail, et n'ont aucun génie et peu de pénétration d'esprit.*' Shame! Sachlikis is more credible.

All this early Cretan poetry of the fifteenth and sixteenth centuries – the dialogues, consolations, complaints, narratives of earthquakes, and so forth — may be seen as a preparation. During this time the Cretan poets were learning two things; the mastery of rhyme, and the use of their own Cretan dialect. Around 1600 the great period of the Cretan renaissance began.

The works are as follows: *The Shepherdess*, a charming pastoral idyll; three tragedies, *Erophile*, *King Rhodolinos* and *Zeno*; three comedies, in the tradition of the New Comedy of Menander; a pastoral play, *Gyparis*; a miracle play, *The Sacrifice of Abraham*; and an epic-romantic poem, the *Erotokritos*. In all these works there are Italian influences; in some of them the Cretan author is following an Italian model. But the resulting works are Greek in feeling.

I don't intend to say anything about most of these. Contemplating a three-line précis of the gruesome plot of *Erophile* is no pleasanter than digesting the pre-act summary of a Wagner opera on the Third Programme. I shall stick to the two masterpieces, *The Sacrifice of Abraham* and the *Erotokritos*.

The Sacrifice of Abraham is a little gem. This play of something over one thousand lines is not primarily a religious play at all; its point is not the mystery of God's command to Abraham. Rather, it takes the command, which is delivered by the angel in the first scene, as a datum, and proceeds to explore the characters concerned: Abraham, Sarah and Isaac. *The Sacrifice* is therefore unlike the English plays of the same name; it is neither a mystery nor a morality. I can vouch for its effectiveness on stage, since I saw it at the Athens Festival. It was played, quite rightly, fast and naturalistically, and despite the disadvantages of confining scenery, consisting of a set of rocks based on the iconography of Cretan painting, and some over-acting from Katina Paxinou as Sarah, it held the multi-racial audience. But then the story, with its miraculous dénouement, is a 'natural' for the stage; and especially moving in the Greek because of the beautiful speech of young Isaac – played by a girl – as he waits bound for his father to sacrifice him. He moves from prayer to resignation. He asks Abraham to kill him gently, caressingly. He wishes his mother were there for him to kiss and say goodbye:

> Mother, no more will you come to my bedside to dress me,
> To wake me tenderly and to caress me.
> I am leaving you and you are losing me – like melting snow,
> Like a candle which you hold and the wind blows it out.

He tells Abraham to come near, to leave off tightening the rope, and for a moment he seems to take courage – for his mother's sake. 'And tell her how I go to find Hades full of joy.' Then the last request: whatever of mine is left in the house, clothes, papers both written and unwritten, and the basket which contained them, give them all to Eliseel, our neighbour, because he is my playmate and companion and best friend at school. I have nothing more to say, he says, just my goodbyes. But at the last moment his nerve breaks:

> Sir, you fathered me, can you not pity me?
> God who created me, help me! O Mother, where are you?

The Sacrifice of Abraham is almost certainly by Vincenzos Kornaros, the author of the *Erotokritos*. (Apart from the superiority of these two works over all other Cretan literature, their linguistic similarity makes it likely that one man wrote both.) *Erotokritos*, more than ten thousand lines long, is the heroic romance of modern Greece. The epic *Digenes Akritas* and the *Erotokritos* have to be for modern Greece what the Iliad and the Odyssey were for ancient Greece. *Parva componere magnis*: nevertheless the *Erotokritos* is beautiful and important, not only because it ties in with Greek nationalism.

It is an astonishing poem. The model is the extremely popular French romance 'Paris et Vienne'; Kornaros knew an Italian version of this (the work was translated into nine European languages!). The whole of the *Erotokritos* is a paean to courtly love, which is a western invention. And yet the *Erotokritos* is not only Greek in spirit – it has been a major force in preserving the Greek spirit. Bury called it 'a long and tedious romance saturated with Italian influence'. In my opinion it is much better than this, though I grant the longueurs.

What happens? Heracles, king of Athens in ancient times, had a daughter Aretousa. Erotokritos, son of one of the king's counsellors, loves her. To win her heart he serenades her at night; and she begins to love the unknown singer. The course of their love does not run smooth. The king has marked down the Prince of Byzantium as a suitable husband for Aretousa. But in the end, when the king of Vlachia declares war on Athens, Erotokritos comes back incognito from his exile and saves the day by winning a single combat. King Heracles is overwhelmed with gratitude, and the marriage can now take place. That is the story, reduced to the thinnest of skeletons. It does not sound particularly Greek. The king is king of Athens; but the story is set in no particular period of history. Intentionally it takes place in an 'ideal' place and time.

Listen to the first words of the poem:

> The turnings of the circle, which come and go,
> And the turnings of the wheel, sometimes up, sometimes down,
> The changes brought by time, which have no ceasing,
> But keep moving and running for better or for worse,
> And the turmoil, enmities, heaviness of arms,
> The powers of love and the joy of friendship;
> These things have moved me this day today
> To tell the actions and the fortunes of a girl and a boy,
> Who were involved together in an affair of love
> Without repose but without ugliness.
> Whoever has toiled at any time in the grip of desire,
> Let him come and listen to what is written here.

From this easy, courteously didactic beginning, the rhymed couplets flow smoothly on, unfolding the long tale with a leisurely wisdom. The girl Aretousa, reflecting on the suitor who sings below her window, expresses this wisdom:

> From whatever beauty there is in man, words have their grace
> To make each heart take encouragement;
> And whoever knows to speak with knowledge and with style
> Makes the eyes of men to weep and to laugh.

The Cretan Renaissance

And this is what Kornaros is after – to speak with knowledge and with style.

The poet George Sepheris, whose flexible fifteen-syllable line has its origin in the *Erotokritos*, wrote a masterly study of the poem, which illuminates not only the value of it and its meaning for the Greeks, but also Sepheris's own views on poetry. He tells how he first came across the poorly printed pamphlets which circulated in the later years of the last century.

[The *Erotokritos*] circulated among the humble classes, in the islands, in the eparchies of the Greek state, in the great metropolises of the nation. Usually it was sold by pedlars. I remember, as a boy in Smyrna, every afternoon at the same time, the same voice in the street: 'I have all sorts of books! Erotokritos and Aretousa! The story of Halima! . . .' In those days these wretched publications delighted me. On the cover, Erotokritos, a young hero with a savage and somehow cross-eyed look. . . . For me, he was the same soul as Digenes and Alexander the Great – triplet brothers. If I had been asked I could not have distinguished one from the other, nor could I have found anything to distinguish Aretousa from Alexander the Great's gorgon-mermaid. Both of these women were tormented by a great lack. What sort of lack it was, I could not then have understood. I understood however that it was enough to make them naturalized citizens of the world which surrounded me. And this world – workers at the vine, seamen – was tormented, I saw, by a great lack: later I understood how it was the lack of freedom.

I quote at length to show how Erotokritos works on Sepheris, and other Greeks, on more than one level. As well as being a poem it is a national poem. Sometimes I think that a nation which has not been oppressed cannot get this sort of pleasure from poetry; for as a nation it has no 'lack', no yearning or wish, to be fulfilled or embodied in poetry. The English have no characters in whom they see embodied the aspirations of the race. (The nearest equivalent to Digenes and Erotokritos and Alexander would be Robin Hood and the characters of Dickens!) For us, therefore, poetry is a personal affair. But for the Greeks works like the *Erotokritos* have been a powerful force for unity, since they have cut across class barriers; and they do this because in them the Greeks see their national aspirations fulfilled – as when Erotokritos defeats the terrible Caraminite, who represents the forces of darkness threatening Hellenism, in particular the Turks.

Of course the fact that the *Erotokritos* is a 'national epic' does not make it a good poem. It just means that some of the Greeks will overvalue it for non-aesthetic reasons. Indeed nationalism has been one of the forces most responsible for silliness and bad judgement in modern

The Great Island

Greece. And even Sepheris, I think, speaks too well of the *Erotokritos*, for he is intoxicated by the history of the poem. He makes out the best possible case for it, however – so that in the end one finds oneself agreeing, yes, it is a marvellous poem. Even so, I wish it were not quite so long and repetitive. But, as Sepheris says, there is no proving a poem is good. 'Poems are like the ancient hetairae: they appear naked in court.' So:

> Let the days go by, let time pass,
> And in time the wild beasts grow tame in the forests.
> In time difficulties and hardships are lightened.
> Necessities, suffering and disease are cured and made well.
> In time the storms and turmoils recede
> And the hot grows cold, the icy comes to the boil.
> In time the clouds and mists dissolve,
> And in time curses turn to great prayers.

The *Erotokritos* quickly established itself in Crete as a folk poem as well as a literary epic. It acquired its own special tune for performance by *rhymadori*, many of whom knew large chunks of it by heart. Some almost certainly knew all ten thousand lines. George Psychoundakis claims that his father, who was illiterate, knew the whole poem. Many of the couplets of the *Erotokritos* are now part of the common Cretan repertoire of *mantinades*; it is difficult to know whether Kornaros took them from the folk or *vice versa*. In any case this popularity of the *Erotokritos* is one reason for its rapid transmission and its place as the national poem. And parts of other poems – *The Fair Shepherdess* and *Erophile* – found their way into folk poetry as well.

The *Erotokritos* was written probably not many years before the Turks took Crete, and left the island in 1669 with the refugees. 'Should all the Cretans be gathered together,' wrote Marinos Bounialis in his poem on the Cretan War, 'There are not, I judge, ten thousand left alive from that time, for they were killed and enslaved and parcelled out, poor things, to various lands. . . . And if two meet, they don't recognize each other, only when one says, "From what place are you, stranger?" and the other says, "From Crete", they take each other's hands and weep.' Such exiles, and Bounialis himself was one, carried Cretan art and learning and literature away from the doomed island. In 1713 the first edition of *Erotokritos* was printed in Venice. The editor wrote that he had decided to print the *Erotokritos*:

an old poem, which is so praised and honoured in the islands of the Adriatic, and in the Peloponnese, and indeed in the famous land of Zakynthos, where are still to be found the descendants of the wretched Cretans who found a friendly refuge there after the capture of their country. It was these who popularized the poem, which is composed in the natural Cretan tongue, and spread it throughout the island, and to other places, where it appears most pleasant and graceful to all such as read it.

The natural Cretan tongue. This is the importance of Cretan literature, and this is what caused trouble. One Dionysius Photinus in 1818 decided to translate the *Erotokritos* with its 'barbarous and almost incomprehensible words' into the sweeter language of his day – by which he meant a stilted neo-classical Greek. Such tampering was not uncommon; the prologue of *Erophile* begs that those who dislike the Cretan expressions will compose their own poem instead, and *not* corrupt the natural, genuine idiom of the poem as it stands. Luckily the philistines who wished to take away the Cretan flavour were an intellectual minority. The people went on listening. In fact the glory of Cretan literature is that it forged an expressive, flexible, rapid language, dignified yet unstilted, and the fifteen-syllable line which could contain it (the two things are inseparable). It took the poets to recognize this – Solomos and Palamas, who cried shame on the nation which had still not realized that the poet of the *Erotokritos* was the great and immortal poet of the Greek nation.

'The fact that has tragic significance,' writes Sepheris, 'is that after a few years the blossoming which had given Theotokopoulos and the line of the *Erotokritos* is cut down suddenly and finally. Such is the fate of the race. Always at the frontiers of places and of epochs; as soon as there is a blossoming in preparation, some destruction threatens it. The endless dialogue of Greek history.'

The *Erotokritos* is full of a sense of the fragility of human aspirations, as if Kornaros knew the destruction which threatened the Cretan blossoming. And probably he did.

> Whoever seeks the great things of this world,
> And does not know how here he is a traveller on the road,
> But takes pride in his nobility, boasts of his wealth,
> I hold him a cipher, he is to be accounted mad,
> These things are blossoms and flowers, they pass by, they are gone,
> And the times change them, often they destroy them.
> Like glass they shatter, like smoke they are gone,
> They never stand unshaken, but they run away, they go. . . .

Alongside this sense of change and time, there is light. Like Vergil, Kornaros floods his poem with light.

The Great Island

With this light I see the *Erotokritos* circulating among the enslaved race ... going from door to door, from ear to ear, filling souls with hope; and Erotokritos coming to free Aretousa from prison, and the world shining to the very corners of the sky; and the little boat travelling, loaded with the music of a whole world, with this epic of the Greek seashore; and the romance of chivalry turning into a history of the troubles of *Romaiosyne*, the troubles of the Greeks.*

Thus Sepheris expresses the debt of the Greeks to Kornaros and the Cretan renaissance.

* *Romaiosyne* means Greekness. The Greeks have been called *Romaioi* (Romans) ever since the country became Christian. Since that time, until fairly recently, the word Hellene carried a slightly pedantic flavour. In the vernacular it came to mean 'pagan': one of the old order. 'Hellene' so far lost its original force that in the fifteenth century the church of Santa Sophia was for the Orthodox 'a haunt of demons and an altar of the Hellenes', in the words of Doukas.

Now of course the wheel has come round again and the Greeks are Hellenes. The shift of meaning was bound to take place as soon as the war of independence increased the Greeks' preoccupation with their identity. It is *Romaios* which is now used pedantically or self-consciously.

6
The Fall of Candia

An Ottoman empire established in the Aegean could not fail to covet Crete. It was perhaps the fall of Cyprus in 1571 which brought home to the Venetians how precarious their position was, and how Crete, the last surviving Latin principality, was become a magnet that must attract the Turks. For in the years following 1571 the island saw not only the extraordinary appointment of Foscarini as Proveditor, but also a rigorous attempt to strengthen the crumbling defences of Crete. A Venetian document of 1593 tells how since the war, that is since the fall of Cyprus, garrisons have been installed, fortresses built or repaired, at Palaiokastro on the harbour of Frascia (this on the ruins of Pescatore's Genoese castle), at Suda on the island of Fraronesi, on the island of St Theodore off Canea, on Spinalonga and on Grambousa. There is something almost desperate about this activity. For without total domination of the sea, the Venetians could not hope to remain in Crete except as unwanted guests, pinned down in their castles, harassed on one side by a sullen population and on the other by the damaging incursions of their enemies. For those who could see, it had been evident for thirty years that Crete was no longer safe.

Khaireddin Barbarossa, the pirate, commander of Suleiman the Magnificent's fleet, visited Crete in 1538. This was no insignificant private adventurer scouring the coasts for plunder. Suleiman had lent the pirate nearly two hundred warships, with which he had sailed through the Greek waters capturing islands almost without opposition. Aegina, Paros, Naxos, Santorin, Mykonos, Chios, Amorgos and, on a second expedition, Karystos and Siphnos fell. Barbarossa then turned to Crete. Starting near Canea, his fleet sailed along the north coast towards Sitea. The pirates stopped frequently to devastate crops, to carry off animals and slaves in thousands. Rethymnon was sacked. But Crete was too big an island to succumb to these methods which had worked well enough in the Cyclades. Barbarossa's methods were haphazard. If his assault had been better organized, more determined, he might well have taken Crete. The fortifications of Candia were undergoing one of their periodic reinforcements at the time, which partly explains the extreme terror of the inhabitants. The populace was hostile, for though there were many who assisted the Turks in the next century, the formidable pirate inspired only panic and loathing among the majority. He sailed away. But the expedition served as an example, and for months the coasts of Crete were not free of marauding Turkish or pirate ships.

The only novelty in Barbarossa's attack was its magnitude; for, as the reader will have guessed by now, hardly a decade could elapse in Cretan history without the appearance of raiding ships. Turkish pirates had ravaged the Sitea area in 1471; destroyed Toplou monastery in 1498. A few years before Khaireddin came, the Venetian Proveditor Canale even succeeded in capturing a pirate chief off Canea, with four of his ships, and in releasing the slaves on board. Khaireddin's attack however was unprecedented in scope.

It is hard for us, whose shores have been comparatively secure for so long, to appreciate the menace of these corsairs. Invasion from the sea presents peculiar terrors to the mind. Coasts are so long. Not every village can be near enough to a Martello tower or Frankish castle. Mothers could terrify their children with the threat that Boney would come; how much worse were the corsairs, whose nocturnal and unheralded descents were a present threat for over three hundred years. The Barbary State, forged by the brothers Barbarossa, had no *raison d'être* other than piracy. Material and human plunder supported the economy. Algiers, the headquarters, contained more than twenty-five thousand slaves in the mid-sixteenth century.

The activities of the corsairs extended beyond the Mediterranean. The Rev. Devereux Spratt, ancestor of the Captain Spratt who travelled in Crete in the last century, was actually taken prisoner just off the Irish coast, after the Protestant rebellion of 1640: 'before wee were out of sight of land, wee were all taken by an Algire piratt, who putt the men in chaines and stockes. This thing was so greivious that I began to question Providence, and accused Him of injustice in His dealeings with me, untill the Lord made it appear otherwise, by ensueing mercye; upon my arrivall in Algires I found pious Christians, which changed my former thoughts of God.' This story had a happy ending. Spratt was freed on the paying of a ransom, but elected to stay with the other English captives in their misfortune; two years later, on the issue of a proclamation that all free men must be gone, he returned to England. For the Cretans, who lacked influential friends, such fortune was rare. There is a church in the Mylopotamos district which was erected in gratitude by a priest and his wife who came home after many years' captivity.

The Fall of Candia

It is these years of slavery in distant places, and banishment for rebelliousness which reinforced the Greek preoccupation with *xeniteia*, 'being-abroad', a major theme in the folk poetry, and one which has been transmitted into the modern poetry. It is not uncommon to find references to Cretans in exile who have 'died of homesickness', like some of those Sphakians who were banished after the rebellion of 1571.

This gloomy picture is relieved by two stories, both from much later, whose interest must excuse their irrelevance. Both are of Cretan girls who, in different ways, made good. The first was carried off to Constantinople when the Turks took Canea in 1645, and in consequence of her great beauty was presented to the Sultan Ibrahim, who gave her to his Grand Vizier. Her young son remained in Crete, was brought up in the Orthodox faith, and went to Padua to take a degree in law. When Tournefort visited Rethymnon he stayed with this son, Dr Patelaros, who told him how on his return from Padua he had set out for Constantinople to see his mother, who had become vastly rich. A traditionally Greek recognition scene took place. 'He made himself known to her by a wart behind his ear; this wart, which he took care to show us, is crown'd with a blackish spot, not unlike a half-moon in form. She presently remembered this mark, and would fain have made use of it as an argument that he was ordain'd to be a Mussulman; which to bring about, no sollicitations were wanting.'

They even offered the doctor valuable property in Wallachia, so he later claimed, to get him to change his faith. But in vain. He resolved to die in the religion of his forefathers, and, says Tournefort, 'he leads an agreeable life, under the protection of France'.

The heroine of the second story was captured by Muslims in 1821. The villagers of Apodoulo, when they heard of the approach of the enemy, retired up Mt Ida, leaving behind only two centenarians who were killed despite their age. One Captain Alexandros, however, having lost four children in a recent epidemic, and wishing to isolate his remaining two from the contagion, put them in a hut outside the village and told them to keep quiet at all costs. The main body of Muslims passed the hut without action but a straggler looked inside in the hope of loot. The two children were abducted; the girl sold into slavery in Egypt.

Pashley met this Alexandros when he visited the village and heard the happy sequel; how in 1829, eight years after the girl's disappearance, an Englishman, with his wife and several domestics, arrived in Canea. The party of visitors made haste to Apodoulo to find Alexandros. The wife was the lost daughter. 'It would be as difficult to describe as it is easy to conceive the joy experienced by the parents on receiving this full proof . . . of the happy fortune which had attended their child. She who had been for years deplored by them as dwelling in Egyptian bondage was the wife of an English gentleman.'

By 1571, then, the Cretan question gave Venice pause. In this year not only did the Sphakians revolt, but also the Turks descended again on the west of Crete, and burnt the unfortunate city of Rethymnon, which seems to have suffered the same fate for the third time in 1597. While the Turkish fleet was in Suda bay, Cretans of Rethymnon, afraid of reprisals for the murder of a local Venetian nobleman of the domineering and oppressive Chiosa family, sent and asked for the Turks' support, hailing them as deliverers. This was ominous of disaster. In their alarm the Serene Republic sent Giacomo Foscarini as Proveditor General with extraordinary powers – 'Dictator of the island Candia' as he is designated in a memorial inscription – to restore the waning fortunes of Crete. Foscarini, a man of prodigious talents and energies, of justice fired by austerity, stayed more than four years. His report is the most valuable document in existence for the study of the condition of Crete in the sixteenth century.

Foscarini soon after his arrival in 1574 issued a proclamation inviting all those with grievances to appear before him and obtain justice. He then studied the condition and organization of Crete, finding evidence of inefficiency and abuses at every point in the social structure. They merit attention, for they show the rottenness at the core of a feudal system of this sort.

In 1574 Crete was divided into 479 fiefs. Of these 394 belonged to Venetian families, 25 to the Roman church, 25 to the Serene Republic, and the remaining 35 to Cretan families. Originally, the Venetian feudarchs had well-defined obligations in return for their privileges; each knight had to maintain a horse and complete equipment and had to be ready to turn out at any time in defence of the island. Smaller fiefs belonged to landowners who constituted the infantry. But as time passed the laws fell into disrepute and Venetians, despite the rule that fiefs were inalienable to Greeks, began to sell secretly to native Cretans. Many returned to Venice. Those who remained were more and more assimilated with the Greeks, in customs, language, even religion. When Foscarini arrived he found that this debasement of the nobility had gone so far that the island had no defence. In country areas the fiefs had been divided into small lots, whose owners would share the military obligations; few, as individuals, could afford to maintain a horse and equipment. Foscarini describes how at the biennial parade of the feudarchs at Candia, the so-called knight would borrow a horse from a friend, and send some farm-labourer into the parade, ignorant of the arts of horsemanship and of bearing arms; the crowd would run to see this ridiculous spectacle, and pelt the riders with stones and rotten oranges. Such knights, now totally Hellenized, recalled their origin only by their resounding Latin names; Dandolo, Cornaro, Venier, Grimani, Sanudo and the rest.

Those fiefs assigned to Cretans were no better. The fiefs had originally been granted to the aristocrats of Crete, the *archontopouli*. But this privileged class had increased; in 1573 there were four hundred well-attested descendants of the *archontopouli* entitled to call themselves feudarchs. But the number of fiefs remained the same, thirty-five. Hence a subdivision of the fiefs, and those bitter rivalries among the impoverished Cretan aristocrats which led to blood-feuds like that between the Pateroi of Sphakia and the Papadopouloi of Rethymnon; a feud bitter and destructive, for the Pateroi's descents to the lowlands caused enough damage to invite Cavalli's punitive expedition of 1571.

It was not only the Cretan feudarchs whose numbers had swelled. Signal service to the Republic earned its reward: either elevation to the Cretan nobility, or for the very few, like the Kallergis family, to the nobility of Venice itself. With the passage of time it had become possible to buy one's admission to the 'Nobilitas Cretensis'. Substantial privileges, too (exemption from service in the galleys or on the coastal fortifications), had been distributed recklessly, sometimes even to serfs or to whole communities, which therefore attracted the inhabitants of other villages. The balance of the population was thus affected.

The peasants, *contadini*, were the ones who stood to suffer from the feudal system and from every abuse of it. Liable for service on land and sea, exploited by the feudarchs at home; living, most of them, in the words of Corner, 'without bread, with only olives, carobs and water'. Foscarini reports that the Venetian *cavalieri* had reduced the peasants to a condition worse than that of slaves, so that they dared not even complain of any injustice. They were tyrannized in such a manner that all their produce was appropriated by the knights. '*Sono di piu i contadini obligati et aggravati di tante altre angarie che cosa incredibile.*' The *angarie* are compulsory services.

Such was the state of Crete revealed by Foscarini. Without energetic reform the island would be like a rotten fruit ready to fall into the lap of the waiting Turks. Foscarini did what he could. He purged the catalogue of feudarchs, made military service compulsory again, and disposed of an effective force of 1,200 cavalry before he left Crete. He purged also the inflated order of the Cretan nobility, and imposed austere restrictions on future grants of privileges or titles. He cunningly made use of the 'privileged' class, those who were exempt from the galleys, rather than cancelling their exemptions outright; for he enrolled them in a gendarmerie – *ordinanza* – in detachments under local captains. These techniques worked well so long as Foscarini stayed in the island.

There was nothing for which Foscarini, as Proveditor, was not responsible, and there was no part of Cretan life and business which he did not touch. As well as restoring the old feudal military system he attempted to increase the revenue by imposing higher duties on foreign importers, and by improving the land. But he must have seen that all his reforms stood or fell together; a weakness at any point in the intricate structure would spread like a cancer through the tissues; if the nobles would not co-operate, then the peasants would revolt again, the land would go unproductive, the coasts undefended. Foscarini was therefore particularly harsh to two classes whom he regarded as dangerous trouble-makers; the Orthodox clergy, and the Jews. Some of the priests were banished. The Jews were repressed. Foscarini held the Jewesses responsible for the increasing laxity of the city of Candia, with their easy morals. Candia, he thought, was becoming full of semi-Jewish bastards. From now on, a man caught in intercourse with a Jewess was liable to ten years in the galleys, or banishment for life with a fine; the woman to death by fire. Christians were forbidden to work as servants for Jews. Jewish women could now hardly stir from the ghetto.

The fortunes of the Jewish colony are an interesting sideline to the history of Crete. We know very little about the Jews until the second half of the fifteenth century, when Jewish immigrants arrived to reinforce the original Jewish stock. They lived in the three big towns; most of them in Candia. Relations with both Greeks and Latins were bad. The Greeks were used to accuse the Jews of despising the Christian religion, and sacrificing Christian children in their barbarous rites. They also considered physical contact with Jews to be dangerous; if a Jew touched something which was up for sale in the market, he could be forced to buy it at an inflated price. Anti-semitism was so prevalent in the sixteenth century that the Patriarch of Constantinople issued an encyclical in 1567 recommending to the Cretans that they treat the Jews better. In the war of 1538 (Khaireddin's attack with the Turkish fleet) the Jews had to ask Venetian protection to escape massacre; the

The Fall of Candia

Cretans thought they were harbouring Turks in the Candia ghetto.

Jewish policy was to lie low and avoid trouble. They suffered from Venetian discrimination as well as Greek prejudice; for instance, their share of the taxes was unfairly high. In Candia, where in the early 1600s there were eight hundred Jews out of a total population of about 11,500, they paid usually over 20 per cent of the taxes. The Jews made their living by moneylending and the export of wine and household goods. There were complaints from the Greeks about a Jewish 'monopoly' in the wine trade; and from the nobles about the extortionate practices of Jewish usurers.

Dapper reports that among the few who remained in Candia when the Turks moved in in 1669 were three Jews. By 1700 there were about a thousand Jews in Candia again.

After four years of unremitting labour in which he tried to restore not only the pristine military defences and discipline of Crete, but also its antique morals, Foscarini returned to Venice and was duly thanked. His work did not last; for even though he himself was in most respects a humane and prescient man, the system he re-imposed contained the evils which must cause its own destruction. Only ten years later the Proveditor Garzoni found the same evils rampant; he reports of the peasant *contadini*:

The women are dressed in rags, the children naked, the men half-naked. Yet these wretched men are obliged according to ancient custom to perform two *angarie* per annum for their feudarch: (i) a twelve-day stint of unpaid work, and (ii) further work for as long as the knight requires at the same rate as was paid two hundred years before.

The peasant pays his feudarch every year the *terziaria* – a fixed amount, whether the harvest succeeds or fails. And on top of this, he is forced to pay so much else in kind that the feudarch appropriates almost all his oil, wine, produce and even livestock.

For the government of the island, Castellani, Secretaries, and 'Captains against robbers' (*capitani contra fures*) are sent to the eparchies. All these are vultures insatiable . . . devouring whatever remains over from the extortions of the feudarchs.

The peasant is in constant fear, day and night, lest he be taken and thrown into the galley and sent to do service far away; a service from which few return; most are slaughtered in battles, or drowned at sea, or die from epidemics and privations. The peasant is forced, if he has some small property, vines, land or livestock, to sell them at knockdown prices in order to raise the amount required to buy him off this terrible *angaria*. If he cannot raise this fee, he takes to the mountains. . . .

Thus Garzoni, reminding the Republic that under the present

The Great Island

conditions the Cretans will support the Turks when it comes to war, recommends a new deal for the peasant, and punishment for the oppressive civil servants and capitani. But again, nothing was changed. In 1592 the unfortunate island was swept by another bout of the plague; according to Filippo Pasqualigo, Capitano di Candia, it carried off over half the population of that city. In all some 14,000 died, and thus, while the people were subdued, the defences were weakened. A paragraph in the 1610 report of Dolfin Venier, duke of Candia, shows how nervous the Republic had become. Ships have been landing on the South Coast and meeting with a hospitable reception; the sailors pay for what they take in the way of provisions, etc., and win the hearts of the islanders. All this for a purpose as yet unknown. And these ships are armed – '*galeoni armati di diversi Principi*'. This could provoke Turkey, says Venier; for these ships are clearly hostile to the Turks and are being succoured on Venetian land. He therefore recommends 'five years at the oar with irons on the feet' as a deterrent punishment for the next offenders.

And this nervousness induced further brutality. Thus Fra Paolo Sarpi, in his address to the Serene Republic in 1615; 'The surest way is to keep good garrisons to awe them, and not to use them to arms or musters, in hopes of being assisted by them in an extremity; for they will always shew ill inclinations proportionably to the strength they shall be masters of, they being of the nature of gally-slaves . . . wine and bastinadoes ought to be their share, and keep good nature for a better occasion.'

Sarpi represents those forces against which Foscarini and Garzoni had to fight. Those Cretans who, alarmed by these forces, fled to Constantinople, were able to inform the Turks of the state of Crete's defences; also of the state of mind of the inhabitants, who would eagerly support anyone who should come in the guise of liberator. There was not long to wait.

A Turkish convoy was attacked by a squadron of the Maltese Knights of St John; among the captives was the nurse of Sultan Ibrahim I, a favourite of his. The marauding ships in their escape put in at a Cretan harbour. This was the pretext for which the Turks had waited. Ibrahim himself spurred on his men in their preparations. For a time, despite the religious scruples of the Mufti, the fiction was maintained that these preparations were for a punitive expedition against the Knights of Malta; but the Venetians could not be deceived for long. Soon the Proveditor Andrea Corner was strengthening the forti-

The Fall of Candia

fications of Crete; and the Republic was requesting the help of friendly states all over Europe – and in Asia – in the defence of this bastion of Latinity. But Venice's own record in the Levant was not one to inspire Christian states to lend arms; and besides, the great nations of Europe had pressing engagements of their own in 1645.

As so often, the attack came in the west. Canea fell after two months' siege; the unfortunate Turkish Commander, Ioussuf Pasha, was strangled at the Sultan's orders after his return to Constantinople, whether for his prodigious wealth or because of the terrible losses sustained by his army (estimated at over 40,000). Rethymnon fell soon afterwards. In 1648 the Turks were before the walls of Candia. During the next twenty-one years, the duration of this most gruelling of wars, all the resistance of Venice was concentrated in the city. The country areas did not count; in any case they favoured the Turk. Candia was defended with a despairing tenacity. At home, the Republic imposed extraordinary taxes, sold peerages to raise money. To divert the enemy she launched expeditions against Turkish parts in the Aegean, Paros, Melos, Chios. Her ships attacked Turkish convoys on their way to Crete as they left the Dardanelles. The war dragged on; Venice was holding out, but it was impossible to say with what prospect of gain.

The Grand Vizier Ahmed Koprili arrived in 1666 to take command in person and risk his reputation, perhaps his life, on a successful outcome. Soon the garrison was in difficulties. They were a motley collection, less than 10,000 strong, of Venetians, Greeks, and foreigners, whether volunteer or mercenary, including Savoyards, French, German, Italian, and Knights of Malta. It was not easy to feed them and the civilian population, nor to keep up the incessant supply of powder and shot; even though until the end Venice kept open her communications by sea. Her fleet lay off the island of Dia (then called Standia) opposite the town.

Francesco Morosini, who was to do further good service to the Republic in the Peloponnese many years later, organized the defence. The town, by 1669, was a shambles; the streets strewn with bullets, cannonballs, and débris; the earth pitted with craters from the grenades which were consumed so prodigally; there was hardly a building whose walls were not holed by cannon shot. On every side the eye encountered soldiers, killed, wounded or maimed.

At the eleventh hour Europe took notice. The Pope supported the Venetians' pleas for aid; and in response King Louis XIV sent the Dukes of Beaufort and Navailles with a fleet and some seven thousand men. They arrived on 19 June to find the defenders hard pressed. The

The Great Island

Turks were concentrating their attack on two of the seven bastions in the city wall, the Saboniera and the St Andrea, these two being situated at either end of the wall, on the seashore. The arrival of these belated reinforcements inspired an extreme joy in the besieged. Every piece of artillery sounded in salute. All the bells pealed. The towers and ramparts were hung with red banners.

On the 27th in the silence of night the Duke of Beaufort led a sortie from the eastern gate of St George. At first all went well. But after daybreak the explosion of a captured magazine among the Venetian-French troops caused panic and flight. The Duke, disgusted according to Dapper by this display of cowardice, refused to retreat an inch, and was overcome. His body was not recovered. The failure of this sortie signalled disaster; and dissension now sprung up among the defenders, for the Duke of Navailles refused to lead a further sortie unless his French troops were preceded by 4,000 Venetians. They knew better the state of the Turkish works, he claimed. Morosini, wishing to spare his exhausted men, would not agree. And now, after their decisive victory, 'les assiégeants entassèrent toutes ces têtes en un monceau, suivant leur coûtume, et en firent une espèce de trophée. Ensuite pour témoigner leur joie, ils les mirent sur la pointe de leurs piques, où ils les atachoient avec des cordes toutes parées des fleurs; ce qu'ils faisoient par moquerie, prétendant braver le Mars François, comme ils disoient.'

The French, depleted and embittered, sailed home; and were followed by others, volunteers, Germans and Swedes. The garrison now numbered only 4,000. Morosini surrendered on 5 September 1669, wisely sparing his own men and the enemy further expense in bloodshed. Under the terms of capitulation the Venetians were given twelve days to leave, and kept their fortified islands at Suda, Grambousa and Spinalonga as reminders of departed power. Dapper's description of those twelve days is strangely affecting:

Pendant qu'on fût occupé à remettre la ville de Candie entre les mains du Grand Visir, il se fit un grand silence dans le camp des énemis, et l'on ne commit aucun désordre dans la ville. Durant les douze jours marquez pour se retirer, les soldats se salüoient de dessus les bastions et les ramparts, et parloient entre eux des accidents et des aventures de la guerre, comme s'ils n'avoient jamais eu de differend, et ils ne se donnèrent dans tout ce temps-là les uns aux autres aucun sujet de plainte.

Authorities differ slightly on the statistics of this siege. By any account the expense was enormous. Dapper gives these figures with a great show of precision: the Turks lost 118,754 killed and wounded; the Venetians lost 30,985. The Turks made 56 assaults; the Venetians made 96 sorties. The Turks exploded 473 mines; the Venetians exploded 1,173.

The Fall of Candia

The Venetians used 50,370 tons of powder; threw 48,170 bombs of 50 to 500 lb. weight; 100,960 copper and iron grenades; 276,743 cannon balls; and used 18,044,951 lb. of lead and 13,012,500 lb. of wick.

In the Representation [says Tournefort] presented to the Divan by the High Treasurer of the Empire, concerning the extraordinary Expenses for the last three years of the Siege of Candia, there is mention made of 700,000 Crowns, given as Rewards to such Deserters who turn'd Turks, and to the soldiers who had distinguish'd themselves; and to such as had brought in Heads of Christians, for which they were allow'd a Sequin per head. This Representation sets forth, that 100,000 Cannon-Ball had been fir'd against the place; that seven Bashaws had laid their Bones there, as also four score Principal Officers, 10,400 Janissaries, besides other militia.

At the conference to settle the terms of capitulation, Morosini was represented by two men, one of them the Englishman Colonel Thomas Anand; and the Grand Vizier by his adviser, the Greek Panagiotes Nikouses, the first Greek to be Grand Dragoman of the Porte. Later this post became a Greek preserve, as Greeks began to infiltrate more and more the Ottoman administration.

The siege had lasted two years three months and twenty-seven days.

After all the inhabitants had left, except for the two priests, some old and decrepit Greeks, and three Jews, the city was formally handed over. A citizen offered the Vizier the keys of Candia on a silver salver. In return Koprili gave sequins and a robe: and wished to give the same to the gallant Morosini, who politely refused. As the Turks entered through the shattered walls of the St Andrea bastion, the Venetian garrison, two and a half thousand sick men, half naked, left the town by another gate and took to their ships. Eight days later, the Grand Vizier was saying his prayers in St Andrew's Church, now a mosque. The head of St Titus, most venerated relic of the Christian island, left for Venice. The educated Cretans, bearers of a culture which had fed on Italian tolerance and civilization, left for the Seven Islands of the Ionian Sea, where the dim light of Hellenic art and letters was to keep on burning, modestly at first, and finally to blaze up when the poet Solomos from Zante proclaimed free Greece at last. Crete was left to a dark age.

7

Turkish Crete

A dark age.

What can a man say of a country inhabited by Turks, if he is confined to what he sees of it in its present condition? Almost their whole life is spent in idleness: to eat rice, drink water, smoke tobacco, sip coffee, is the life of a Mussulman. The speculative sort (of which there are not many) employ themselves in reading the Alcoran, consulting the several interpreters of that book, thumbing over the annals of their empire; what's all this to us? The things that attract strangers thither, must be a search after antiquities, study of natural history, commerce.

So Tournefort in the first detailed report on Crete under the new master. He saw much to criticize, sometimes unjustly. By 1700 the Turks had had time to make their mark on the island. But Tournefort found that they entirely neglected to repair the ports and walls of the towns, devastated after the war of Candia. Candia itself was the carcass of a great city; hardly anything but rubbish. The only buildings of which the Turks took reasonable care were the fountains, since 'they are great water drinkers, and their religion obliges 'em very frequently to wash every part of their body'.

Tournefort criticizes the gardens round Canea, planted without order or symmetry; the figs insipid, the melons almost as bad. Skills were lacking; the Turks cannot graft, or candy citrons. 'As for those pretended palm trees [in the east, at Hierapetra], they are so bunglingly done, that they may pass for pines'; but this is unfair – there is a grove of excellent palms at Vai on the east coast. The country is in a sorry condition. Even the smells are abominable; for, as the world knows, the Turks inter their dead upon the highways: 'this practice were extraordinarily well, did they dig the graves deep enough. Candia being a very hot country, these smells are very offensive under the wind....'

It is not surprising that a bitter note creeps into Tournefort's account; sixty years earlier, a distinguished visiting French botanist would have been treated with respect; he would have found himself among people he understood. But the Turks were barbarians; when Pococke went out

Turkish Crete

to copy an inscription at Gortyn the Turks gathered around and insulted him to such a degree that he was obliged to give up and retire until his janissary returned. It must have been a shock for Europeans to discover that they were not safe from the arbitrary demands of the pashas. When Ali Pasha, 'that voluptuous minister', was viceroy at Megalokastro, he was troubled by a distemper which did not respond to Greek treatment (syphilis). A visiting French dignitary recommended an Irish surgeon he had aboard, and the Irishman put the pasha in the powdering tub. At the height of the salivation, the great man, thinking himself about to die, summoned his council and sentenced the surgeon to have a hundred bastinadoes. The council demurred and the pasha recovered. Thus the story ends happily; but the unfortunate surgeon Teague gained such a reputation that he had to spend nearly twenty-four hours a day in '''nointing the Mussulmans'.

Most of the pashas were rapacious. One having been given a rich brocade vest by the French demanded another on the grounds that he had two wives. 'The toppingest lords think it no shame to beg.'

All this by the time of Tournefort's visit, when Crete had been Turkish for only thirty-one years (dating from the fall of Candia in 1669). In general, what can be said about one period of Turkish domination can be said about another, for the Turks were at least consistent in their extortion and indifference to reform; until 1821 at any rate. If we see, then, the chief differences between Venetian and Turkish rule we shall have a fair idea of how the island was administered from 1669 to 1821.

The first difference we have seen: under the Turks the cultural and artistic life of the cities Candia, Canea and Rethymon stopped. The Ottoman Turks were nomad fighters, uninterested in the arts, cunning to adopt the talents of their subject peoples in their own interests. Thus Greeks were prominent in administration and trade throughout the empire. But there was no need for art; and so the cultural centres of Hellenism were Venice and the Ionian islands.

The second difference, and it is crucial, was over religion. Very rarely – it happened once during the war of Candia – fanatics meditated the extermination of Christianity throughout the empire. Usually however the Turks were much wiser. Since the fall of Constantinople the Turks had used the patriarchy; Mohammed II, by engineering the election of Gennadius II as patriarch and confirming his rights and privileges as ethnarch of the entire Orthodox community, set a pattern which lasted throughout Ottoman suzerainty. Certainly the Turks manipulated the patriarchy; the office, like every other office in the

The Great Island

Ottoman Empire, was to be bought, and a recalcitrant patriarch might be deposed by the sultan. Nevertheless, the main tenet of Turkish policy was stable: religious toleration. One might rather call it indifference; outside a very limited area of social and economic activity, the Turks were literally not interested in what the Christians were doing.

This religious toleration, indulged at first as an insurance against the Catholic states of western Europe, had its effect on the Cretans; they were induced by Turkish promises to support the Venetians only half-heartedly, or even to assist the conqueror. Theory and practice differed. Many of the churches of Canea and Candia were converted into mosques as soon as those cities fell. Still, the Turks made what looked like a good start by expelling the Latin priests and returning the sees to Orthodox bishops. The first Metropolitan under this new dispensation, Neophytus Patellaros, was installed at Canea while Candia was still in the hands of the Venetians.

Theoretically, therefore, the Orthodox church now existed once more in Crete in its pristine form, with its own bishops. In fact, however, the Turkish assurances soon were seen to be delusive. In theory, and according to the Koran, Christians were not to be forced to renounce their faith; they were people of the Book, one stage better than outright heathen. In practice, however, there are other ways of inducing conversion than putting a pistol to someone's head. The material advantages of the Muslims were so great that conversions took place on an extraordinary scale.

Under the Venetians society was classified into 'peasants', 'serfs', 'nobles', and somewhere apart stood the original Venetian colonists who formed the nucleus of the nobility. Against this last class the others might revolt. Society under the Turks was not classless; but the divisions cut at different points in the social structure. Most fundamental was the religious difference. The world, for Muslims, was divided into the House of Mohammed and the House of War. Within the Muslim world, all men were divided into believers and infidel, and the infidel had no rights. Christians were Rayahs, human cattle who belonged to the Sultan and had to buy all their privileges, including the very right to live. Thus every Christian was liable to the capitation-tax or *haratch*, which secured safety of life and limb; and to property taxes; and to import and export duties heavier than those paid by Muslims. The Muslims were exempt from such humiliations as the *haratch*. They had the advantage over Christians in every way; at law, for instance, a case between Muslim and Christian was tried before a *cadi* who could penalize the Christian far more severely than the Muslim – even by enslavement or confiscation of property for quite minor offences.

This great divide of faithful and infidel cut right across racial barriers; a Greek convert to Islam was at once, and automatically, one of the chosen, able to bully and oppress his old co-religionists and compatriots. Hence the multitudinous apostasy in Crete. Not only in Crete, of course; but on a much greater scale in Crete than in, say, the Morea. Pashley compares Sicily under the Saracen conquest, where 'such was the docility of the rising generation, that 15,000 boys were circumcised and clothed, on the same day with the son of the Fatimite Caliph'. The Cretan peasants could not afford to remain Christian; as more and more turned to Islam, the burdens on the remaining Christians must have become correspondingly more crushing. But curiously it was the Muslim philosophy itself which ensured that Christianity should never be ruthlessly and systematically persecuted; for as time passed the Muslims saw that they were dependent on a hard core of Christians for their taxes. A world-wide universal House of Mohammed was a noble and inspiring conception; but it would entail burdens on the followers of the Prophet which fell now only on the infidel.

The apostates were the bane of Crete. They are often called Turks, which adds to the confusion of Cretan history of these times. The evil was rife even in Tournefort's time.

The Turks throughout the island are mostly renegadoes, or sons of such: the true Turks, take 'em one with another, are much honester men than the renegadoes. A good Turk says nothing when he sees a Christian eat swine's flesh, or drink wine; a renegado shall scold or insult 'em for it, tho' in private he will eat and drink his fill of both. It must be confessed, these wretches sell their soul for a pennyworth; all they get in exchange for their religion, is a vest, and the privilege of being exempt from the capitation tax, which is not above five crowns a year.

Tournefort may be right in deprecating the advantages of conversion; but only in those early days. The more renagadoes there were the more insolent and oppressive they became, so that by 1821 the Christian peasant was worse off than at any other time in Cretan history.

The Christians naturally had a hearty dislike for the renegadoes, and an extreme hatred of the Muslim faith. It was Muslim practice, in war, to kill prisoners. The Christians did the same. When Nicephorus Phocas recovered Crete for the Byzantine empire in 961, the inhabitants of Candia were butchered; and Theodosius the Deacon praises the Emperor Romanus II for his fatherly care for the souls of his own flock, in that by this massacre he prevented the pollution of his soldiers by unbaptized women. Hartley in his *Researches in Greece* reported that

The Great Island

Turkish women had been the downfall even of Greek bishops, thereby causing incalculable injury to these ecclesiastics themselves; and also bringing infinite scandal on their profession. 'These inconveniences', says Pashley, 'the Cretan mode of warfare effectually prevented.'

Once the island settled down under Turkish rule, however, there was no time for perpetual animosity. Certainly, even until the end of the nineteenth century, the latent animosity could be fanned into flame, as in the 1897 rebellion. Certainly renegade Muslims were often intolerable to their brother Cretans. Still, behind the quarrels, revolts and bitternesses, the two creeds got along together. It was in any case the privileges that went with Islam which caused the animosity, more than religious differences. The soil was not fertile for religious quarrels. The entire rural population spoke Greek, and Pashley found that even among the aghas Greek was usually the mother tongue. Gibbon's words apply to Muslim as well as Christian: 'In the East, as well as in the West, the Deity is addressed in an obsolete tongue, unknown to the majority of the congregation.' Cretan Mohammedans drank wine. Their knowledge of the Koran was minimal.

There was no objection to the Mohammedan marrying a Christian woman. The objection came from the Christian side; such a woman would be refused the sacrament until and unless she renounced her husband, it might be on the deathbed. She could hardly be prevented, however, from attending church. La Motraye in 1710 described a happy mixed-marriage: *'Ce couple vivoit fort bien ensemble: Ali-oglou alloit à la mosquée, et sa femme à l'église. Pour les enfants, ils étoient élevez dans la Mahometisme. Il ne faisoit point de scruple d'allumer pour elle la lampe les samedis, devant l'image de la Panagia.'* A hundred years later Mohammedans were still paying their respects to the Virgin, and standing godfather to Christian children.

Thus when we are told that in the eighteenth century the Mohammedans outnumbered the Christians by 200,000 to 60,000 we must remember first that the vast majority of these Mohammedans were Cretan, second that their faith was of a peculiar, bibulous Cretan nature. There were also a few crypto-Christians – probably not many. Pashley traced the history of one distinguished family, the Kurmulidhes of the Messara, whose children were secretly baptized with Christian names; then later circumcised and called Ibrahim or some such Mohammedan name. The family had influence, which they used with the Turks on behalf of the Christians in the Messara. But sometimes they were troubled with doubts about the propriety of this game. Eventually one of them went to the bishop of Jerusalem and asked his advice; he told them they were damned unless they confessed their faith openly. Thirty of the family then decided to confess to the pasha that they had been Christians all the time. The Metropolitan dissuaded them, pointing out how they would compromise other crypto-Christians and by assuring them that they were in no danger of damnation.

The family hardly survived the 1821 revolt; out of sixty-four men of the Kurmulidhes, only two were left alive. Their reputation was glorious for years afterwards; and portents attended the death of two of them. These were two brothers executed with a cousin in 1824 by Mustapha Bey. As always they were offered their lives if they would change their religion. The question was formulaic. 'Do you turn Turk or not?' 'No, I will not turn Turk. I was born Antony, I shall die Antony'. During the three nights following their beheading, the bishop of Rethymnon claimed to see a light descend on the two brothers' bodies. Fragments of their clothing, if burnt in the bedroom, were said to cure the sick.

In the social structure of Crete under the Turks the Christians represent the lower class, liable to taxes, impositions and even insults from the meanest Mohammedan. The open restrictions on religious freedom, however, were minimal. Perhaps the only one was the ban on church bells. Early on the Christians were ordered to deliver up their bells; many gave in a substitute and buried the real bell, handing on the secret of the hiding-place down the generations. This practice gave the Turks a convenient means of extortion. A rich man would be arrested and accused of concealing a bell on his land. He would have to buy his way out of prison. Permission to build and repair churches was needed from the City. Apart from such minor restrictions, the church could function as it wished, and indeed the Turkish archives at Heraklion show that there were severe penalties for anyone who violated the integrity of the monasteries. Except in time of war. Then, of course, the niceties of mutual respect went for nothing, and monasteries and churches were burnt, their occupants slaughtered. The Cretan clergy were peculiarly bellicose; their record as insurgents, martyrs, and fighters for freedom, as notable as that of any other province of the Greek world.

Crete was divided into three pashaliks, Heraklion, Rethymnon and Canea, the pasha at Heraklion being as a rule supreme over the other two. Since the pashas rarely stayed long, they had little interest in reform and just administration. 'The generality of the bashaws are rapacious, and in regard they buy their places at Constantinople, where everything goes by auction, they spare nothing to lick themselves whole.' In any case, a just pasha could hardly survive the pressure exerted on him from below by the aghas and janissaries. It was they who set the tone; if a pasha stood up to them they had him deposed, as happened in 1819.

Below the pashas were the landowners; beys who owned great estates, and perhaps commanded one of the garrisoned fortresses, and the aghas who owned the numerous small fiefs formed out of lands taken over from the Venetian noble feudarchs and the Latin church. It was they, and the janissaries, who ran Crete.

The janissaries are important. As founded in the fourteenth century, they were a corps of troops recruited from Christian children only. One boy from every Christian family might be snatched away to be brought up as a Mohammedan member of the Sultan's bodyguard. These tribute-children were a kind of praetorian guard. The tribute of children stopped in the seventeenth century, so the Cretans never suffered from it. But the janissaries, mercenary, arrogant and undisciplined, continued to be the military trustees of empire. It must be remembered that in theory all the Turks belonged to some military body.

Since all land belonged to the Sultan – with rare exceptions such as the island of Chios which belonged to the Sultana-Mother – every proprietor had originally to buy his fief from the Grand Signor. The purchaser could not then be dispossessed, and the land could be given in bequest. But a heavy tax was payable on it every year. Thus, as under the Venetians, the peasant producer was supporting his conqueror. The burden fell, ultimately, on the lowest class. In return for the taxes paid in cash and in kind the Christians received almost nothing in the way of public services, roads built, communications improved; at best, the slothful indifference of the Turks allowed them usually to conduct their own affairs, to educate their children in the customs of their ancestors for the coming of freedom.

The history of Crete under the Turks is the history of her revolts; sung by folk poets, by novelists like Kazantzakis and Prevelakis; regarded by the mountain Cretans as the natural state for the *palikari* (hero). As with the revolts against Venice, not all merit the telling. There is a uniformity in blood and heroism that in the end fatigues. Some years, however, cannot be ignored – 1770, 1821, 1866, 1897. The first of these, 1770, the year of Daskaloyiannis's revolt, is, together with 1866 and 1941, the most glorious year of Cretan history.

8

The Revolt of Daskaloyiannis

The Cretan heroic myth is rooted in the revolts against the Turks, of which there were not less than ten between 1770 and 1897. Of these the most magnificent was that of Daskaloyiannis, whose grand conception was to re-establish the old order, to restore *Romaiosyne*. He failed, of course, as did all the other rebel chieftains until the time of Venizelos. But, unlike those others who have gone down to history in comparative anonymity, like puppets mouthing the invariable formula 'Freedom or Death', Daskaloyiannis was lucky in having a chronicler. The revolt took place in 1770. Sixteen years later a shepherd from Sphakia copied down the story of Daskaloyiannis from the dictation of a master bard. In a personal epilogue to the poem the scribe left us his name, Siphis Skordylis, son of the priest Skordylis, and thus a branch of one of the twelve great families of Byzantine aristocrats sent to Crete by the Emperor Alexius Comnenus.[1]

> I began, and wrote a little every day . . .
> I held the paper and I held the pen
> And he told the story and I wrote it bit by bit.

'He' is Barba Pantzelios, the bard.

> His eyes filled with tears as he narrated,
> As he told me the plight of Daskaloyiannis.
> His speech was cut short, he was gripped by thoughts
> And from his entrails he uttered dark groans. . . .
> He told it me in rhyme, being a *rhymadoros*,
> For he has been given by God His greatest gift –
> What he did not see he knew, and what he saw he remembers,
> For he has a memory better than anyone.
> Many things his eyes saw and his ears heard,
> Trials, suffering and troubles sent his hair white.

The scribe adds a rider of a certain condescension to this sympathetic picture:

> But if these lines are at fault, the words graceless,
> If the lines are at fault, the words all confused,
> Have sympathy, you who listen – they are not by me!

The Great Island

It is pleasing that his own verses are not noticeably more polished than those of Pantzelios, the illiterate cheesemaker.

The poem, consisting of rather more than a thousand lines of the 'political' fifteen-syllable verse – in fact, about as much as could comfortably be recited and taken in in one evening – has a double interest, historical and literary. It is the fullest source for a badly documented episode. In his humdrum, pedestrian way Pantzelios manages to cram his song full of information, some of it mistaken. And it was a good story.

Daskaloyiannis was one of the wealthiest men in Crete. His name means 'John the Teacher', 'teacher' being a mark of the respect which the Greeks accord to learning rather than a literal description. He spoke foreign languages; also, and this probably impressed his compatriots more, since it is unlikely that he had much opportunity to practise languages in Sphakia, he wore European clothes. He owned a fleet of ships which traded throughout the Mediterranean, and in the course of a commercial expedition to the Black Sea he met the Russian Count Orloff and became, without realizing it, a pawn in Russia's strategy.

For Orloff, representative of Catherine the Great, Daskaloyiannis's appearance was providential. The Russo-Turkish war had just begun. Orloff was to foment rebellion against the Turks wherever it were possible. He found in Daskaloyiannis a willing, credulous ally. At two meetings they discussed plans. It was decided that the Cretan revolt must coincide with the proposed rising of the Peloponnese; and Orloff was to support the insurgents from the sea. The scanty documentary evidence we possess shows that the Russians deceived Daskaloyiannis. However, the Russian fleet entered the Mediterranean in November 1769, the Mani rose in March 1770, and Daskaloyiannis was able to convince the Cretans that rebellion was feasible.

The bard Pantzelios calls on God for enlightenment as he begins.

> God give me thought and a mind in my head,
> To sit down and call to mind Daskaloyiannis,
> Who was the foremost in Sphakia, the foremost chieftain;
> With his heart he wished Crete to be Greek again.
> Every Easter and Sunday he put on his hat
> And said to the priest, 'I shall bring the Muscovite . . .
> And those who wish to stay in Crete
> Shall worship the Cross and become Christian.'
> The priest said, 'Teacher, what are you thinking of?
> You will enslave Sphakia with these plans of yours. . . .'
> 'Silence, priest; be it sooner or later
> I shall take the Cross to the gate of Canea
> I shall take the Cross to the gate and fix it there. . . .'

The Revolt of Daskaloyiannis

The promise to bring the Muscovite did the trick. Daskaloyiannis raised his standard of revolt on 25 March, the day of the Feast of the Annunciation.

The Turks retired within the walls of Canea, and Daskaloyiannis with his pitifully inadequate force of eight hundred pushed down to the Malaxa ridge, his plan being to hold the enemy in Canea until the Russian fleet arrived. Had Orloff kept his promise, the Turks could have been shot to pieces; (though this would by no means have ensured that Crete became Greek again). As it was, as soon as it became clear that the Russians would not be coming, Daskaloyiannis must have seen the rebellion was doomed. The depressing story of retreat before the Muslim army, which outnumbered Daskaloyiannis's force by about thirty to one, is told in detail by Pantzelios. Twice the Turks called on Daskaloyiannis to surrender. The first time, the Teacher wished to give himself up but was dissuaded by his fellow chieftains, who held that surrender was pointless and shameful. The second demand for surrender came when the Cretans' position was desperate; their last line of defences, the Aradaina ravine, had been crossed. Some traitor must have revealed the only path across it. In Pantzelios's song:

> But the Pasha wrote again to Daskaloyiannis . . .
> 'Daskaloyiannis of Sphakia, come and meet me,
> And see that you tame the birds you drove wild. . . .
> Trust my letter, whatever they may tell you,
> And so leave Sphakia with men to live in her.
> When you come and we talk together
> All will be settled and we shall be friends.'

This letter was accompanied by another which the pasha extorted from Daskaloyiannis's brother, who had been captured in the fighting. The brother, having assured Daskaloyiannis that the pasha's invitation was made in the best of faith and should be accepted at once, succeeded in adding three *M*s at the bottom of the page; these, a prearranged code signal, showed Daskaloyiannis that he was to pay no attention to either letter. He can therefore have had no hope of saving his own life when he decided once again to surrender.

This time the other Cretan leaders cannot prevent him. Even his cousin the priest is moved by his courage, for, though Pantzelios offers no explanations, it is clear from what Daskaloyiannis tells the assembled company that his only motive is a desire to obtain the best terms he can for his followers when defeat finally comes. He says goodbye to his wife and children.

The Great Island

> He said, 'My dear wife, my faithful partner,
> Listen with attention to the news.
> I shall go to the Pasha, to speak with him,
> And I do not know well whether I shall return.
> Care for the children, as you know how to do,
> Waking and sleeping think of them. . . .
> Let us trust in God, and pray to Him
> To see again those who live, to meet together again.
> Come to my arms, children, for me to kiss you,
> And be wise until I return again.
> Listen to your mother and your own people –
> You have my prayers. May God help you.
> And you, my friends, my people, brother Sphakians,
> Listen to the advice I give you.
> Do not trust the Turk, whatever he orders,
> He will fight with lies to cheat you all.
> Avoid the Turk, let no one approach him.
> Our fate, our destiny, have not changed yet.'

And Daskaloyiannis gave himself up. He was taken to Heraklion, where the pasha greeted him effusively, offering food, wine, tobacco and coffee, and then subjecting him to a most courteous and reasonable interrogation. What was the cause of the revolt? The Sphakians, compared with other Cretans, were privileged. If there were any complaints, you should have brought them to me, not risen in rebellion. I am pasha, it's my job to sort things out.

Daskaloyiannis blew smoke out of his mouth, and replied:

> 'The cause – you are the cause, you lawless Pashas. . . .
> That's why I decided to raise Crete in revolt,
> To free her from the claws of the Turk.
> First for my fatherland, and second for my faith,
> Third for the Christians who live in Crete.
> For even if I am Sphakian, also I am a child of Crete
> And to see the Cretans in torment is pain to me.'

The pasha then asked, again politely, about Daskaloyiannis's contacts with the rebels of the Peloponnese. Unfortunately Daskaloyiannis lost his temper. 'Silence, Pasha, you are wasting your words; your net is cut and you will not catch the fish. . . . Do what you like with me, but harm no one else.'

Soon after, according to the poem, he was flayed alive, without uttering a single groan, in the main square of Heraklion.

The story proper ends at this point. But the poem suddenly and

The Revolt of Daskaloyiannis

mysteriously comes to life. Pantzelios, like other greater poets, was more concerned with the pity of war than the fighting of it. The two of Daskaloyiannis's four daughters who were captured ask after their father.

> 'He is down at a feast, and other chieftains with him.'
> (And all the time the fishes were devouring him.)

And from the girls, 'the envy of the Maytime cherries, dear princesses, fresh as foam, the envy of the April flowers', Pantzelios moves into a long, long dirge, contrasting the old Sphakia, prosperous and happy, with the new. It is an exact picture, closely and lovingly observed, of a way of life. If you walk through Sphakia you will no longer see long-haired girls dressed up in their Sunday best or young men with silver-crusted armour, tall and wasp-waisted, like violins, or old white-haired men sitting at the table, eating and drinking, singing their songs till the table rings. Where are they? All gone. And Uncle Pantzelios says goodbye to the great Sphakian families, calling on them by name, and dismissing them with a question – 'Where are you?'

He was right to dismiss them, for though the names survived, Pantzelios's old society was gone for ever. Greece, which is the cradle of democracy, as the people are reminded by some newspaper every day, could justly claim to be at least a playpen for oligarchy as well. Daskaloyiannis's society was oligarchic, led by a few pre-eminent families, prosperous as never since. (Before the revolt Sphakia had a fleet of over forty ships, whose activities are unfortunately badly documented. But for this premature uprising, Sphakia might well have figured more largely in the 1821 war, as Hydra did.) Sphakia was thus ideally suitable for the heroic oral poet like Pantzelios, who could count on a sympathetic, aristocratic audience. Provided the rules were observed, that is the patron's name mentioned from time to time, the poet could earn a living. Pantzelios was just one of a long line of Cretan *rhymadóri*, who, always poor and often blind, wandered from village to village peddling songs. Outwardly, the 'Song of Daskaloyiannis' is quite like a Homeric lay, in its heavy reliance on formulae, its invocation of an inspiring deity, and its philosophy. Virtue for Pantzelios is akin to Homer's *arete*: in modern Greek, *levendia*, gallantry –

> Joy to the man who meets his death in battle.
> He who dies in battle is the winner, not the loser.
> He wins a deathless name, a garland of honour.

But there are puzzles; the chief of them concerning Daskaloyiannis himself.

The Great Island

Was he a fool or a hero, or both? To the poet he was a hero; but when we look closely we find that a fair amount of what the poet tells us is misleading, and can be corrected by documents from the Turkish archives in Heraklion.

For instance: Pantzelios states, perhaps for the first time, what has become an article of faith with historians of Sphakia – that the eparchy was free of taxes. This is completely untrue. From early in the Turkish occupation Sphakia was subject to the *Vakouphiko* system, by which all householders had to pay an annual tax towards the upkeep of some holy building or some good cause. Sphakia's money went to the poor of the two holy cities, Medina and Mecca. From 1690 Sphakia was subject to the capitation tax as well. The area was thus as badly off as any other in Crete, and worse off than many. Naturally the Sphakians resisted as best they could; in the year of the revolt they threw the tax-collector out of the eparchy. But it was not till after 1760 when Sphakia was assigned by the Sultan to the protection of Fatma Hatoum, grand-daughter of Sultan Ahmed III, that there was any relief from these burdens. (Pantzelios wrongly says that Sphakia was granted to the Sultana-Mother.) Thus the popular theory of Sphakian independence, of an island of wild Hellenism hardly violated by Venetian or Turk during seven hundred years, must be modified. In 1672 there was a *soubashi* – an agha's representative or steward – living in the town of Sphakia. In the eparchy the agha or his representative was rarely absent.

Pantzelios's first mistake, then, is to exaggerate Sphakia's autonomy. He also exaggerates the strength of the Turkish forces used to crush the revolt; the impression is of a steamroller cracking a nut. The revolt was a serious threat to the Turks; strict security measures were imposed even in distant Heraklion, where the pasha put a ban on gunshots at night time, ordered the Christians to wear distinctive clothes and to place a distinctive mark on their house doors, and prohibited the sale of gunpowder. Nevertheless, the Turks did not send – they did not have at their disposal – the sort of armies Pantzelios talks of – imperial armies under the command of five pashas! The pasha of Heraklion in fact remained at home. The secretary to the Turkish army wrote to him in May 1770: 'When they [clerics from Preveli monastery and Tymbaki sent to collect information and parley with the insurgents] went over to the place and were apprised of the situation of the disloyal inhabitants of the eparchy, and spoke with them, Daskaloyiannis gave them the following answer: "In no way are we to be at peace. We are ready for war; we are prepared for the battle. In no way do we submit." '

The Revolt of Daskaloyiannis

Of this the folk poet says nothing; in his account Daskaloyiannis offers to give himself up.

Pantzelios is wrong too about the *protopappas*, who in the poem starts hostile to the revolt and ends up voluntarily accompanying Daskaloyiannis to the pasha. A further letter from the army's secretary, written a fortnight after the preceding one, tells how the priest was captured and gave the Turks much information. The secretary quotes the priest's words:

Daskaloyiannis sent a message to the Muscovite: 'The Mani, like Crete, is inaccessible land; and we have many men; we shall master Crete on our own.' On the basis of this the Muscovite sent powder and shot . . . and said that soon he would send cannons, shells etc.; 'For the time being, prepare yourselves and collect your army.' . . . But instead of coming first to Crete, the Russian ships sailed to the Mani. . . . After some time Daskaloyiannis sent another man to the Morea: 'Why haven't you appeared? Send us two ships. With them we could do wonders.' The Muscovite general said in reply: 'You are inferior to the Maniot army. They told me I could take Mani in three days, but I can't. . . . Mani must be taken first, and then I will come in person to Crete.' So the Sphakians prepared, and they're still waiting for the Russian ships.

Lastly, Pantzelios gets the date of the execution wrong. In fact Daskaloyiannis lay in prison for about a year and was put to death in June 1771. In the poem his martyrdom immediately follows his defiance of the pasha.

Now all these points, where Barba Pantzelios departed from the historical facts as we know them from Turkish documentary evidence, serve one purpose; they help to make a heroic story. We can see just how Pantzelios does his own primitive plot-making. He rounds off the jagged corners of real life and constructs, half unconsciously, a story of irony and tragedy. The ingredients – a prosperous, untaxed, privileged community taking up arms for the sake of the Christians of Crete; the Christians' representative forsaking his materialism, his arguments of expediency and compromise, at the last minute, and joining the rebel leader: and the rebel leader, Daskaloyiannis, showing the priest what his duties are.

The plot is good. In Daskaloyiannis the poet portrays a character who took a step beyond the conventional *arete* – or simply, extraordinary bravery – to which his audience was accustomed. Christian self-sacrifice is part of his character. Daskaloyiannis, unlike his colleagues, who are typical Cretan *palikaria*, cannot see the point of fighting on when his surrender might save lives. Yet in the end, having made the noble gesture of surrender, he fails to see the implications of it; for if he had agreed to the pasha's terms instead of turning stubborn and losing his temper, lives might have been saved. Thus with his final and futile defiance, his actions conform exactly with the conventional heroic philosophy which he earlier transcended. Which seems psychologically quite probable.

Probable, but no more. In some of the short folk versions of the story Daskaloyiannis is a much less heroic figure. But Pantzelios's picture is the most detailed, and there is no other more reliable. Daskaloyiannis has come down in the memory of the Cretans as the archetype of the Hero. He corresponds in real history to Digenes, Alexander the Great and Erotokritos in folk-tale, legend and romance. As time passed, however, even Daskaloyiannis took on legendary features. Glorified by later generations, and magnified by folk poets, he is to be found in one short poem struggling with the enemy single-handed for three whole days – like Digenes struggling for his soul with Charos on the marble threshing floor.

9

The Nineteenth Century

Turkish rule is marked by a uniformity which enables one to pass quickly over the last hundred and fifty years. Before 1821 Crete was, in Pashley's words, the worst governed province of the Turkish empire. The reports of contemporary eye-witnesses confirm his judgement. Thus, the French consul at Canea, in 1820: '*L'autorité du Pacha est, pour ainsi dire, nulle en ce pays, les Agas et les Chefs de régiments font des avanies qu'ils veulent sans que personne n'ose s'en plaindre : les malfaiteurs de chaque corps se livrent a toute sorte d'excès, et se permettent même d'entrer d'autorité dans les maisons des Rayas, et s'en disposer entièrement à leur gré.*' At one time these turbulent janissaries were in the practice of sending to some unfortunate Christians a bullet wrapped in a paper which carried the message that a certain sum must be paid by a certain date. Failure to pay meant death. They would take Christians, too, for target practice on the ramparts of Canea, and wager on which way they would fall. It is proved beyond doubt that the janissaries at this time were beyond control, taking the Christians' money and their women at will; in 1819 they deposed an obnoxious pasha, and disobeyed the orders which came from the Sultan at Constantinople. Once again, it must be emphasized that the worst offenders were Cretan renegades from the towns.

Thus Crete was differently placed in 1821 from mainland Greece. For among the causes of the War of Independence which started in 1821 the oppression of the Turks was only one. In fact, in many parts of Greece conditions before the war were not desperate. Turkish rule had improved in the eighteenth century; the tribute of children had stopped even earlier; and the Greeks had established themselves as the masters of Levantine trade. Rather than systematic oppression, it was the ferment of new ideas which spread after the French Revolution and were propagated in Greece by Koraes which aroused latent nationalism.

25 March 1821 is the date conventionally assigned as the beginning of the War of Independence; on this day Bishop Germanos raised the standard of revolt at the monastery of Agia Lavra in the Peloponnese.

The Great Island

The Cretans did not follow at once. In June the Austrian consul at Canea reported, 'The bishop of Kissamos has been delivered over to the fury of the people, who without regard for his character have dragged him through the town, half naked, by the beard, and have cruelly hanged him.' This incident was followed by the massacre of some thirty Christians in Canea. In Heraklion the Metropolitan Archbishop and five bishops, together with other priests and laity, were cut down at the altar of the cathedral, where they had sought sanctuary. After this, a major uprising was inevitable.

Thus the Cretan insurrection was caused by an unprovoked and murderous attack on the Christians. The Sphakians rose. Soon the Turks were penned within the fortified towns. In 1824 the revolt was crushed due to the intervention of Mehmet Ali, Viceroy of Egypt, who was called upon by the hard-pressed Sultan and sent a powerful expedition.

This revolt had three characteristics. First, the savagery displayed by both sides. The people of Melidhoni, with their livestock and valuables and enough food for six months, took refuge in a great cave near the village. Khussein Bey, the Egyptian commander, required them to come out. The herald who made this demand was shot. Khussein then sent in a Greek woman to promise the villagers safe conduct. She too was shot, and her body thrown out of the cave. Twenty-four of the Egyptian troops had been killed in an attempt to force the cave. Khussein then directed his men to block the mouth by throwing stones into it; but overnight the Greeks succeeded in opening an air-hole. After trying this method on four successive days, Khussein put down brushwood and lit it, smoking the cave. All 300 occupants were suffocated. The Mohammedans waited eighteen days to make sure, before sending in a Greek prisoner who reported, 'They're all dead inside, boss.' Other incidents of this type are reported by Pashley, who 'collected' Turkish (and Cretan) atrocities. Xan Fielding describes the cave at Vaphes in the White Mountains, which has this inscription: 'Here in this coldwater cave on the ninth of August 1821 the Pashas Resit and Osman put to death by suffocation 130 men women and children of Vaphes, Christians fleeing from a Turkish onslaught after three days of valiant resistance.' The method was again asphyxiation.

The second feature of the '21 was the religious enthusiasm displayed by the Cretans, which, if we are to trust Pashley's impressions gained from conversations with survivors in 1834, was excessive. All over Greece the war was in some sense a sacred war; Greek church and state were the same, and it was the church which prepared the Greeks for the struggle; but in Crete the church seems to have avoided the mistrust which attached to its higher dignitaries in other parts. Cretans are not anti-clerical; probably because the Cretan hierarchs preserved a greater independence than some of their colleagues on the mainland. After their initial successes, says Pashley, the Cretans believed themselves to be under the especial protection of the Deity; their every banner was accompanied by a brave priest, 'who celebrated, with an unheard of frequency, the most solemn ordinances of their religion'. And for about a year some fanatical Christian husbands avoided intercourse with their wives as a pollution which would bring them death in battle. Pashley also found that many Sphakians had become 'Brothers' according to a religious ceremony which dated from the time of Justinian and had been forbidden by both ecclesiastical and imperial authority. This brotherhood, like gossiprede, was a sacred tie; to marry your 'brother's' sister would be incest. 'Better the brothers of the church than the brothers of the womb' went the tag.

Thirdly, the '21 revolt was marked by dissension among the Cretans themselves. The two most prominent leaders, Roussos of Sphakia and Melidhonis of Central Crete, were bitter rivals; (Melidhonis was in the end murdered). And apart from these local chieftains, whose small guerrilla bands carried on the only sort of warfare which could profit the Greeks, there was one Michael Comnenus Aphendoulief, a Russian-Greek who claimed descent from the Comnenus dynasty of Byzantine emperors, sent by Ypsilandis to direct operations – at the Cretans' request. The Russian eventually retired to Malta; for the Cretans found they did not want him after all. With such disagreements at the top, the revolt had no hope of success.

After Navarino the Cretans rose again; a Council of Crete was set up on the islet Grambousa, which had become a stronghold of patriot pirates, as it had been before. But this new insurrection collapsed with the defeat of Hadzimichalis at Frangokastello, in 1828.

Things could never be the same again, however, after Navarino. Greek independence was now a fact which must be recognized; there was now a 'Cretan Question'. Crete had entered the sphere of Great Power politics. Yet due to the lunatic machinations of the powers, *enosis* was to be delayed for another eighty-five years. Britain must bear a large share of the blame. Prince Leopold of Saxe-Coburg, whom the Powers chose as a suitable king for the new principality of Greece, recognized the impossibility of the proposed frontiers. He wrote to Lord Aberdeen that he could see no way of pacifying Greece without including Crete in the new state. But Leopold never actually became

King; Capodistria dissuaded him. Hence the unsatisfactory Bavarian Otho; and when he ascended the throne of Greece, both Crete and Samos were excluded from the kingdom. Already British diplomacy was scheming to support the sick men of Europe, and to avoid building up a strong Russophil Greece. Cretan deputies, however, had attended the Greek National Assembly; the forces of nationalism could not be for ever suppressed.

For the time being Crete was attached to the Egyptian pashalik of Mehmet-Ali. His troops had quelled the revolt; and he was better placed to govern the island than anyone else. Mehmet made a good start, announcing through his Governor-General Mustapha Pasha that his sole object was 'to establish the tranquillity and cause the prosperity of Crete, and to deliver the Christians from the vexations to which they were formerly exposed'. A likely story! Two judicial councils were established, one at Heraklion and one at Canea, of mixed Christian and Mohammedan constitution, and for once the Christians got a fair deal; indeed, rather more than a fair deal, since the Egyptians knew that the Cretan Mohammedans, accustomed to tyrannize over the island, would never accept Egyptian rule. Many of those who had left Crete after the last revolt returned. After every revolt many were forced to go into exile. (As early as 1692 we hear of two thousand Cretans, who helped the Venetian Captain-General Domenico Mocenigo in an attack on Canea, leaving in Venetian ships for the Peloponnese, where they encountered great hardship.)

Within a year, however, the new Viceroy began to squeeze Crete, imposing heavy new duties and shackling the councils, where from now on the views of the president, an Egyptian-Turk, prevailed. In 1833 a measure which would have enforced the cultivation of all land in Crete, thus tending to 'reduce independent mountaineers to the wretched condition of the fellahs', provoked the Mournies incident – something quite new in the movement for independence.

Several thousands of Cretans assembled at Mournies a few miles from Canea, to demand redress for their complaints. They sent deputations to the consuls of the powers, Great Britain, France and Russia. The consuls, as one would expect, recommended peaceful dispersal. Instead they constituted themselves a permanent assembly composed of both Christians and Mohammedans. They were unarmed. A solitary misdemeanour – the theft of some fruit – was publicly punished.

This remarkable peaceful demonstration met with no more success than bloody revolt. The peasants' memos to representatives of the powers in Constantinople and Nauplion went unanswered. Mustapha

Pasha, the Governor-General, wisely attempted no violence, and the Assembly's numbers gradually diminished as more and more drifted home to work. But some remained, unsatisfied with the assurances they had received. Two months after the Assembly had met together, therefore, Mehmet ordered the execution of some of these who remained; and the pashas, having vainly interceded with Mehmet for mercy, had ten of the demonstrators hanged on 3 December, while twenty-one others were executed in different parts of the island simply to strike terror into the inhabitants.

Robert Pashley's travels took place shortly after this incident. Curiously enough, although the picture he paints is a grim one, of a land desolated almost beyond repair by the recent war, the times were not too bad; Mustapha Pasha (1832-55) was one of the more humane and farsighted of governors. But it required more than a reasonable governor to set right such a multitude of wrongs. The population was halved between 1821 and 1834. Think of this through people and not numbers; at Vithias, 'the only male inhabitant . . . is a young Mohammedan. . . . The rest are all widows. In many places in Crete the number of widows is large; and in one village of Lassithi they actually form the entire population.' Charred ruins, roofless houses told of the recent destruction.

The island was a strange, colourful place in the middle of the nineteenth century. Mehmet Ali's intervention had brought in new races. His fighting men were Albanians, who could be distinguished from the Cretans by their dress, as well as the muskets they carried and the pistols hung from their girdles. 'Idle and licentious' Pashley calls them. Long after the suppression of the '28 revolt they lingered on, small groups of them quartered in the villages as a kind of militia; with nothing to do except to 'attend to their horses, smoke their pipes, and visit the house of any villager when he is absent . . .'. At the same time there sprang up an Arab community of between 2,000 and 3,000 strong on the shore west of Canea; the inhabitants, most of whom were boatmen, porters and servants, came from Egypt and Cyrenaica. This African village was fringed with Bedouin tents.

Then, in 1859, the most extraordinary incident in the modern history of Crete. Of the powers, England was least favourable to Cretan aspirations. Russia's attitude fluctuated; although Orthodoxy was a strong tie with Greece, the Tsar had recently suggested that should the Ottoman Empire break up Crete should become English. The French had generally shown themselves friendly to Crete; and their com-

The Great Island

mercial interests in Crete were stronger than those of any other power. France had always been better represented in Crete than England. After 1765 the French consul in Canea was the only European representative allowed by the Turks to fly his country's flag. And whereas the French consuls were Frenchmen, the English until a late date were not Englishmen. Even in 1834 Pashley found that the English consul at Heraklion was a Greek born in Malta, an ex-Barbary slave, who spoke no English.

The French, therefore, had had representatives in Crete for hundreds of years; including a few Capuchin priests in Canea and Heraklion. It was through one of these Capuchins, Seraphim, that the trouble started. A peasant from Kalyves went to him and complained about the oppressions of the Turkish garrison in Kalyves; Seraphim told Du Tour, the French consul, who interceded with the Turks. The garrison was moved. Precisely what happened is doubtful. But somehow the Capuchin now gave the Cretans to understand that if the Cretans turned Catholic they would qualify for French protection in similar cases; and the peasants were allowed to assume that this protection would come from the French Government.

The Cretans rushed to be converted. The pressure in western Crete was so great that the Capuchins demanded reinforcements of Greek-speaking priests. Even some Orthodox priests made the change. From a Capuchin letter in January 1860: 'More than a dozen priests came to . . . recognize the Pope as St Peter's successor. And till now more than 30,000 have been enrolled . . . who would not only be good Catholics but also would attract the rest of the island.' The movement snowballed; the Capuchins were talking optimistically of importing their first bishop from Corsica, where there were many Greeks 'reconciled' to the Roman church.

As soon as it was clear what was happening, the reaction came. The Metropolitan Dionysius issued a proclamation explaining the Catholics' aims, and the impossibility of the French guarantee of protection. The Turks, hostile to any form of change, supported the Metropolitan; and according to the Capuchins, some Orthodox priests were seized on leaving the Catholics' house, taken before the pasha and the Metropolitan, and beaten up. There were protests from the Greek government and from the Ecumenical Patriarchy in the City.

The French had got themselves into a fantastic predicament – some thousands of would-be Catholics on their hands, all ready to be converts for political reasons only, and fraudulent reasons at that – and Consul Du Tour, who perhaps did not at first realize the implications of the Capuchin's promise, must have been seriously embarrassed. Wisely he extricated himself by pinning up a notice in the Catholic monastery; '*Le Consul de France rappelle que ceux qui embrassent spontanément la réligion Chrétienne Catholique apostolique, comme ils sont libres de le faire, accomplissent un acte qui n'a rien de politique et qu'à aucun de ceux-là il ne permet en aucune manière de se dire ou de se croire sujet ou protégé français.*'

Scandal was avoided. But both Du Tour and the pasha were compromised, and were replaced soon afterwards.

In 1840 Crete was restored from Egyptian to Turkish rule; the Albanian Governor Mustapha Pasha, however, remained. In 1841 the island rose again in revolt, which was quickly suppressed. Thereafter there was some peace until the great revolt of 1866. The preceding years were filled with Cretan petitions and complaints, and Turkish promises. There is something comprehensive about these complaints; in 1866, for instance, they covered excessive duties, tax-farming, the lack of bridges and roads, the lack of schools, the Mohammedan bias of the lawcourts, and the closing of most of the ports; among other things. But the desire for *enosis* was behind all this. From now on no European power would be allowed to remain ignorant of Crete's just desire; the islanders petitioned the Great Powers represented in the persons of Queen Victoria, Napoleon III and the Tsar.

The General Assembly of Cretans at Sphakia proclaimed *enosis* in September. The longer the revolt held out the better for the Cretans; for while open victory might be impossible for the small guerrilla bands operating from the mountains, prolonged warfare must attract the attention of the powers and might in the end demand their interference. Lack of food and arms was a problem, despite the little *Panhellenion* which ran the Turkish blockade. The problem of organizing a Cretan revolt would have driven a western officer to despair. The *palikaria* would descend from their mountain villages with a few days' provisions in their packs; harass the enemy; and when the provisions were exhausted, return home. Jules Ballot, a French volunteer, wrote, '*L'insurrection était d'ailleurs sans la moindre unité, sans la moindre organization, et chaque chef de bande combattait séparément.*' Only a slight exaggeration.

Then suddenly, on 21 November 1866, Crete, which until then had been just a name vaguely familiar to progressives and Philhellenes, and a pawn to politicians, entered the consciousness of Europe. Crete was divided into three commands. The commander of the centre, Koronaios, set up his headquarters in the solid, ornate monastery of Arkadi near Rethymnon. Mustapha Pasha, having defeated the westerners at Vaphes, turned his artillery on the monastery. For two days the monks and soldiers defended Arkadi. Finally the Turks forced the gate and rushed into the courtyard. Down below the *hegoumenos* Gabriel, surrounded by fighters, monks, women and children, put a match to the powder-magazine. In that tremendous explosion both Turks and Christians died. A year later their bones were still to be seen scattered round the ruined monastery.

Crete could not be ignored after this. In Athens King George's attitude was of sympathetic neutrality; for open support would have meant a war with Turkey. Nevertheless Piraeus was busy with the to-and-fro of ships carrying Greek volunteers and supplies, and bringing in refugees from Crete. Moscow called for donations for those Cretans who had taught the Russians how to practise their holy religion. In England newly-formed Philo-Cretan societies subscribed enough money to raise a ship, the *Arkadi*, which started to run the blockade with food and supplies and volunteers in 1867. A Greek Relief Committee was formed, in America, and the Senate publicly sympathized with the insurgents. In Italy Garibaldi was in touch with the Cretans; 'Rejoice then, brave children of Ida . . . learn that our spirit suffers because of your sadness, and our heart beats during your triumphs.'

Victor Hugo, the greatest rhetorician of them all, was indefatigable in his published support, and magnificent in his exposure of Great Power politics. He wrote in a reply to the Cretan leader Zymbrakakis: '*Hélas, la politique de retraite du gouvernement a deux résultats, refus de justice pour la Grèce, négation de sympathie pour l'humanité. Oh Oui! Un mot sauverait ce peuple. Un mot seulement de l'Europe est si facile à dire. Dites ce mot.*' The word will not be spoken; among the powers there is a conspiracy of silence.

Mais la foudre ne participe pas à cette conspiration. La foudre vient de haut, dans la langue politique, elle s'appelle insurrection. La porte pressée par la hache est près de tomber. Le vieux prend une bougie dans le sanctuaire, il voit les enfants et les femmes, il la plonge dans la poudre et se sauve. Intervention effrayante, l'explosion aide les lutteurs, l'agonie se change en triomphe, celui du monastère héröique, après avoir lutté comme une place forte meurt comme un voleau. Psara n'est pas plus épique, Missolonghi n'est pas plus grand. Tels sont les faits.

The practical results of this heroic sacrifice, this new pan-European interest? Nothing except the concessions embodied in the organic statute of 1868. The French now recognized the truth; that prudence as well as justice demanded *enosis*. The Marquis de Moustier declared that Crete was lost to Turkey; she was a sore limb of the Empire, and better amputate it than allow a gangrene to start and spread. Russia was in favour of *enosis*. The French proposal of a plebiscite to decide Crete's future was crippled only by Britain's obstinate refusal to agree. At this moment the powers could have ensured a just solution to the Cretan question. The Tory Foreign Minister Lord Stanley was therefore responsible for the forty-seven-year delay of independence and union. Among the blows this country has delivered Greece this is not the least. The Cretan insurrection petered out.

In 1878, more concessions in the Pact of Halepa: Christians were to outnumber Mohammedans in the Assembly: Greek was to be the official language in the lawcourts: revenues for hospitals, harbours, roads. Under a Christian governor the island was reasonably content: so content that when Turkey actually offered Crete in 1881 and the Greek government refused, preferring concessions on the mainland, there were no disturbances.

But public works were not carried out on any grandiose scale even now; in 1897 there was only one proper carriage-road, from Suda to Canea, about five miles long. Veli Pasha, who had tried to build a road from Rethymnon, was soon recalled in 1858; ironically he had become exceedingly unpopular with the Cretans because of the extra labour and money required for the construction. This is a solitary example of Turkish public works; at first they devoted money to the upkeep of Venetian fortresses, but even these fell into disrepair in the nineteenth century. The harbours stagnated. Social services were minimal. Spratt notes the humane gesture of the Turkish government (under the enlightened Veli Pasha again) in allowing a ration of half an oke of bread per day to the unemployable inhabitants of the leper colonies outside Heraklion, on Spinalonga, and elsewhere. Spratt blames the whole community, as well as the government, for the neglect of lepers, undoubtedly with some justice; and doubts in consequence whether the Cretans are ready for self-government (1851). They were not more callous, however, than their masters. And their callousness was a product largely of ignorance about the disease. The Cretans' attitude to spastics today is rather similar.

The grim story was nearly over. The Turkish tactic had too often been to promise reform and do nothing, and more recently to hamstring the Christian governor in his office; as if to demonstrate that, even if the days of Turkish rule were numbered, government by a Christian would not work. The last great insurrection broke out in 1896. In Athens

The Great Island

public opinion was at last too strong for neutrality. Prince George of Greece left Piraeus amid scenes of wild excitement with six torpedo-boats; and Colonel Vassos landed near Canea, with orders to take possession of Crete in the King's name. Meanwhile, the Powers occupied Canea, and at one time bombarded the Cretans in their efforts to keep the peace. The Greek action precipitated a Greco-Turkish war. And when this ended in May 1897 a solution was 'imposed' on the Cretan question.

That is to say, for some eighteen months the Powers looked for a suitable High Commissioner, canvassing the merits of various Frankish candidates. In the meantime, once again, the situation on Crete was extraordinary. The island was divided into spheres of influence, administered by the powers. The English garrisoned Heraklion; the Russians Rethymnon, the French Sitea, the Italians Hierapetra; while all four held Canea, and the fleet under the Italian Admiral Canevaro lay off in support. The Mohammedans were confined for the most part to the large towns where foreign troops offered some protection.

Independence had been unnaturally delayed some seventy years. It came now, for though she remained under the suzerainty of the Porte Crete was to be autonomous. Violence broke out in September 1898 and among the Christian victims were some British soldiers and the vice-consul. Within two months the Turkish forces had left Crete, and the Powers had offered the job of High Commissioner to Prince George, second son of the King of Greece. He landed at Suda on 21 December. From the pealing bells, the guns sounding the salute, the wild cheering, enthusiastic crowds, you could have guessed that Crete's troubles were over.

And, more or less, they were. Hellenization proceeded peacefully under Prince George. The foreign admirals left immediately after his arrival, and a year or two later the British troops could leave too. The Mohammedans, many of whom had left – and were encouraged to leave by the Porte – had a favourable proportion of seats in the new Assembly: 50 to 138 at the first meeting. There were internal troubles; a quarrel between Prince George and the young lawyer Eleutherios Venizelos led to the prince's resignation. Under the new Commissioner Zaimes, Crete proceeded on her unalterable course towards *enosis*, which came in 1913.

The 'Cretan Question' belongs to recent history, and because the Great Powers were involved, is well documented. Whole books have been written about it. The spectacle of European politicians intriguing and bargaining for plots of land they had never seen, whose people they did not understand, in the name of some sacred principle ('the integrity of the Ottoman Empire'), is not a pleasing one. It is true that without the intervention of the Powers, Cretan independence would have been still further delayed. Nevertheless, concessions had to be squeezed out of the Powers one by one, just as they had to be squeezed out of the Turkish rulers. Thus autonomy was bought with Cretan blood; the blood shed after 1828. Once Greece was an independent kingdom, and once the Great Powers were interested, it was only a question of time; and every revolt, by weakening the hold of the Porte, brought independence nearer.

In a sense, then, these *palikaria* did not die in vain. Why is it, then, that nineteenth-century Cretan history is so depressing? Why the overwhelming feeling of waste? Partly, I think, because to us who look back on it autonomy seems so inevitable. Need so many lives have been lost for something which had to come? But also, because the profits of each revolt – and this is true of all Cretan history – were so meagre; and the distant goal, liberty, poor comfort to the wives of those who had died.

That period when Crete was governed by the four Great Powers, and the fleet with its four admirals rode at anchor in Suda bay, is one of the oddest in the island's history. The English in Heraklion, under Colonel Chernside, seem to have left a favourable impression. They succeeded in pacifying their zone of influence and in increasing the revenues; and to judge from Mr Elliadi's delightful account, they administered justice with an ethic which would have been incomprehensible to the Cretans. For instance: 'A person having discovered that his servant was stealing from him, he discharged her without giving notice to the police, with the result that, to the great astonishment of all, he was fined, the reason being that though he rid himself of her, she was thus allowed to continue her bad practice elsewhere, whereas a good citizen should not only be a guardian of his own property, but also that of others.'

Down in the west meanwhile, in Suda bay, the admirals were behaving in a very different way. In Kazantzakis's *Zorba the Greek* there is a pathetic, old and ever-hopeful character named Madame Hortense, whose fondest memory is of the time when she was wined and dined and treated as a queen by all four foreign admirals. This French Madame, young and beautiful in 1897, had pulled the admirals' long silken beards and implored them not to bombard the wretched Cretans – 'Oh, Canevaro, my little Canevaro, don't go boom! boom!';

and had distinguished them at night by the scent which clung to her in the morning: Cologne for the Englishman, violet for the Frenchman, musk for the Russian and patchouli for the Italian. They drank champagne from her slipper, showered her with roubles, pounds and francs and when the order came to leave they sounded a salute of cannons as she was rowed ashore.

I had always thought this extravagant character was invented by Kazantzakis. But she crops up again – or at least her prototype crops up – in Prevelakis's *Chronicle*. Hortense was born in Provence, enticed away at the age of sixteen and set to work in the brothels of Marseilles. In 1897 she was thirty, and decided to go with a ship that was sailing to join the British and Russian fleets off Crete. No sooner did they arrive in Suda bay than she was captured and taken on board by the Russian Admiral Andreyev. For some weeks she went from ship to ship, delighting admiral after admiral. I had always imagined these four as the austere upholders of the decisions of the Great Powers; it comes as a pleasant shock to find them pouring champagne between Hortense's breasts and drinking it from her navel. 'I was naked nine hours out of ten,' the poor girl complains.

There is a sequel to this chapter – a sequel which had to be written to the Turkish occupation. After Constantinople fell in 1453 the Greeks never ceased to regard the City as Greek. The Turkish occupation was temporary; and some day the interrupted mass would be completed in St Sophia. The 'Great Idea', based on reclaiming the City for Greece, was the strongest force in Greek politics after independence. The idea of Greater Greece, the 'Great Idea', was shattered in 1922 when the Greek forces in Asia Minor were utterly defeated by the Turks, in their attempt to realize the dream. The Smyrna disaster is beyond dispute the most important event in modern Greek history – a Suez on an incomparably larger scale. It forced the Greeks to reassess not only their foreign policies but also their whole lives, their identity as a nation (as we would put it), their national destiny (as they would put it).

The immediate consequence was an exchange of populations on a colossal scale. Refugees from Asia Minor flocked into Macedonia. In Crete alone some 30,000 Muslims left. Prevelakis in his *Chronicle* gives an extraordinarily vivid picture of the Turks' departure from Rethymnon. He was about fourteen when they went. Prevelakis tells how those who grew up after independence bore no resentment against the Turks despite the big talk of their elders; and the Turks themselves had come to regard Crete as their own country. They had a tag – 'Me too, my guts are Cretan'. After the Smyrna disaster the refugees started to pour in; somehow they were accommodated, and everyone thought that was the end of the matter.

Then, like a thunderbolt, came the news that there was to be a complete and compulsory exchange of populations. The Turks and Christians were staggered – 'like a couple whose divorce is pronounced at the very moment when they have buried the hatchet'. The Turks were being torn away from land and property, from olives, vines and orchards. 'From one end of the island to the other the groans of Turks preparing to leave were heard, mingling with those of the refugees who had just been uprooted; and one asked oneself what profit could there be in such distress for the monsters who held human grief at nothing.' When the ships arrived to take them away a kind of madness possessed the Turks; they tore down the shutters from their houses, ripped off doors and woodwork, intending to take with them these scraps of their former life. The Greek refugees meanwhile, who were to occupy these Turkish houses once they were vacated, took fright and rushed furiously into the Turkish quarter. The militia was called out to restore order. At last the Turks began to wind down towards the quay in a long dejected queue. All night they were embarking, and in the early morning the queue was still there. It was not till about midday that the steamers hooted, the anchors were weighed, and, as the ships began to move away, a great cry arose from thousands of Turkish mouths – 'Wild and full of entreaty, bitter and menacing, carried by the wind in great surges to the shore.'

In Heraklion Elliadi watched the Turks kneeling in their cemeteries before the time came for them to go. One of the transport ships, the steamer *Ujid*, was wrecked outside the old Venetian harbour in a gale, so that many of the Turks had to wait, having packed their things and worked themselves up for departure, for new transport. Eleven thousand Muslims left Heraklion alone; thirteen thousand Christian refugees took their place.

Very few Turks were able to stay. Among those few who did was one Fatme who worked in the Turkish baths; but then, it turned out that she was not a Turk at all. She was Madame Hortense, the old French courtesan, who after her admirals left Crete had spent twelve years in a brothel in Canea – 'with those Cretan wild beasts' – and then become an honest woman, her past shrouded in mystery, in the baths of Rethymnon.

With the departure of the Turks a long chapter of Cretan history

The Great Island

came to an end. They were soon forgotten. There are now only a few minarets and fountains left as a reminder. As for the refugees, they were soon absorbed, they soon adopted Cretan customs; and some of the customs and practices they brought were woven into the fabric of Cretan life – among them, a new method of fishing by lamplight; so that now on a calm night the sea is dotted with little pinpricks of light.

10

The Death of Pan

> Pan is dead. Great Pan is dead.
> Ah! bow your heads, ye maidens all,
> And weave ye him his coronal.
> *Ezra Pound*

> The ancient spirit lives within us
> Unwillingly concealed;
> The Great Pan did not die,
> No; Pan does not die!
> *Kostis Palamas*

It happened like this. Aemilian the rhetorician told Cleombrotus the Spartan a marvellous story concerning the mortality of demons. Aemilian's father was voyaging to Italy, and, the wind falling, the ship drifted late in the day toward the islands of Paxi. After supper, as the passengers were drinking, a loud voice was heard coming from one of the islands and calling on one Thamus. All were amazed. Twice the voice called and there was no answer. The third time Thamus replied. And the voice then said:

'When you approach Palodes, announce that the great Pan is dead.'

Thamus resolved that, if there were a following breeze, he would sail past the spot and say nothing; but if the sea were calm he would transmit the message. There was no wind. So when they were off Palodes, Thamus looked toward the land and proclaimed, 'The great Pan is dead.'

There arose at once great cries of lamentation and amazement, from many throats. And since the strange news spread, Thamus was later sent for by the Emperor Tiberius.

This marvellous story, from Plutarch's *On the Cessation of Oracles*, succeeds by the mention of Tiberius in putting the death of Pan intriguingly close to the Crucifixion of Christ; and therefore it has struck poets from Spenser to Pound as a mystical allegory of the destruction of paganism.

The Great Island

> The lonely mountains o'er
> And the resounding shore
> A voice of weeping heard and loud lament;
> From haunted spring and dale,
> Edged with poplar pale
> The parting Genius is with sighing sent;
> With flower-inwoven tresses torn
> The Nymphs in twilight shade of tangled thickets mourn.

So Milton. And even Swinburne accepted the general terms of this picture, though he reacted against it – the picture of Pan dying, withering away as it were from shame, but mourned by thousands of lamenting voices and defiant always, at the coming of Christ. Though those that were Gods are dead, he wrote, 'Yet thy kingdom shall pass, Galilean, thy dead shall go down to thee dead.'

Of course Pan never died. Nineteenth-century folklorists seized on this fact and proved it, understandably, at great length. But they went too far in attempting to show that the basic dogmata of Christianity had never had a grip on the mass of the Greek people, nor indeed on any people. My favourite among these controversialists is Mr John Stuart Stuart-Glennie, who tangled with the splendid Neo-Hellenist Tozer in the pages of the *Academy*. Stuart-Glennie succeeded in fitting the survival of paganism into a theory of general Progress according to his own law of Mental Development, which deserves quotation: 'Thought, in its Historic Development, advances from the concrete conception of One-sided Causation, through successively less concrete Conceptions of Differentiated Agents, to the abstract conception of Reciprocal Causation; and this advance is effected in Forms and Periods determined by, and corresponding to, Physical and Social Conditions.' Stuart-Glennie found proof of this in laws of Functional Races, Periodicity, and Correlative Unity. And he thought that, ignored and suppressed as his theory had been by editors, the results obtained in twenty years' verification of it justified the prediction that it would be the basis of all future scientific histories of civilization. But this was not surprising, for the facts used to verify were chosen to fit the theory.

Stuart-Glennie thought that Pan's survival showed that Christianity had been as it were imposed on the Greeks, a naturally pagan people, by cunning propaganda which happened to coincide with peculiar temporary conditions. Pan was a good type of pagan divinity to choose, since he was so unarguably pagan and primitive. (He was a bad choice, though, in that there is less evidence of his survival than there is for many other ancient gods and spirits.) Originally a deity of the Arcadian mountains, the most primitive part of classical Greece, he wandered goat-legged through the woods, guarding the flocks and herds, seducing nymphs, spending the lazy afternoons in sleep. Responsible for the herds, he was also the cause of those sudden inexplicable thrills of communal fear which went shivering from beast to beast and set them madly running. Panic. Unsuspecting travellers in rural Arcadia would be shattered by his sudden mischievous shout. He caused the groundless terror that walks in desolate places. In other ways the cult was down to earth; if the Arcadians failed to get a sufficiently large bag of game, they would thrash Pan's image with wild squills, which by removing evil influences strengthened the god for his proper function.

There is a survival here too. The squill is an irritant and was used as a purgative before certain ritual acts. Lucian tells how Menippus was purged and cleansed with leeks before being allowed to consult the oracle of the dead. It is natural that such purgative plants come to be regarded as potent to expel evil influences. Thus in Pythagoras the squill is a charm to be hung over the doorway, and will avert evil from the house; and it has exactly the same function in Crete today, though to this has been added the more positive property of promoting good. For the squill is now regarded as immortal; age cannot wither it, and it will ensure good luck to the household. This agelessness is explained in the story of Alexander the Great so well known to sailors[1]; and although it is a digression, it is too good to be left out:

King Alexander when he had fought many battles and taken the whole world, so that all trembled before him, called his wise men and asked:

'Tell me, you who possess the writings of Fate, can I succeed in living for many years, so as to enjoy this world where I have made everything my own?'

'King, your powers are great, but what the fates have written cannot be unwritten. Only one thing can make you enjoy your kingdom and glory, so as to become immortal. But it is difficult, very difficult.'

'I'm not asking if it's difficult, only what it is,' said Alexander.

'Ah, then, my king, according to your command. . . . It is the water of immortality. If anyone drinks it he need no longer fear death. But he who goes to fetch it must pass between two mountains which close in on each other like a vice. Not even a bird can get through. The number of princes and lordlings who lost their lives in that fearful trap! And if you do get through the two mountains, there's a sleepless dragon who guards the immortal water. Kill the dragon and you've got it!'

So Alexander went and mounted his noble horse Bucephalus, flashed through the jaws of the two mountains, killed the sleepless dragon and took the glass of water.

But oh, the blessed man, when he got back he didn't manage to keep it. His sister saw it and poured it away, not knowing what it was. It fell by chance on to a wild squill, which is why squills never wither.

Later, Alexander goes to drink the immortal water, but – where is it? He asked his sister, who explained what she did. In his rage he cursed her: 'May you turn into a mermaid, fish from the waist down, and suffer tortures till the world stand in the middle of the sea!'

God heard his curse, and since then voyagers can see her suffering amid the waves. But she doesn't hate Alexander. When she sees a boat she asks, 'Does Alexander live?'

And if the ship's master is ignorant and unwise, and answers, 'Dead', the girl in her excessive grief churns up the sea with her hands and her tresses of hair, and swamps the boat.

Those who know better say, 'He lives and reigns!', and then the much-tormented girl takes heart and sings sweet songs. And thus sailors learn the new tunes.

That is how the squill became immortal. The story is also the most common piece of merfolk lore to be found in the area of the Aegean and the Cretan sea. But we must return to Pan.

His worship spread late. He came to Athens in the Persian wars, intercepting the runner Pheidippides on his way from Athens to Sparta to ask for Spartan help in the imminent battle of Marathon. Pan appeared to Pheidippides, or so the athlete claimed, on Mount Parthenium, and told him to ask the Athenians why they had been so unfriendly to him in the past, since he had helped them and would do so again. The Athenians believed the story and instituted a cult. It was later that he was regarded as the 'All-God', owing to a mistaken derivation of his name. For Alexandrian mythologists he was a symbol of the universe. And it was in this universal aspect that he was announced by Thamus to have died; as the story was understood at the time, and later by the poets, that is. The probable explanation of the story, not that it affects the strange beauty of it, was first pointed out by Reinach. Thamus simply heard the ceremonial lamentation for the Egyptian god Tammuz. The Greek for 'The all-great Tammuz is dead' and 'Thamus, the great Pan is dead' is phonetically exactly the same.

The Death of Pan

But that indefatigable geographer Pausanias, when he travelled round Greece in the second century A.D., found evidence of Pan's cult in shrines, caves and altars which were not neglected. And the cult continued. The case of those who hold that the Greeks have always been pagan, that Christianity never touched the roots of their lives, begins to look plausible. But it is a case that must be approached warily, for several reasons. First, we must not forget those who lived in the towns, who mixed with the Venetians, who doubtless often looked down on the country folk just as the modern townsfolk often do: the folk songs are not good evidence for their beliefs, yet they are just as much Cretans as the 'folk'. Second, there is abundant evidence from outside the songs of the hold Christianity has had on the Cretans – evidence from the countless churches all over the island, from the stories of Cretan sacred wars against the Turks. Third, we must not fall too easily for the theory that folk songs show what a people *really* believes, that they contain the distilled wisdom, the hard core of a race's philosophy; and that therefore the paganism of Greek songs shows that the Greeks have in some way always remained crypto-pagans. For although it may be granted that any major theme in a country's folk song is important to the race's life and interests, it does not follow that everything which is important to a race's life and interests finds a place in folk song.

To take one obvious example. The sea is physically closer to most Greeks than to most Englishmen. It supplies thousands of them with a livelihood. The Greeks are a nation of sailors and merchants. Yet the sea, which is a major interest of literary poets and writers, hardly figures in folk poetry. There is only one important ballad about the sea: '*O Kyr Vorias*' (Mister Northwind). In one form of this a ship is engulfed by a tempest. A Jew who is on board swears that if he is saved he will become Christian; but thinking, in the lull that follows, to have escaped, he goes back on his oath, and the ship is lost after all. There are some variants on this theme. But if we had to judge from the folk songs alone we should never have guessed how important the sea has always been to the Greeks. Thus even in folk poetry one must beware of the argument from silence.

It may be then that sincere beliefs in the doctrines of Christianity just do not happen to form a suitable subject for folk poetry. But the case for paganism is not just that the songs contain non-Christian elements, as we shall see; it is that the system of beliefs contained in the folk songs actually contradicts Christianity in several important ways – for example, over the question of life after death. This being

The Great Island

so, one need hardly bother oneself with unanswerable questions, such as 'Which is their *real* system of belief? Which do they believe *harder*?' For they believe both, at different times and in different ways. And if we appreciate the facts of the situation, that is enough.

After all these reservations and qualifications it is time to look at the folk song itself; it has already cropped up from time to time in this book.

The Greeks are perhaps the oldest ballad-mongers in Europe. Arethas of Caesarea, who died in 932, refers to the *agyrtes*, mountebanks like the accursed Paphlagonians (i.e. Cappadocians) who make up songs about the feats of distinguished men and sing them from house to house at an obol a time. These ballads, now called the Akritic cycle, arose out of the wars on the borders of the Byzantine Empire, where the borderers had to defend themselves against the Saracen menace – often without help from the imperial armies. Thus there existed the best possible conditions for balladry: an unsettled aristocratic society, and a series of wars in which great feudal chieftains had opportunities for magnificent personal exploits. *Akra* means an edge. The Akritic cycle is the cycle of ballads from the edges of the Empire – border ballads – and one of the heroes who features most prominently in it was named Akritas, the Borderer: Digenes Akritas, the hero also of a long narrative epic poem.

What have these Cappadocian borderers to do with Crete? Plenty. For the Akritic ballads are the beginning of Greek folk song as we know it, song which is almost always in the fifteen-syllable 'political' verse, which sounds like our Barbara Allen:

> In Scarlet town where I was born there was a fair maid dwelling
> Made every youth cry well-a-day; her name was Barbara Allen.

Only rhyme came into Greek folk poetry from contact with the 'Franks', long after the Akritic ballads were born.

Thus all Greek folk poetry stems from the Akritic cycle, songs from which have been collected from all parts of Greece and the islands. Certain elements of Greek song are much older even than this. The swallow song, for instance, where the swallow flies in from the sea and announces the coming of spring, is found in ancient Greece, and other themes are survivals from the ancient world. But the form is comparatively young.

Now ballads, and especially good ballads, travel quickly. The best of them cross linguistic frontiers. There are at least two cases where

The Death of Pan

this has happened with an originally Greek ballad. In one case the song has reached England, and in the other the belief embedded in the song is found in England even if it did not come from Greece. The Greek ballad of the Dead Brother who rises from the tomb to ride home with his sister, is transformed into the Suffolk Miracle. And 'The Bridge of Arta' embodies the same primitive and horrifying belief as a nursery rhyme of ours, 'London Bridge is Broken Down'. When the bridge falls down, and wood and clay will wash away, and bricks and mortar will not stay, and iron and steel will bend and bow, and silver and gold will be stolen away, then

> Set a man to watch all night,
> Watch all night, watch all night
> Set a man to watch all night,
> My fair lady.

The Greek song 'The Bridge of Arta' illuminates this rhyme. In it the master mason has to immure his own wife in the bridge he is building in order to make it strong and firm. There is little doubt that the 'guardian' of London bridge is a victim. It is a belief common to Indo-European folklore that bridges demand human sacrifice. The Bridge Gate of Bremen, which was demolished in the last century, was found to have the skeleton of a child embedded in the foundations.

Only a very few Greek songs had the mobility of 'The Dead Brother' and 'The Bridge of Arta'. But within the Greek world almost all the ballads circulated freely. Thus in a sense one is bound to talk about all Greek folk poetry if one talks about a part – hence this general introduction. Still, it can be kept short. For Crete was a creative centre in its own right; and Cretan poetry can usually be distinguished from ballads of alien origin which passed through Crete. In any case, the origin of a song is only of academic interest. The important fact is that it is sung in Crete; for songs and characters which came from Rhodes or Cyprus or Asia Minor were usually adapted or domesticated by the Cretans.

Digenes Akritas himself, for example. The man who lurks behind the legends, songs and epics of Digenes is a shadowy figure, very likely never to be firmly identified. One suggestion is that he was the turmarch Diogenes, 'a competent officer', who fell in 788 fighting the Arabs. Whoever he was he has become one of the archetypal heroes of the Greek nation. The poet Sepheris links him with Erotokritos and Alexander the Great, and Grivas in Cyprus could think of no better *nom de guerre* than Digenes. In the epic poem, Digenes is the son of an Arabian Emir, Mousour, and a Greek girl, Eirene, the daughter of a

The Great Island

Byzantine general of the Doukas family. The Emir carried off the girl, settled within the Empire, and was himself baptized. A son was born to them, named Basil, and later, because of his birth and calling, called Digenes Akritas; for Digenes means 'twyborn' – of double birth. The best of both defender and invader was combined in him. His task was to pacify the marches of the Empire; and the epic describes how he accomplishes this, how he marries, and how he finally dies.

There is little of this to be found in Crete. The short ballads of the Akritic cycle, transmitted from Pontus and Cappadocia through Rhodes and Cyprus to Crete – all the way from mouth to mouth – preserve a different atmosphere: an atmosphere of the magical and the marvellous, where Digenes's fists smash rocks, and birds can speak human words, and horses can weep, and Digenes himself is only one among many heroic borderers – Porphyrius, Andronicus and so on. Many of these ballads are found in Crete. But Digenes has caught the imagination in a way other heroes have not. He has become the giant hero of Cretan folk lore, and the countryside is dotted with his memorials.

The Cretans are fond of giants anyway. They call them the *Sarandapechi*, the 'forty-cubit ones', and they associate them with a legendary heroic age, as in this story preserved by the novelist Kondylakis.

On Psiloreiti and its roots there lived originally the Sarandapechi, who were tall, very tall, and strong. When the flood came, they went up to the top of Psiloreiti to avoid drowning. They were tall, the mountain was tall, the water didn't come up so high as to envelop them. Many days they stood up there, water up to the neck; and worms emerged from the mud from under their footprints, and gave them no rest. And where they bent to catch them, they slipped and fell and drowned, because they could not raise themselves up again, whether from their great weight or because their backbones broke.

Of these giants, who are sometimes regarded as ancestors, Digenes is the greatest. A saddle on a mountain will be 'the saddle of Digenes'. The marks on a rock are the prints of his horse's hooves. There is a tradition which I heard repeated by a boy on the Messara plain that the great saddle above Kamares on Psiloreiti (Mt Ida) marks the place where Digenes rode the mountain. Further down the mountainside there is a cavity – the spot where Digenes put his foot when he was thirsty. One foot here and one foot on the mountain opposite (right the other side of the Messara) and he would bend over the plain and drink from the river that ran below him. But his beard blocked the river, so that it would overflow and flood the Messara.

The Death of Pan

So Digenes is familiar in Cretan legend. But he hardly features in Cretan song except in his death, which is one of the most popular themes in Crete. The theme, which is found also in Rhodes and Cyprus (and started of course in Asia Minor), is treated differently in each area; it is a good example of the way themes are incorporated into a local tradition. The Cretan song is thus quite different from the Cypriot. In Cyprus various episodes from the Akritic cycle are woven into a longish, dramatic account. Charos, dressed in black, comes to Digenes's house and finds him eating and drinking. They wrestle together for the hero's soul, and in the end – but only with God's help – Charos wins. Digenes on his deathbed tells the friends who stand around of his life's exploits; and when he dies he takes his wife with him in his crushing embrace.

This makes a good story. The Cypriot *poetares* is a professional and goes from village to village reciting his work and selling it in pamphlets afterwards. He combines the function of poet and journalist – very like those accursed Paphlagonians. So he is merely treating the Digenes themes in his usual style. That is, he is primarily interested in the story, which he puts over with a wealth of formulae to help him. You can see in the first four lines of a version recorded by Professor Notopoulos how the bard's aim is to catch the audience's attention for a *narrative*:

> Schoolmasters and schoolmistresses have told me to begin
> To sing the song of Digenes the brave.
> Let us start the song which they have praised so much,..
> And thanks to my Creator it has not a lie in it.[1]

That is rapid and fetching enough.

The Cretan mountaineer treats these themes in his usual style too. So he compresses and reduces and distils, and the result is a short lyrical heroic piece.

> Digenes lies dying and the earth trembles at him.
> The heavens lighten and thunder, the upper world is shaken,
> And the lower world has opened, the foundations grind,
> And the gravestone shudders – how is it to cover him,
> To cover the eagle, the brave one of the world?
> Houses could not cover him, caves had no room for him,
> He straddled the mountains at a stride, he jumped the peaks,
> He played quoits with the rocks.
> He beat hares at speed of movement, and hawks at flying,
> At racing and jumping he beat deer and the ibex.
> Charos is secretly envious, watches him from far off;
> Wounded him to the heart and took his soul.

The Great Island

This is of no great value, but it illustrates the method. The whole struggle on the marble threshing floor is gone; Charos dares not come close enough to fight. The song hints at one of the burdens under which Cretan poetry labours – the burden of shortness. Most Cretan songs are heroic; but the heroic, if it is not to be naked and chilling, needs expansive treatment. It needs to be embodied in a story. Too many Cretan songs are statements, not stories – which is all right for the lyrical, but not so good for the heroic.

II
The Song

Digenes has taken us unobtrusively right into the heart of Cretan song. And since Cretan song, like all folk song, is a social art, one might say a practical art, it is time we looked at the social background and context of these songs.

They are called *ta rizitika tragoudia*, which means 'the songs from the roots'. And the roots, *rizes*, are the roots of the White Mountains in the west, which is the most fruitful area for the collector of songs. They are divided into two categories: songs of the table, and songs of the road. The songs of the road are those sung while the villagers go to fetch the bride for a wedding, while they transport the dowry from her old house to the couple's new house, and on other such occasions which involve a march. The songs of the table are exactly what you would expect. All these songs are closely associated with the *glendi*.

A *glendi* is a party. It takes place whenever a few people, or many, gather together for the sake of good company, and this happens in honour of saints' days, baptisms, weddings, visits of important visitors, etc. If you go to Crete you will very likely attend quite a number of *glendia*. They are exhausting but fun. When your spirits are aroused, when the wine and food and company give you cheer, you sing the *rizitika*, and also the couplets called *mantinades*. In between songs you drink a lot – partly because if one man wants to drink he clinks glasses and then everyone drinks, so you will be keeping pace with the fastest – and you eat chunks of lamb, bread, slabs of cheese, honey, hot pilaf.

Descriptions of these performances have an odd sound to our ears. 'One side of the table sings a phrase which is then repeated by the men on the other side. The melodies are many and the singers never achieve unison for each man sings in his own pitch and in such a way that his own voice is not lost in the group singing.'[1] It is exaggeration to say that each man sings in his own pitch, thank heavens; but certainly they often fail to observe strict unison. Another account, by a Cretan, throws valuable light on the way such songs may be corrupted and shortened in the course of time.

At the weddings, baptisms and so on, at which these songs are principally sung, since all the villagers gather together with the women and children, and everybody wants to sing not only one or two songs but the whole repertoire (as well as the *askites*, the products of momentary inspiration), they are compelled to perform only half or less of each poem; justifying themselves with the adage 'His mother will die, who sings to the end.' It should be noted that the curtailment of these songs is assisted too by the attitude of the persons at these gatherings who sing only for exhibition, so that others may not say 'So-and-so doesn't know how', and not from any real urge to sing. Again, whoever plays an instrument, lute or lyra, does not sing, but plays almost continuously: for the musicians remember that their payment depends on the dancing, and whoever dances pays. Finally the songs are curtailed by the common interchange of tune. . . .[2]

This is fascinating, both as an account of the conflict of wills at a *glendi*, and as a suggestion, which is supported on other grounds, that the songs as we have them are relics of longer songs. And this suggests that the reasons why a folk song is what it is, and not another thing, are not primarily aesthetic reasons. You could tell this from internal evidence; many Cretan folk songs are bad, but some are even senseless, and must be the remnants of something longer. Yet they continue to be sung in their condensed form, in defiance of aesthetics.

Musically the *rizitika* are unlikely to please Frankish ears. There are some thirty tunes, each of which is now attached to certain of the songs. They are slow dirges in minor keys – some in the Dorian, some in the Lydian mode. It is difficult for us to listen with pleasure to unaccompanied song unless it is relieved by harmony, or delivered by voices of great purity. I once heard a commercial, 'unauthentic' record of a *rizitiko* sung by a woman to the accompaniment of, I think, the *santouri*. It was most moving. But usually the *rizitika* are roughly sung. They must be heard in context, at a *glendi* in the Cretan mountains, where the roughness ceases to matter and the performance is a social thing.

The *rizitika* take for their subject the themes usual to folk song, and have also some peculiar ones. The index of Papagregorakis's collection lists 565 songs: 146 are patriotic, including 14 of what the Cretans call 'allegorical' songs, in which the Turks are disguised as rabbits and so forth; 96 love songs of various sorts; 43 convivial songs; 38 shepherds' songs; 36 dirges and songs about death, Charos and Hades; 31 songs about mothers; 23 songs of the German occupation; 20 songs of the house, the countryside and the hunt; 19 satirical or humourous songs; 17 religious songs; 16 songs of separation or *xeniteia*, which means exile; 3 baptismal songs; and the rest are miscellaneous.

The Song

The peculiarities of this list are obvious. Not many peoples could boast such a high proportion of patriotic songs, which would seem to be the antithesis of art. (Papagregorakis includes in this category 'heroic, war and historical songs'; it is of course those songs which are overtly 'patriotic', rather than personal or narrative, which fail.) The mother fixation is illusory; many of these songs merely begin with an invocation to the mother. Most important, there is a whole class which is missing in many folk cultures – the songs of *xeniteia*. We in England have songs of separation (a lover goes away to sea, etc.) but we do not have this nostalgia, this homesickness of the Cretans.

Xeniteia is part of the stock in trade of Greek folk song for simple historical reasons. The Greeks are, and always have been, indefatigable travellers. There are large expatriate colonies nowadays in America, Australia, West Germany and elsewhere. Under the Ottoman Empire there were Greek colonies all over Europe, in Venice, Paris, Marseilles, London, Manchester and other great cities. But the Greek does not usually travel for pleasure, nor because he dislikes Greece. He travels because his own country seems to have become too hard for him, and life is easier elsewhere; and usually he returns in his old age with money. When he is away he sends money to his family. He is continually thinking of his home. There is more than one apparently serious report of Cretans exiled for revolutionary activities by the Venetians *dying* of homesickness; and they were always petitioning to be allowed back. Travel means homesickness. There are no songs which exalt the excitement and joys of travel for its own sake, in the 'Give to me the life I love' manner. That is sophisticated.

The Greek sings of *xeniteia*:

> To be abroad, to be an orphan, to be sad, to be in love,
> Put them in the scales, and the heaviest is to be abroad.
> The man who is exiled abroad should put on black,
> For his clothes to match the black fire of his heart.

And a typical Cretan song combines the fear of 'abroad' with the Greek insistence on proper burial:

> I beg you, my fate, do not send me abroad,
> And if you send me abroad do not let me die there;
> For I have seen how they bury them abroad
> Without incense and candle, without priest and deacon,
> And far from church.

The idea of *xeniteia* is not confined to folk poetry. It has eaten its way into the Greek psyche, and permeates their literature, as a kind of nostalgia which comes across most movingly in the poems of Sepheris.

Some songs of love:

- Mother, it is snowing on the mountains, it is raining in the foothills,
  There's a stranger passing our door, wet through from the snow;
  Mother, let us open up and let the stranger in.
- Child, we have no bread, what do you want of the stranger then?
- Mother, they sell bread at the bakers; send me to fetch some.
- Daughter, we have no wine, what do you want of the stranger then?
- Mother, there is wine in the neighbourhood; I'll go buy some.
- Daughter, we have no blankets for the stranger to lie down.
- Mother, my skirt covers the two of us . . .

> It was cold last night and the birds were in pain.
> And I stayed on the seashore naked and was in no pain.
> Why was I in no pain, why no pain?
> I was holding a slender body in my embrace, and white breasts
> Were in my hands, red lips were on my lips.

To a girl who drives men mad:

I've told you once, I've told you twice, I've told you three, five times, haven't I?
You mustn't walk with that wiggle, shaking your breasts.
You've sent all the young men mad, you know, and all the heroes
AND . . . one priest!

> Three years are gone today, the fourth is on its way,
> And I am not of good heart, nor would I be.
> A stranger kissed me, passed by and left me.
> He said: 'I shall come back in March with the swallows.'
> I watch March and it passes, April and it is gone.

I pass and say nothing and the girl greets me.
- Where are you going, kiss-stealer, cheat-in-love?
- If I am a kiss-stealer, a cheat in love,
  Why did you give me your lips and I kissed them sweetly?
- If I gave you my lips and you kissed them sweetly,
  It was night, who noticed us, it was dawn, who could have seen us?
- The Morning Star, the brilliant, he saw us
  And came down low and told it to the sea;
  The sea told the oar, the oar told the sailor,
  And the sailor babbled the news to the wide world.

The Song

For the characteristically Cretan heroic conceit:

> If the earth had steps, and the sky had links,
> I'd tread those steps, I'd grasp the links,
> And climb up to heaven, and sit down there –
> I'd make the skies quake, and belch black clouds,
> And rain water and snow and priceless gold –
> Snow on the mountains, water on the plains,
> Priceless gold at the door of my well-loved girl.

And best of all, in the Greek, because it is precise and unassuming and the twelve-syllable line gives relief from the incessant fifteen syllables:

> A graceful girl, fair and dark-eyed,
> Let down her hair beside a brave man's tomb.
> Her hair covered the gravestone.
> Her eyes, dropping tears, turned earth to mud.
> Her hands prayed to the Lord.

The characteristic tone of the *rizitika* is the tone of heroic poetry, and the world of heroic poetry is alien to us. It is a world dominated by the hero (*palikari*) who is tall and dark and like a cypress. His virtue is *levendia*, which is the ancient Greek *arete*, a gallant attitude to living and dying – courage. His girl is also slender, like a lemon tree, sometimes fair and sometimes dark, but always dark-eyed. The world is deceitful. Life is short. Soon Charos the reaper, the black knight of death, will come, and the women will be in mourning.

Pride figures high on the list of virtues. The *palikari* and his womenfolk despise not only the enemy but also the Cretans who live below on the plains, in comparative luxury, on terms with the occupying power.

> Fie on the young men down in the plains
> Who taste the good things of the world, the choicest foods,
> And are base to look at like the creeping lizard.
> Joy to the young men up in the hills,
> Who eat the snow and the dew-fresh air
> And are fine to look at like the orange tree.

The girl who is married to a plain-dweller says the same thing in symbolic terms:

> Mother, you've made a poor match for me in giving me to the plains;
> I don't hold with the plains, I don't drink hot water.
> My lips will wither, will turn to yellow leaves
> From the warm water, the great heat of it.

The Great Island

Here the nightingale sings not and the cuckoo does not speak.
The plains nourish horses and the mountains heroes,
And the girls waste away and become husks.

The heroic can easily become a bore. It is most likely to avoid the danger of bombast when there is something to be heroic about. The majority of Cretan songs have little or no poetic merit at all, and that includes the best known of them, 'The Rebel'. All Cretans know this song; it describes how when the starless nights return and February comes round, the hero will take his gun and go on an errand – to make wives into widows, and little children into orphans. 'The Rebel' caught the imagination of the oppressed Cretans. Poetic merit by our standards of course has little to do with the popularity of a song, since folk songs serve plenty of non-poetic functions. But of those songs which are worth repeating, it is no accident that some of the best concern death; for this is something in the face of which heroism is not out of place.

Others have written of the place of Charos in Greek folk lore.[3] He is no longer the grim ferryman who conducts souls across the Styx. He has taken the place of Thanatos, Death itself, and of Hades, the ruler over the dead. He comes to abduct the souls which are due. Sometimes he is sent by God – sometimes he is even called St Charos – but usually he acts on his own. For his kingdom has nothing to do with God. It is the 'lower world', peopled by shades of the departed. A few songs will make quite clear the Cretans' attitude to this twilight kingdom of Hades (which is now a place) with its cobwebbed gates.

> Why are the mountains black and filled with tears?
> No wind assails them, nor rain beats them;
> Only . . . Charos is passing, sweeping the dead.
> He sweeps the young in front, the old behind
> And the poor babies in rows on the saddle.
> – Stop Charos in some village, stop at some stream,
> For the old men to drink water, and the young to play with ball
> And the little babies to gather flowers.
> – But I do not stop at villages, I do not stop at a stream,
> For mothers to come for water and recognize their children,
> For man and wife to see each other and avoid separation.

Tell me who it was that threw the apple into Hades
And the golden sword in the earth down there, and the silver ribbon.
Young men run for the sword, young girls for the ribbon,
And the little babies run to take that apple of Paradise.

The Song

    Eat and drink, captains, and I shall tell you,
    I shall tell you the story of a brave man,
    A young man whom I saw on the plains hunting,
    Hunting the hares and chasing the ibex.
– Put off your clothes, young man, lay down your weapons
    And bind your hands high in the air and I'll take your soul.
– I'll not put off my clothes or my weapons.
    You are a man, I am a man, both of us brave –
    Come let us wrestle on the marble threshing floor,
    For the mountains would crack and the countryside be spoilt.
    They went and wrestled on the iron threshing floor.
    And nine times the young man threw Charos,
    And Charos rose up again nine times, and took the young man.
    Grasped his hair and forced him to his knees.
– Let go my hair, Charos, and take me by the arm,
    And then I will show you what heroes are made of.
– I take all heroes just like this,
    I take beautiful girls and fighting men
    And I take little babies with their mothers.

    A slender girl met me on the three steps of Hades
    And I thought she would ask me of her mother
    Her brother or sister or her first cousins;
    But she did not ask me of her mother
    Her brother or her sister or her first cousins,
    But she sat down and asked me of the upper world.
– Does the sky still hold up, does the upper world stand?
    Do brave young men and women still get married?
    Do they build churches, do they build monasteries,
    Do they baptize children?

In other songs Hades is a place of denial and negation, where there are no children playing, no targets to shoot at, no weapons, no musical instruments. Sometimes the dead make vain plans to escape. In Greek folk song as a whole the iconography of death is extraordinarily rich – for it is pictures which these songs put into the mind, miniature, poignant pictures. The view they embody is primitive and anti-Christian. There are glimpses of Christian elements; Charos sometimes appears dazzling with golden hair like the rays of the sun, his eyes flashing lightning – in other words with the attributes of the Archangel Michael, who is Charos's shadow-minister in the Christian tradition, and carries off the soul at the moment of death. But this is little comfort when his kingdom is as it is. It is a place of nothingness. It is the abroad from which you do not return. And there is a perpetual, frustrated dialogue between the imprisoned homesick dead and the free who live. 'Do they still get married up there?' 'Do you celebrate Easter down there?' 'Send us weapons to get out.'

Death is the arch enemy.

> Even with so many trials, still life is sweet.
> And anyone who wants Charos to come, he must be mad.

In tone this is Homeric. 'Don't comfort me about death,' said the shade of Achilles to Odysseus among the meadows of asphodel. 'I'd rather be a serf and work for hire for some poor man than rule over all the corpses of the dead.' The shades of ancient and of modern Greece are the same hopeless creatures. And it need not surprise us that Death is regarded as a malevolent, active and personal enemy in an island where Charos has regularly swept through decimating the inhabitants in pestilence, earthquake and bloody war.

As well as the *rizitika* there are the long historical narrative poems, like the song of Daskaloyiannis, and the *mantinades*. *Mantinades* are at the root of Cretan song. They are simply rhymed couplets.

> Whoever hears me sing, says this is to be happy –
> He no longer sees the withered leaves of his heart.

Every Cretan, even in those areas where the heroic tradition is less strong, knows *mantinades*, for the good reason that the *mantinada* is, less perhaps today but still indubitably, a form of language as well as a song.

Couplets or distichs are sung all over Greece under various local names. They are the liveliest form of Greek folk song: that is, they continue to be created after other longer forms become ossified. But this does not mean that the couplets are a decadent 'late' form. There is every reason to believe that something like the *mantinada* is very old. The Cretan *mantinada* for instance is certainly older than its Venetian name. The name is a simple corruption of *matinada*, the morning song, the song of the after-midnight hours which corresponds to the *serenata* of the early night. The *matinada* was what you sang under your sweetheart's window in the still time before dawn, with lute or guitar. The original function survives:

> Wake up, my love, the day is already dawning;
> Give your little body up to the clean air.

And the *mantinada* is still primarily a love song. It embraces as well every subject in the deceitful world – birth, baptism, marriage, death, burial, dance, food, drink, eulogies of places and people, oaths, curses, jokes, lampoons, homely philosophy – but most *mantinades* are of love. In the couplet the Cretan can get away from his heroic strait-jacket for a moment, and sing, like folk singers everywhere, of love in personal terms. Over the *rizitika* hovers the shadow of Venetians, corsairs, Turks. If it is a lover, he cannot reach his beloved because the enemy has blocked the road. He asks the cuckoo to pass on his message, since he has had to flee the country. But in the *mantinada* these obstructions have been stripped away, leaving just the singer and his love, and the Cretan countryside, a frame in which the beloved is set, a rich source of similes for her description.

> Why does your mother want a lamp at night
> When she has in her house the August moon?

> Your marble hands, your sweet eyes,
> Your coral lips have broken me in pieces.

> Your eyes are like olives on the branch,
> Your brows like a two-day-old moon.

> Clear-weather eyes, light-filled, like the sky;
> Sometimes raindrops fall but there are no clouds.

Mantinades are sung unaccompanied; also accompanied by the lyre and the lute. Many Cretans know thousands of them, and some can improvise them.

There are not many who have this gift. Those who do are helped in two ways. While the assembled company picks up and repeats the first half of the line, they have a little time to prepare the second improvised half-line. Also there is a rich collection of formulae on which they can draw. (One example: the phrase 'Leaves of the heart' which occurred in the *mantinada* at the top of this section is a formulaic cliché – just one of a large stock of phrases on which the singer can draw in order to fill out a line.) When two such gifted rhyme-spinners meet at a *glendi* there may be a competition. They will sing *mantinades* at each other; the first must sing one, and the second must cap it, sticking to the same theme. And if one of the contestants recognizes his opponent's couplet, he sings scornfully, 'My mother knew your *mantinades*, but mine came right from the guts.'

This is amoebaean verse. The singing contests of Sicilian shepherds in the pastoral poems of Vergil and Theocritus are similar. Two shepherds meet. They challenge each other to a match, often boasting about their own prowess and denigrating the opponent, and they appoint a third as judge. One of them then sings a few verses (not always just a couplet) and the other answers in the same number of verses, sticking strictly to the theme set by his opponent. Thus Vergil's shepherds –

Damon: The wolf is the ruin of the sheepfold, rainshowers of the ripened crops, winds of the trees, and Amaryllis's temper of me.
Menalcas: Water is the pleasure of springing crops, wild strawberry of the young kids, supple willow of the mother goats, and only Amyntas of me.

And so on. Now Theocritus's *Idylls* and Vergil's *Eclogues* are highly sophisticated compositions written for a cultured, even a jaded audience to whom real folk music would very probably have appeared barbarous. It is therefore dangerous to jump to the conclusion that the artificial shepherds' contests in the pastoral poems are similar in this or that particular to the verses actually sung by Sicilian (or other) shepherds. The most that can be said is this: there is *some* genuine folk song contest which lies behind the *Idylls* of Theocritus. And since there is no evidence to be had, we might as well accept these Cretan contests (and similar contests of the Cypriot bards) as the nearest we are likely to get to the verse-matches with which those shepherds whiled away their long days.

In primitive societies inspiration is recognized as a force which sweeps through the mind, implanting poetry. Barba Pantzelios, in the prologue to the song of Daskaloyiannis, invoked God and asked for inspiration, in the same way that ancient poets invoked, and believed in, their Muse. The instrumentalist, as well as the singer, is entitled to respect as the recipient of unusual gifts. The *lyraris*, player of the three-stringed Cretan lyre, is the central figure at many festivals, together with his partner who plucks vigorously at the lute with a quill. They do quite well, since anyone who wants a dance will pay them to play it; and what with electric loudspeakers and amplification, they raise the roof. One feels that the old legend of how they get their inspiration may be out of date in the days of these mechanical aids.

Whoever wishes to learn to play the lyre well, it is said, must go at midnight to a deserted crossroads and there carve a circle on the ground, with a black-shafted knife. Then he must go inside it and sit down and play. Soon Nereids will come from all directions to surround him. They mean him harm. But they cannot enter the charmed circle, and so they try to entice him out with sweet words and lovely songs. If he is prudent he will make his heart of stone, and continue to play. When the Nereids see that all their ruses are failing, 'Don't you realize,' they say, 'You're wasting energy playing like that?'

The Song

'That's how I learnt, that's how I play,' he says. 'What's it to do with you?'

'Nothing,' they say. 'But if you want we can teach you to play so the rocks will dance.' And they beg him to come out of the circle and be taught. He goes on playing. They ask, at any rate, for the lyre. He hands it over taking care not to put his hand outside the circle – for they would cut it off. A Nereid takes the lyre, plays it for a few moments with ravishing skill, and gives it back: 'Take it. You don't trust us.' But they go on trying to trick him into putting at least a hand or a finger outside.

Finally the cock crows. It is the signal for their departure. They cannot teach him without some payment. So now, carefully, the lyrist puts just the tip of his little finger outside the circle, and the Nereids cut it off. In next to no time they have taught him to play like themselves – and then they are off, to hide during the daylight hours.[4]

Cretan instrumentalists have no false modesty. Why should they, when they are members of an honourable guild? There are probably less of them now than there once were – it is difficult to be sure of this – but they are far more mobile than before. A pair of professionals based on Canea can cover the whole of western Crete, playing at festivals, and, if they are well known, making records and playing on Canea radio.

Among the lyrists, singers and poets of Crete, one stands out if only for his versatility. This is John Dermitzakis, the bard of Sitea. He keeps a draper's shop, but is happy enough to put work aside and listen to his own records with any interested visitors. He plays the lyre, the guitar and the violin, and composes and sings his own *mantinades*. As well as making records he has published his verses, together with a few pithy moral aphorisms – 'Death is the fate common to all of us, but we conquer it with what we create' – which illustrate the self-confidence I spoke of. This is particularly well marked in Dermitzakis. His little book is full of pats on the back from men who approved of his verses. There is a letter from Spyros Markezinis the political leader; a postcard from Nikos Kazantzakis in Antibes ('With much pleasure I read your *mantinades* which reminded me of my beloved Crete'); a postcard from Samuel Baud-Bovy the musicologist; and an intriguing message from 'Angelika Farmer, Great Missewden'.

Most of Dermitzakis's verses are of no great interest. I mention him here because he is typical of the *rhymadori* who have kept the tradition going. Each of these creators left something behind him; and doubtless some few of Dermitzakis's better *mantinades* will enter the repertory.

Personally, I like best some of his verses which will not last – the ephemeral and political. For Dermitzakis is the poet laureate of his area, and he sees it as his job to comment on the small and great events of the world. His booklet contains lines in praise of Fix beer, lines about Khrushchev and Kennedy, lines in honour of Gregory Lambrakis, the deputy who was murdered by thugs in 1963, and some exceedingly vigorous, threatening and optimistic lines about Cyprus.

'Cypriots, you are far off and the sea divides us, and we cannot strike a blow at the wild beast who torments you, at his filthy body, so as to lay it low with Greek fists. England! Know well, the wheel turns, your time is up, the hour is approaching. . . . And you Turks, know well that the Christians will complete the Mass in the City!' This, and there is plenty more of it, is in the best abusive tradition. The *mantinada* is as well suited to abuse and to obscenity as it is to love.

The lineaments of Cretan song are now clear. It is a fascinating and frustrating subject. Frustrating because with the best will in the world one cannot get worked up about the music. It is possible while you are in Crete to persuade yourself of its virtues, mainly because the atmosphere of performance is so exciting. And the dance music is pleasant enough. But Cretan folk music cannot compare in melodic richness and rhythmic vitality with, say, our own.

The words compare, however. Cretan poetry does not thrill like the best of English folk poetry, with an intensity which stabs:

> There's not a swish goes round my waist
> Nor a comb goes in my hair.
> Neither firelight nor candle light
> Can ease my heart's despair.

Those lines, and others from our folk songs, produce in me the Housman effect, or something like it. A shiver goes down the spine. I would not swap these lines for any in Greek poetry. Indeed in singing the despair of love the English poet has no peer. And the language with its monosyllables, its flexibility of metre, seems forged for the direct expression of the simplest and most painful feelings: 'For love it is a killing thing did you ever feel the pain?'

The Greek poet does not aim at this sort of stabbing thrill. The effect of his fifteen-syllable line is cumulative (and sometimes monotonous; the fifteen-syllable may be the glory of the Greek language – it can also be a liability). If he sings of love he can sometimes be reflective, impersonal, in a way which the English poet rarely could; as in this quiet poem (which is not Cretan):

The Song

> Go out, young men, to the dance, and girls to your songs
> Tell and sing how love is caught.
> It is caught from the eyes, it goes down to the lips,
> And from the lips to the heart – takes root and will not go.

But as a rule, if British folk poetry expresses the despair of love more surely than any other, the Greek expresses best the despair of man in the face of the most elemental facts of life; especially death. Thus the *mantinada*:

> The world's a tree and we the produce of it,
> And Charos is the reaper and takes the fruit of it.

And the song:

> The Lord made the earth and founded the world,
> But three things only He did not make in the world –
> A bridge over the sea and a return from Hades
> And a ladder up to heaven.

And the mainland couplet associated with the death of the hero Diakos in 1821:

> What a time Charos has chosen to take you,
> Now when the branches are blossoming and the earth putting out grass.

12

Sphakia – Impressions

Sphakia. The name is always cropping up in the pages of Cretan histories and books of travel, and has cropped up often enough already in this one. Sphakia, they all say, is something special. But the reader must be warned, if he is to visit Crete; Sphakia is not so special as it once was. Many of the distinctions which marked it off from the rest of Crete have disappeared. The traveller today will find similar clothes, customs and language throughout the west of Crete. There are local variations, but less marked than before the days of radios and buses. The whole area of the White Mountains, however, remains distinct from the rest of Crete, and is the most interesting part of the island. A few jottings made on a trip through these mountains, and now expanded and edited, may give the flavour better than a formal description. Julie du Boulay went with me on this trip.

27 May. Canea to Lakki, where the people leave you alone. The question of the donkey arises here. (We had decided if possible to buy one.) Julie is very keen. Of course they all think us mad. Eventually an old man, Georgioudakis, speaks up; he has a beast which he might sell, for 2500 drachmas (about £30) since it is a good beast, so we arrange to inspect it later and meanwhile go down to Meskla. Much better. Friendly people. A bustling *papas* is sitting under a clambering vine, unscrupulously extorting money for the church.

'Come on now, the church needs money. Look what it does for you. Everyone has a duty to give.'

An old man: 'Yes, but . . . I have nothing, next year I'll give an extra lot', etc.

Most of the villagers are working on the new church. In the old one we are forced to eat olives and drink wine, and apparently it has ceased to be holy ground, because we are all smoking cigarettes in there in front of the *papas*. The church they are building – the children all helping – will be the usual concrete affair. There are three other churches in the village, one of them old, containing excellent frescoes. They love new things.

Sphakia – Impressions

Conversation in Lakki: the sort which is quite frequent here. The host: 'All men have in them a good disposition even if it is hidden. The strongest forces in the world are Truth, Justice, Humanity. But the world is a jungle, we are caught between two wild beasts – Communism and Capitalism. When these two beasts die, or devour each other, and the democrats remain, *all will be well.*'

'I am not so confident,' say I, talking like a Greek too. 'They are just symptoms of our nature, of *physis*. They are not themselves the roots of evil.'

'No. They will disappear. We look to England for a lead. That is why it is so important for the world that the Labour party should win your next election.'

From there we get on to Gregory Lambrakis, hero and martyr, the left-wing deputy murdered by thugs of the extreme right in Salonika on 22 May 1963.

31 May. Kollyva: one of the days of remembrance for the dead.[1] The word *kollyva* comes in Aristophanes, meaning small round mealy cakes. It now signifies a dish of boiled grains of wheat, with seeds or nuts on top, and spice. At the end of the service each member of the congregation takes a little of this and offers a prayer for the soul of the dead; but since I didn't go to church I missed this. There is a tradition that Julian the Apostate determined to annoy the Christians by defiling all the grain in the market with the blood from heathen sacrifices. The Patriarch Eudoxios was warned of this in a dream and told to set apart some special grain for the faithful, which had not been defiled. And the *kollyva* are offered in memory of this. But it looks like a ritual offering for the dead man.

The *kollyva* are offered on certain special days in the year, and also on certain fixed days after the death of a man: usually the third, ninth and fortieth. Dawkins found a Cretan version of the apocryphal Apocalypse of the Virgin which has a unique bit at the end throwing light on the *kollyva*. There are various theories as to the significance of these days, e.g. that the third day is chosen because Christ rose on the third day. But this apocryphal Apocalypse proposes that the days mark danger points in the progress of the soul towards salvation. When the Virgin's visit to the next world ends, a monk asks an angel to reveal the mystery of what happens to the soul after it has left the body. The answer given is that angels carry the soul up towards Christ, but he must climb a ladder, and countless demons try to drag him down, producing written evidence of his sins. The angels help him, and the memorial prayers on the third day after the death help him in his three-day struggle. Prayers on the ninth day help him and fortify him after his visit to the scene of his good and evil deeds on earth. Prayers on the fortieth day fortify him for the moment when he pays homage to God.

This is a late explanation. (It is a sixteenth or seventeenth-century manuscript.) I suspect that the memorial *kollyva* are offered not only to help the soul but also to placate it; for a person may haunt the earth until the fortieth day after his death, and if he is not properly buried he may become a vampire.

The baby we saw last night cried all through the night, so this morning we had to spit on her in case one of us had put the evil eye on her. (Blue eyes or over-complimentary remarks may affect a child even without any guilty intent.)

In the evening, one of those rather childish conversations about the desirability of our marrying Mesklans. The naïveté of it is a bit irritating. Perhaps I am envious because I imagine them to be shielded from some of the peculiar horrors of this century. Their horrors are the age-old ones, things that they can touch and feel, like cracking bones and disease and the last war, with its hunger and death. Ours seem to be more creeping, abstract things, and in the last resort annihilation. Their peace correspondingly is something which they can touch and feel, like warm earth. And ours, it seems, is hovering always just out of reach, and if we catch it it is as fragile as a butterfly's wing.

(And yet the incidence of mental diseases in poor and primitive societies is generally higher than in sophisticated ones. The paragraph above suffers from what might be called Arcady disease.)

1 June. The doctor tells me the etymological legend. Meskla was the headquarters of Kandanoleon, and some of the unfortunate Greeks who were executed after the wedding were buried here. A bush called *mousklia* grew from their tomb; and this word, corrupted, became Meskla, the village.

Julie heard from Antigone, our hostess, a story of the powers of St Nektarios, who died quite recently on Aegina. A girl from Meskla – it turned out later to be the hearty Antigone herself – had a bad cough. She became so ill that she decided to go to Aegina to get help from the saint. She promised him presents of oil, but without effect; she returned to Crete just as ill. The cough had troubled her now for over a year, and her mother forced her to go to the doctor at Heraklion. Just as he was about to give her an injection, the needle broke. A sign from the saint that he had taken notice at last! Since then she has had perfect health.

There is a sequel. Some time later a blight fell on her brother's sheep in the hill-pastures. They were dying, two of them every day. He was sceptical but intrigued by Antigone's experience, and he was persuaded to take the icon of Nektarios up the mountainside and bless the sheep with it. From that moment on they flourished.

(There are fashions in saints just as in clothes and pop singers; and Nektarios is popular at the moment, being fresh in the people's memory. I met a woman a few days later who had a three-month-old baby, as yet unbaptized. When she bore him in Canea, there were complications. It was thought she might die. So: 'I prayed to God, since He is the greatest, and then to Nektarios, and the baby is all right.'

I also saw a boy in Kandanos wearing a Nektarios badge on his lapel – a plastic badge with a picture of the saint, as if he were a Beatle or a film star.)

2 June. We had seen a donkey three days before. Georgioudakis's animal up in Lakki was much too expensive, although sweet and mild-tempered. I think the old man was really a little reluctant to sell him to us; as he said, charmingly, 'Men are of many kinds – some good, some bad, some steal animals, some are honest. I don't know you, you don't know me. One must take care.' The second donkey belonged to a store-keeper in Meskla, a morose, weary man with asthma – one shelf in his store was devoted to his own medicines. As soon as this donkey saw us he rolled on the ground. A sign of healthy disrespect. We made test runs up the village street on his back.

Today we bought him for 1000 drachmas (about £12). After deliberating on Ajax, Jason, and Bellerophon, we called him Alexander; Aleko for short. He has a mealy nose, white belly, brown body with black patches where the hair rubs off. He is very healthy and has a rigidly straight back. The saddle is a wreck. His voice is tremendous and rises to a tormented shriek on the breathe-in; he gives sound when he sees another donkey. Their voices are all different. He likes sniffing donkey mess. He has to be pulled sometimes. He nips.

(In the end he had to be pulled almost always. We were too soft with him; the Greeks were much tougher.)

3 June. Overnight near Lakki Aleko was tethered to a sturdy root. At about 2 a.m. he tore free and clattered off through the vine terraces. Julie woke up, felt that something was wrong, got up and inspected the root; by which time Aleko had disappeared. I woke up, and immediately went to sleep again, having ungallantly decided that nothing

The Great Island

could be done until morning. Julie made a brief search without success. She went back to bed and lay sleepless with worry till first light, when she went out again. Aleko was in the middle of a vineyard, entangled in his own rope. He had stripped three vines clear of leaves, and looked ashamed of himself. When we found the owner later in the day, he would not hear of repayment.

(Some days later we tethered Aleko at blackest midnight to the only available tree, and woke – or rather Julie woke – to find that he had eaten two or three square yards of a field of barley. The *agrophylax* (country warden) arrived immediately, as if by magic, and was quite rightly annoyed. In the end, however, his natural courtesy towards mad foreigners overcame his anger. A Cretan would have copped it. Putting a donkey on to your neighbour's land would be as malicious as slyly moving his boundary stone.)

So we had acquired a donkey. I must admit I was a little uneasy. Stevenson only had to deal with Modestine's whims and tantrums; but in Crete there are other dangers – beasts are not always what they seem. Inside the body of a dog may lurk the soul of an infidel Turk. The hare changes its sex every year. The crow has a hole pierced in its throat. The donkey may be an *anaskelas*. I remembered a story about one Statheroyiannis of Voriza and a donkey.

This *palikari* was going one night from his village to another, when he saw a donkey standing loose in the middle of the road. The donkey looked tired. Statheroyiannis resolved to ride him.

He mounted. They hadn't gone ten paces when the donkey began to grow taller.

'Hey!' shouted Statheroyiannis. 'To the devil with this donkey I've got here!'

The donkey laughed and enquired, 'Does the devil himself go to the devil?'

A sinister reply. Statheroyiannis at once realized he was dealing with an *anaskelas*. He kept his grip on the monster despite its diabolic size. He drew his knife (which had a black handle – the magic colour for evil things) and pinned it to the beast's rump. Immediately the *anaskelas* shrunk and became a normal donkey again.

'Devil-believer!' said Statheroyiannis. 'Now see who you're up against. The very devil of devils!' And blow by blow he beat it all the way to his destination, riding on its back.

As a matter of fact the *anaskelades* (upside-down-ones) do not seem ever to have been really dangerous, in the way that vampires can be.[2] The fear that they inspired was never excessive, simply a part of that general fear of the dark which holds unaccountable mysteries. Methods of dealing with the upside-down-ones abound. If your donkey expands and takes you past your destination, it needs only the sign of the *pent-alpha* (the five-pointed star of Solomon, infallible against demons) to put him on to the right track. And a prayer to the Virgin will take you back to where you started from with your foot raised ready to mount. The donkey will then vanish from before you, filling the air with fire and sparks from his unrestrained farting. As usual the devil turns out to be somewhat ludicrous.

But the best way of coping with an upside-downer is to unmask him before you even mount, by an obscene threat. Seize him by the tail and shout, 'Thus shall I f. . . you!' Again, if he is diabolic, he will disappear in a sulphurous cloud, farting as he goes.

Needless to say, we did not test Aleko in this way when we first met him, or at any time later. It would have been an insult to the owners, and to Aleko, who looked so gentle, sweet, yet lively, that any spirit which possessed him must surely have been saintly, not devilish. Besides, if I remembered rightly, the upside-down-ones, like vampires, Nereids and other supernatural phenomena, appear at night. It is only Pan, the midday demon, who disturbs the unwary at noon.

We came on to the Omalos in the evening, passing shepherds and distant goats whose tinkling music of bells sounds like spring-water in the poets' descriptions. Up here the stink lilies are still in bud – purple spear-like flowers a foot long. The bearded barley rustles; the asphodel shimmers in the late sunlight. Tucked away beside the road on the way up there are cheese huts where rich *graviera* and creamy *mizithra* are squeezed from the milk of thyme-fed sheep.

The Omalos ('the level') is the strangest of the upland plateaus which distinguish Crete; such as the Nidha plain on Mt Ida, the plateau of Anopolis, and Lassithi. Lassithi is large, fertile and beautiful; especially in springtime when the upland grass is of Alpine greenness, the flowers are manifold, and the snow on Dicte is gashed by black outlines of ravines. Then at the beginning of May the windmills start to turn, pumping water to irrigate the plain. If you look down on Lassithi from the cave where Zeus was born you can see thousands of white-sailed windmills riding the plain like tall ships. The Omalos is different; it is much smaller, and lacks the cultivated apple trees, the mills, the populous villages which fringe Lassithi. It is a simple patch of productive land, a thousand metres high, ringed with mountains. In the winter it is uninhabited. Snow covers the plain, and for some time after it melts the land remains flooded and unworked. In summer, from May on, the dry stone huts round the edge of the Omalos are occupied by men from Lakki and Agia Eirene. Cereals and potatoes make up the crop. Some 30,000 goats and sheep pasture on the surrounding slopes.

In the café on the Omalos where we slept on the floor, there is an astonishing photograph of the local *palikari* Hadzimichalis Iannaris, looking exactly like W. G. Grace except that he is cradling a gun instead of a bat. Beside him there is a second photo of Cretans who fought in Macedonia (1906-9) with just the moustaches, the stern faces and stiff poses of nineteenth-century cricketers: hands on hips, or arms folded, and in front one captain lying, reclining on one elbow, with his legs crossed. But again it is guns, not bats.

Hadzimichalis, who was prominent in the '66 revolt, first distinguished himself in a brawl. After the fall of Sebastopol in 1855 the Turks of Canea held three days of festivities on the Sultan's recommendation. Some Turks met in a little café to drink and celebrate with music; and turned to insulting the Orthodox Russians and Cretans. 'Now that the devil has taken the Tsar, he will soon take you too.' Hadzimichalis, with a cousin, entered the café and was invited to drink; filled with anger, he proposed the health of the Emperor of Russia. A brawl ensued, in which several Turks were wounded.

The Turks took relatives of Hadzimichalis as hostages and imprisoned them; but soon Mustapha Pasha released them and promised an amnesty if the two miscreants gave themselves up. They did; and were imprisoned. After some months Hadzimichalis was allowed out on paying a sum of money towards the hospital bills of those he had beaten up. But seven years later he was back in prison. A group of Lakkiots came down to Canea to release him. Passing a church of St Panteleimon on the way they prayed for help, promising him a chapel. And after his successful release Hadzimichalis raised a little chapel to the saint on the Omalos. He is buried next door.

Local tradition is rather different. Aphrodite Drakoulakis, the wife of the café keeper, told me that when the two heroes were in prison, Hadzimichalis and his Lakkiot friends all prayed to the saint at the same time. 'Help me, St Panteleimon, and I will build you a chapel.' Hadzimichalis was scratching a hole in the wall, covering it up each day with his bed. 'And God enlightened him.' He managed to send a letter out of prison, saying 'allegorically' that ten men were to go to work his vines at such and such a time. His friends understood, and were there. At the agreed moment, Hadzimichalis broke through the wall and jumped down into the blankets they held below. His friend jumped but broke his foot. 'What could they do? There was no time.

Sphakia – Impressions

They left him behind.' Back on the Omalos, Hadzimichalis erected a house in triumph. And lo, it fell down overnight. So he realized what he had forgotten to do, and built the saint's church. This done, the re-erected house stood firm.

A poem is inscribed over his grave:

> Traveller on the Omalos, turn aside and pass near me,
> So you may see and reflect on what I achieved.
> Learn and assess the story of my troubled course,
> And do not remain deceived and innocent of the world.
> The planet which gave us birth has great sweetness.
> The mighty are struck down, the humble are revealed.

I therefore transcribed these lines to remind readers of the achievements of a typical Cretan captain.

5 June. The gorge of Samaria. We tried to take Aleko through the gorge, but without success. It was difficult to persuade him at first to go down the *xyloskala* (wooden steps) which descend from the Omalos into the gorge. Even after he reached the bottom there were problems; for where the path was narrow the rucksacks which hung on either side of his saddle would bang against the encroaching rocks, and we were afraid that he would twist an ankle from the jolt. After one such incident he panicked. So we decided to return to the Omalos. But more intrepid travellers will find that it is quite possible to take a mule or donkey through the gorge.

We went through ourselves the next day. I don't want to say too much about the gorge of Samaria. It seems to attract exaggeration. For example, 'All who have been through the gorge describe the experience in awesome terms – like some descent into the underworld or back into some past millenium.' Well. . . . The gorge is beautiful, it may inspire awe; but it is no more remote or dangerous (in summer) than many Scottish glens. A new motive for exaggeration is the tourist build-up. The gorge is now a National Park and game reserve. A new metalled road is being built from Lakki on to the Omalos to complete the communication line with Canea. A tourist hotel is being built at the very top of the *xyloskala*, overlooking the gorge itself; God knows why. The top is already prey to trippers in excursion groups who stand on the rim and throw stones over the top. But at least when they have had a look they go away. They might have built the hotel at the other end of the Omalos. There is something paradoxical about the publicity the gorge now gets. Just at the time when it is in danger of being domesticated it must be made to appear savage, majestic and tremendous beyond description (yet safe at the same time, or tourists might be frightened. But this paradox applies to much tourist publicity.).

Let me show restraint then. The *xyloskala*, plunging down off the Omalos into the gorge, is indeed impressive. Standing on the top you can see the inland end of the gorge to the right – a long smooth scree. The gorge winds down towards the sea seven and a half miles away to your left. Mt Gingilos rises opposite, sheer and massive, blocking the view to southwards. Its rock faces, the Rotten Cliffs, are dotted with cliff-hanging trees, scree and gullies where the snow clings all the year through. The *xyloskala* – not really wooden steps, but a zigzag path worn into the cliffside – descends a sheer 2500 feet to the gorge. This is impressive; especially since the gorge is a pocket of strange weather conditions. To come off a sun-bathed Omalos and enter this gloomy cleft, to see vapours rising from the depths – this is what has made travellers compare the descent to a descent into Hades.

Once down the wooden steps you have a seven- or eight-mile walk to the sea. The path winds beside the stream, which (in summer) disappears underground half-way down, reappearing again below Samaria. Samaria, the remotest village in Crete, is the only settlement in the gorge. In the winter it is cut off by the flooding stream. Like many of the Cretan villages it looks depopulated with its crumbling ruined houses – and soon will be, for the government's schemes for the Samaria National Park entail removing the villagers to other sites and leaving Samaria to the ibex. Not far below Samaria, the true gorge begins; the mountain walls close in, and for the last few miles you walk between sheer rock faces a thousand feet high – at one point (the Iron Gates) only about ten feet apart.

Julie, who did a lot of research into the gorge later in the summer, says that the people are quite content, indeed pleased, at the prospect of being moved. They have possibly been led to expect better compensation than they will in fact get; however, what they do get in the way of land could hardly be worse than what they have now. I remember the refrain of Georgia Katsamerakis, the housewife with whom we stayed on the way back through the gorge, and who had made a little necessary money by selling some of her magnificent woven stuffs and embroideries to foreigners. 'I have two daughters. A dowry costs money, a lot of money. There is no work here. Life is difficult here. I have two daughters, you see.' Happily she sold only those pieces which were comparatively easy to replace. The fair-haired Samarians were the handsomest people I saw in Crete; the children, though they looked

Sphakia – Impressions

undernourished and unwell, rivalled only by some of the colony of superb children who congregate round the unofficial mayor of Poros (a suburb of Heraklion), the much-loved Michael Akratos.

I noted: 'Halfway down, while we bathe in a mountain pool, the sun breaks through. If only I knew flowers I could compile quite a list. Fragile rock roses in green beds, flowering yellow mullen, stink lilies, planes with old bark peeling like shavings off a stick, larkspur, coltsfoot, oleanders bursting with pink flames, flowering thyme, saxifrage, purple peaflowers, daisies; olives and mulberries at Samaria; red and orange-flaming pomegranate at Agia Roumeli and crocus-yellow prickly pear. Other ravines slash through the mountains and join ours. Ants in colonies. From Samaria down, many ruined crofts and walls. The stream bubbles up, under planes and oleanders, through slate-grey, blue and green stones and pebbles: no warmth at all. Yet the sides of the gorge glow in russet and ochre; warm walls dotted with trees, rock-whorls, caves, convolutions. We cross the stream by stepping stones and logs. Agia Roumeli is a water garden of oleanders and on either side the cliffs curve down into the Libyan sea.'

Because the gorge is easily defended and difficult of access and, besides, a place which few Greeks would want to visit, since it is not on the route to anywhere important, it has always served as a refuge; to outlaws, to communists at the end of the Civil War, and to the ibex. This animal, of extraordinary rapidity and noble bearing, is mentioned by everyone who has ever written about western Crete – it was mentioned by me in the first chapter – and although I have never seen one in its natural state, I must now say more.

Capra aegagrus, the indigenous Cretan ibex, the Cretan wild goat, the *agrimi* (the common Cretan name), or simply *kri-kri*, has a long and distinguished history. They used to roam all over the island even in Tournefort's time: 'The wild goats mentioned by Solinus, and which Belonius has given a print of, run up and down these mountains in herds; the Greek call 'em Agrimia, a name they give to all deer' – 'these mountains' were the range near Hierapetra in the east. In ancient times they were well known not only for speed but also for their sagacity, being able to cure themselves of wounds through the requisite simples. Thus Vergil, on the wounding of young Ascanius (in Conington's translation):

> Then Venus, all a mother's heart,
> Touched by her son's unworthy smart,
> Plucks dittany, a simple rare,
> From Ida's summit brown,

The Great Island

> With flower of purple, bright and fair,
> And leaf of softest down:
> Well known that plant to mountain goat,
> Should arrow pierce its shaggy coat.

Vergil was following Aristotle on the habits of the ibex. And it was doubtless because of these great authorities, and Pliny, that the obscure herb found its way into the mediaeval Bestiaries. 'The WILD GOAT (*caprea*)' we read in T. H. White's *Book of Beasts*, 'has the following peculiarities: that he moves higher and higher as he pastures; that he chooses good herbs from bad ones by the sharpness of his eyes; that he ruminates these herbs, and that, if wounded, he runs to the plant dittany, after reaching which he is cured.' But the bestiarist does not mean by 'wild goat' specifically the Cretan ibex.

There is traditionally, then, a connection between those two Cretan products, the ibex and the herb. Like the gorge itself, they are in the process of being domesticated. Dittany which tends to grow in precipitous and dangerous spots, used sometimes to cost the lives of Cretans who climbed for it. But now there is enough easily accessible to deter the foolhardy from risking their necks. The ibex, too, is accessible on his preserves, the little islands of St Theodore and Dia, and in the National Gardens at Athens. For only a short time ago he was in danger of extinction. In the last century he was to be found as far west as Mt Ida, and also on Antimelos in the Cyclades. But the assiduous work of huntsmen drove him into the remotest ravines of the White Mountains, so that during this century he has been found only in the gorge of Samaria and the surrounding country and gorges.

The ibex is large, surprisingly heavily built for one so nimble, with a reddish coat and horns that curve back in a long sweep over his shoulders. The Cretans speak with awe of his surefooted course over the mountain crags; but nimble as he is he could not escape the huntsmen, who shot him not only for the tasty meat but also for the sport – and went on shooting him after it was forbidden by law. The ibex is now safe. Preservation has had its effect, and apart from those which are kept on the island reserves, there are thought to be about 500 at large in the gorge. The danger now is not that they should die out, but rather that the race may degenerate through indiscriminate breeding with ordinary domestic goats. There is no fear of the male goat mounting the female ibex, for she runs too fast and escapes him. But the *agrimi* can and does couple with the female goat.

The *agrimi*, an animal at once rapid, surefooted and unapproachable, is monarch of the gorge of Samaria. Penned up in a small enclosure in

Sphakia – Impressions

the National Gardens he seems cowed and uneasy. It would be pleasing if the preservation laws encouraged him to venture outside the gorge – so that one day we might see, as in days past, whole herds of ibex roaming the slopes of Dicte and leaping wind-borne from crag to crag on Ida.

Undated. An old braggart in a cloth cap, his chin stubbly, very talkative. A Sphakian with a dark carved face, deep-set eyes, dark crisp hair just going grey, big eyebrows, headband, very silent. Eventually he admits he left Sphakia because of 'family differences', i.e. a blood feud. It seems to have blown over since he can now revisit Sphakia. The old man suddenly says, 'That is the evil of Crete!' He is rather drunk, but a remark about old age causes him to speak with passion: 'Listen to me. There where I stand, you will stand. Are you listening? This is ancient Greek philosophy, write it down. This is Latin. Listen. Where I am now you will be. There where I stood you now stand. In the end it is the same for all.' And we and the Sphakian nod.

Making cheese: Sheep's milk is heated in a great copper cauldron, to 48° C., before being curdled. If it exceeds this temperature by much the cheese will not take salt and is spoiled. The cauldron full makes three 'heads' of cheese: that is, three whole *graviera* cheeses, each between four and eight kilos in weight. In the cool of winter they can make it all into two or even one head. The milk is stirred perpetually. Eventually you can plunge a hand into the cauldron and turn over the grains of milk-cheese. A third of the contents, enough for one head, is gathered in a cloth, pushed into an open metal cylinder, and pressed into shape. A pail catches the whey. After some hours the head can be laid in the maturing room where it is turned and salted daily.

The maturing room is marvellous – dark and mysterious – row on row of cheeses, over a foot in diameter; at first they are soft and immature, and later as the rind hardens they begin to glow with health. They take a month to mature.

How should one eat *graviera*? Best at a Cretan festival or *glendi*, in large slabs, with cold lamb, or hot pilaff, or honey. And of course washed down with the great local wines.

11 June. An evening's revelry at Agia Eirene ends with Julie and me singing 'On yonder hill there lives a lady', and our doing a waltz accompanied by the village schoolmaster on the comb and lavatory paper – only being Greeks they have no lavatory paper, and so use the tissues from a cigarette packet instead.

The Great Island

We did not actually visit Khora Sphakia (the town) on that trip, though we had been inside the eparchy of Sphakia in the gorge. A month later we were back.

The road to Sphakia cuts across Crete from the north, over another upland plateau, through grey, denuded mountains. By this road the British forces, depleted and exhausted in the Battle of Crete, crossed the island in 1941 to await evacuation from Sphakia. The town is a half-ruined, half-deserted place: a cluster of pretty houses on the shore, dominated by a pine-clad hill with the crumbling ruins of Castel Sfacchia on the top. In July the sea is a sinister sheet of glass and the hint of a warm breeze rustles in from Africa. At night, by a startling change, this breeze turns into a violent offshore wind. In the morning the island of Gavdos (St Paul's island) appears, floating out of a sea of haze, separated from the water by a band of light.

But it is not really the acropolis with its slender aromatic pines which dominates Sphakia; it is the wall of mountains inland, which twist and tumble down to the sea in gigantic folds of rock. Looking along the coastline you can see the cliffs superimposed one on the other, each with a different tone of shade. All bare.

The town is a shell. The Daskaloyiannis revolt ended a period of peace which had lasted two hundred years, a peace originally bought by the Venetians at the cost of certain concessions to the Sphakians, who worried both Venetians and Turks by their natural bellicosity. After the rebellion of 1866 many of the already depleted population left Crete to avoid Turkish reprisals and by now, instead of several thousands, the town supports a few hundred. Pasturage is minimal. There are fish, but not many. One may be sad, but not surprised, at the movement away from the countryside towards the towns, and West Germany.

Julie du Boulay joined us in Sphakia with Aleko. In order to save time she and my sister Elizabeth brought him over from Canea by lorry. Julie had been understandably nervous about this trip but the Greeks assured her all would be well. (I can imagine the scene. When Greeks answer questions they have a wonderful knack of making you feel a fool for asking. Whether the answer is yes or no, the implication is that no one but an imbecile could have conceived that any other answer was possible.) In the event her fears were entirely justified, and not only by the callous way in which Aleko was hoisted on and off the lorry. Passengers were officially not allowed, so that whenever they passed through a village Julie and Elizabeth had to hide. At the same time they had to tend and comfort the donkey, whose moorings gave

Sphakia – Impressions

cause for alarm. (The road to Sphakia is tortuous and rough.) And there was something which made the journey still more hazardous – Aleko was suffering from the same disease as I was – acute diarrhoea.

On his arrival Aleko, overjoyed at being on firm ground again after his first experience of motoring, unwisely ate too much barley and drank too little water. I was sitting in a café when Julie came running up the path faster than any dingbat. Aleko had just collapsed by the village watering place. He had just folded up and sunk to the ground, rolling his eyes horribly, his legs stiff and extended.

At once we were deluged with contradictory advice; or, more simply, with amused comment.

'He's had too much to drink.'

'He's had too little to drink.'

'Give him an onion with salt on it,' says the postman.

'Try so-and-so, he knows all about donkeys.'

The expert, a mountainous man, prescribed exercise. We took turns hauling Aleko along the village street until his eyes lost their fixed, complaining stare.

An itinerant preacher came to Sphakia. A Cretan, just back from the Holy Land, with colour slides to illustrate his lecture. A white sheet was pegged up as a screen on the terrace of a café some twenty yards from the murmuring sea; and most of the town turned up to watch.

Some of the slides were colour shots of the present-day landscape – the Mount of Olives, Bethany, Zacchaeus's tree. As they came up on the screen the preacher interrogated the Sphakian children, who sat in the front row.

'What's that tree?'

'It's a tree.'

'Yes. What tree?'

Silence.

'It's the tree which Zacchaeus climbed to get a good view of Our Lord.'

Others were wishy-washy tinted pictures of biblical scenes, each one illustrating some 'point':

'Here Our Lord washes the disciples' feet. It shows His humility. *Egoism is a great sin!*'

We did not see all the slides, however, as the projector broke down. I think this suited the preacher rather well. He was able to preach a sermon instead, and it was one of the two most rousing sermons I have ever heard.

'The machine has broken down,' he said. 'And there is a reason for it. It is the will of God, you may be sure, for nothing happens without His knowledge and His will; so He has been good enough in His wisdom to *stop* the machine for us.

'Why? I don't know. Nor do you. But I'll tell you what the reason may be. It may be that *you* are at fault! Somebody not attending, whispering, looking round. . . . There's a lesson for all of us here.'

This was extremely embarrassing, since I had been relaying a translation of his words in what I had hoped was an unobtrusive whisper. I shuffled forward and explained this to the village priest, who said that it was nothing – the children were to blame – God was rather pleased than offended by my translation.

After a long pause for the lesson to sink in, during which Elizabeth suggested that we ask my brother Chris to do God's will by mending the machine, the preacher went on:

'Never mind. The machine is unimportant. What is really important is the *message* – what comes through the machine – and we still have *that* available to us. You probably think that the machine is important, that once the motor stops that's the end of the whole show, but nothing could be more mistaken! It's no more important than your own heart!

'Your heart is a motor working away inside you, and it has no importance compared with the *other* heart you have. The first one, the motor, ticks and ticks, and if it stops it stops. Pouff, like that! It only lives inside your body, and your body is just a house, a prison, four walls – *nothing* compared to what is *really* in there – the soul. And the soul too has its heart and the heart of the soul is what matters. . . .'

His arms began to wave. His bald head glowed in the darkness.

'We are all sinners. But there are several different kinds. There are the *molyntiria*, rotten right through, cancerous growths, and where are they going? You know where they are going. To *kolasis*. Hell!

'Then there are the *vatrachi* [frogs] who may repent, and may not. They must make the choice, because there is no middle way. It's either heaven or hell – paradise or *kolasis*. You can't hide. The tallest castle, the deepest cave, the biggest crowd is not enough to hide you from God.

'You know that there is an eye up there which sees everything, and that eye is God's eye. And an ear which hears every word. God's ear. And next door a book in which your record is written – this is symbolical of course, since God and His angels don't actually write – so there is *no escape*!'

Next came harrowing stories about murderers who thought they had gone undetected, sheep-thiefs who faced the prospect of a year or two in gaol with equanimity, not realizing that hell is for all time.

Sphakia – Impressions

There were exhortations to repent at once. And then it was finished. Translation and compression destroy the flavour of this remarkable performance. This bald, paunchy, dynamic Cretan was one of those few who have a natural capacity for terrifying people.

I now see that he was not the first of his type to visit Sphakia. Shortly after the Daskaloyiannis revolt a saintly monk came from the Holy Mountain, a blind man who fasted perpetually. He pointed out the sinners, expelled the renegadoes from his congregation, and preached so powerfully that murder and blood feud came to a halt. Pashley tells also of another saint who appeared in 1811, wearing a coarse garment, an iron chain around his neck, preaching the necessity of repentance, the imminence of earthquake and disease and war. He took no money; but accepted voluntary contributions of sheep. He appears to have astonished the credulous villagers with conjuring tricks. A shepherd's wife broke three eggs into a pan, had to go for a moment to the door, and when she returned found four. 'How is this, holy priest? I only broke three.'

'I blessed them,' he replied, 'and they are become four.'

The terror inspired by this man induced good order which lasted until the 1821 rebellion.

The day after we heard this sermon I was still more embarrassed. We had left our clothes and possessions on the rocks while we swam; and the preacher, taking his morning stroll with his wife, noticed watches and wallets lying in full view. Later in the café, he held us up as models of natural goodness on the strength of this.

'Look at them. Look at that trust. Where they come from you can leave things around without their being pinched. Listen to them. They don't blaspheme like us Greeks, we blaspheme, we steal, we don't trust each other. That's why Greece is in a mess today.'

I could not help pointing out that in England we should have been more careful. The listening Greeks with whom we were contrasted nodded meekly, but it was obvious that they thought us foolish. And maybe they were right, because Elizabeth lost her watch in Sphakia. But probably even this was due to carelessness rather than light Cretan fingers.

13

Sphakia – The Vampires

Les habitants de Spachia . . . surpassent tous les autres en courage et en adresse à manier les armes. Car ils sont des hommes rudes, mal polis et presque sauvages, qui sont accoûtumez à vivre de pirateries et de brigandages.

Dapper

When travellers and historians speak with awe of the Sphakians – *Sfacchioti popoli bellicosi* – they are referring not only to the inhabitants of the town, but also of the mountain villages, Anopolis, Imbros, Askyphou and the rest. This awe has called forth tributes from all who have come in contact with them – to the purity of their blood, the nobility of their bearing, their bravery, beauty, and skill at shooting the bow. Sphakia was the centre of the blood feud, of marriage by abduction, of sheep stealing and lawlessness.

When God made the earth, they say, he distributed to each place its own product – olives to Selino, vines to Kissamos, wheat to the Messara, oranges to Canea, and so forth, until all his good gifts were gone, and nothing remained for Sphakia but the dry stones. The Sphakians therefore paraded before the Creator and asked him angrily how they were expected to live off these rocks. He answered, you've got brains, haven't you? Can't you see that all these people down in the plains are working to grow all these splendid products for your benefit? The Sphakians accepted this. As a result they have been disliked by their own countrymen as well as by the foreigners.

The Sphakians were different because in their easily guarded mountains they were less liable to Roman, Arab, Venetian and Turkish contamination than others. But even they did not avoid it entirely. Of recent years, with the increase of movement from place to place, they have become less and less distinct from other Cretans. Nowadays, for instance, one rarely hears the prevalent *r* sound (instead of *l*) which used to be a feature of the dialect. But even now there is something tough about Sphakia. As recently as 1948 two whole villages, Lakki and Samaria in the gorge, were involved in a vendetta with each other.

The Sphakians are a credulous, godfearing people. Their shepherds

Sphakia – The Vampires

have always had a reputation for divination by the marks on a sheep's shoulderblade. (The abbot of Arkadi told W. R. Halliday early in this century that the 1866 rebellion was foretold by these means. He had been told by a travelling German about planchette, and succeeded in proving to Halliday that it was only impure spirits, and not the souls of the dead, who wrote messages thus. The abbot was of the opinion – like all folklorists at all times – that things were not what they had been; the art of divination was dying. If so it has taken an unconscionable time to do so.)

Demons, evil spirits and vampires haunt these mountains. There is an old story, how two men sat up one moonlit night waiting for *agrimia* near the gorge of Samaria. Their vigil was disturbed by a great noise, caused they imagined by overzealous workmen come to hump snow down to Canea for use in refrigeration. But on going closer they could distinguish lyres, viols, and other stranger noises such as they had never heard. Then they knew that these were no men, but members of a Demons' Council. At last they saw them – phantoms, male and female, some mounted, some on foot: the men white as doves, the women fair as the rays of the sun; winding their ghostly way across the slope.

They were supporting something, as one supports a bier – a girl, it seems, for they were singing, 'Where are we to take her, the bride, the lonely bride?'

When two hunters interrupted them by firing into the company, those in front cried 'Who is it?' and those behind cried 'They have killed our bridegroom, they have killed our bridegroom.' And they wept and fled.

The superstitions survive, even if battered and eroded by scepticism. George Psychoundakis claims to have heard a similar ghostly army, but admits that it can never be seen. When its members are evil spirits, they come to carry off a soul, when good (but this is rare) there is a smell of incense in the air around them. George, returning to Asi Gonia from a neighbouring village, heard the footfalls of a great company approach. He waited until they passed in front of him, and then, dismayed because he could see no man, ran back to Asi Gonia and fetched his relations out to listen. But although he himself could still hear the drumming of feet, for the others there was only silence.

Two days later an old man died in the neighbourhood.

Ghosts in large numbers are hard to cope with. When they appear singly there is more opportunity for the Cretan to show ingenuity in dealing with them; and often the best method is indecent.

There was for instance the vampire in Anopolis, the little village

The Great Island

above Sphakia where Daskaloyiannis's house can be seen – much restored. This demon – again invisible – began to throw stones at a woman who was out walking with her daughter. He also sang what sounded like a song, though the words were indistinguishable. The woman tried saying 'priestly words', but these had no effect. Then they knew that he was a vampire; and therefore crossed themselves, prayed to the Virgin, and repeated thrice over, 'In the beginning was the word, and the word was with God, and the word was God.' Still no effect. The stones continued to fall, and Hail Marys were no better.

On reaching the village however, and seeing friends close at hand, the mother took heart. She shouted vigorously, 'Out devil, or I'll bash your arse with my stick!'

This did the trick. They were molested no longer – though how she could have carried out her threat on an invisible spirit is not explained. The point is, however, that the obscene threat was enough. The same sort of technique can be used on demon donkeys.

Without doubt there were lovers who went in the guise of vampires. It is useful for erring wives to have some ghostly visitant to blame for unwanted pregnancies, and in England the devil has sometimes served. One troublesome vampire who was at large in Anopolis succeeded in convincing a respectably married woman, apparently, that he was her husband; so she did not refuse him. The husband came home late at night and demanded his rights. She looked surprised.

'What's the matter with you?' said the husband.

'You've been at me long enough this evening. I can't.'

'Me? I haven't been here at all.'

'Then . . . it must have been that *vampire*!'

They banished him – the vampire, that is – soon after to Santorin.[1]

The best and most detailed account of a Greek vampire which I know comes in Tournefort's chapter on 'The Present State of the Greek Church', a state which alarmed him. An ill-natured and quarrelsome peasant on Mykonos had been murdered in the fields in mysterious circumstances. He was buried in the town; but two days later it was rumoured that he had been seen to walk in the night; 'He tumbled about peoples' goods, put out their lamps, gripped them behind, and a thousand other monkey tricks.' At first these activities were treated as a joke, but weighty men believed the stories, and it became clear that something must be done; nothing, however, could be done until nine days had elapsed after the internment – because of some musty ceremonial. The nine-day gap accounts for some of the nastier details of subsequent events, which Tournefort relates with that vigorous delight in the exotic – and here gruesome – which informs all his book. He was a professional botanist, erudite and observant.

On the tenth day after the peasant's death a Mass was said, in order to drive out the demon which animated the corpse. After the Mass they took up the body, and the town butcher tried to extract the heart.

The butcher, an old clumsy fellow, first opens the belly instead of the breast: he groped a long while among the entrails, but could not find what he looked for: at last somebody told him he should cut up the diaphragm. The heart was pulled out, to the admiration of all the spectators. In the mean time, the corpse stunk so abominably, that they were obliged to burn frankincense; but the smoke mixing with the exhalations from the carcass, increased the stink, and began to muddle the poor peoples' pericranies. Their imagination, struck with the spectacle before them, grew full of visions. It came into their noddles, that a thick smoke arose out of the body; we durst not say 'twas the smoke of incense. They were incessantly bawling out *vroukolakas* . . . this is the name they give to these pretended *redivivi*. . . . Several there present averred, that the wretch's blood was extremely red: the butcher swore the body was still warm; whence they concluded, that the deceased was a very ill man for not being thorowly dead, or in plain terms, for suffering himself to be reanimated by Old Nick; which is the notion they have of a *vroukolakas*. They then roared out that name in a stupendious manner. Just at this time came in a flock of people, loudly protesting they plainly perceived the body was not grown stiff, when it was carried from the fields to church to be buried, and that consequently it was a true *vroukolakas*, which word was still the burden of the song.

Tournefort attempted rational explanation of these phenomena. It was not surprising that rotting entrails should feel warm: a dung heap if turned over will emit fumes; the blood on the butcher's hands, so far from being red, was a 'nasty stinking smear'.

Despite these arguments, the people decided to burn the dead man's heart on the sea shore; but even this had no effect; he went on with his racket more furiously than ever, and was accused of beating people up, breaking down doors and roofs, tearing clothes, emptying bottles, like a common or garden poltergeist. 'Nothing could be more miserable than the condition of this island; all the inhabitants seemed frightened out of their senses; the wisest among them were stricken like the rest: 'twas an epidemical disease of the brain, as dangerous and infectious as the madness of dogs.' And Tournefort, realizing that if he were to try to check this hysteria he would be accounted a blockhead, atheist and infidel, kept his silence. There were debates night and morning; the priest went into a fast; the zealous rushed around sprinkling holy water over the doors, and even into the vampire's mouth. Tournefort told the magistrates of the town that the strictest watch should be kept at night, and as a result some vagabonds were caught who undoubtedly had a hand in the disturbances. But there were still disorders. Numbers of swords were stuck over the grave of the vampire; and 'an Albaneze, that happened to be at Mycone, took upon him to say with a voice of authority, that it was to the last degree ridiculous to make use of the swords of Christians in a case like this. Can you not conceive, blind as ye are, says he, that the handle of these swords being made like a cross, hinders the devil from coming out of the body? Why do you not rather take the Turkish sabres?' But even this learned advice did no good. The vampire was incorrigible; and it was finally resolved, rather than allow the island to be depopulated and left to the ravages of the unnatural creature – for whole families were packing and preparing to move to Syra or Tinos – to burn the *vroukolakas* entire. What remained of the maltreated carcass therefore was consumed in a great fire on 1 January 1701: and the devil having met with his match, no more complaints were heard.

The priests were just as frightened of this vampire as anyone else; and small wonder, for it would take a strong character, or a rigid set of dogmata to which the village priests at that time did not have access, to withstand from the inside an outbreak of hysteria such as this. It was easy for Tournefort, who was an outsider from a different culture. But in any case, if you are committed to the belief that supernatural powers take tangible form and are not abstractions, it could be argued that it is then a matter of empirical evidence whether strange events are caused by these powers; and the Greeks thought they had this evidence. Tournefort concludes: 'After such an instance of folly, can we refuse to own that the present Greeks are no great Grecians; and that there is nothing but ignorance and superstition among them?'

The vampire, then, which is called in Crete *katachanas*, not *vroukolakas*, is a corpse gone to the bad, for one of many reasons: sudden death or suicide, excommunication, lack of the proper burial rites. The unavenged victims of murder, the unbaptized, the still-born, and those who die under a curse, are all in danger of becoming vampires. They are not ghosts, but animated corpses. The lively belief in these revenants has produced not only horrid superstitions but also one of the finest of Greek folk poems, the very ancient ballad of 'The Dead Brother', which caught the imagination of neighbouring races and spread through the Balkans, arriving eventually in England as the Suffolk Miracle: (though as the ballad moved north a lover-lover relationship substituted itself for the archetypal Greek brother-sister relationship). The ballad is of a mother with nine sons and only one

Sphakia – The Vampires

daughter, Arete, who is sought in marriage by a foreigner. The mother, and eight brothers, do not wish to let her go abroad, but Constantine, the ninth, persuades them, and swears his mother an oath: 'I take the heavens as judge and the saints as witness; should death come, should sickness come, in joy or in sadness, I shall fetch her to you.'

> And the deadly plague fell, and the nine brothers died,
> The mother was left alone like a reed on the plain.
> She wept at all their tombs, she sang her dirge,
> At Constantine's tomb she tore her hair.
> 'Curse on you, Constantine, a thousand curses,
> Since you banished my Arete to foreign lands! –
> The vow you vowed me, when will you fulfil it?
> You took the heavens as judge and the saints as witnesses,
> In joy or in sadness to go and fetch her back to me.'
> From these thousand curses and the heavy oath,
> The earth was disturbed and Constantine came out.
> He made the cloud his horse and the star his bridle,
> The moon his companion. And he goes to fetch her.

Constantine comes to his sister and tells her to return with him; seats her on the horse behind him.

> On the road they travelled birds sang,
> They sang not like birds, not like swallows,
> But they sang and spoke in human speech:
> 'Who ever saw a corpse dragging a beautiful girl with him!'
> 'Constantine, did you hear what the birds say?'
> 'They are birds, let them sing, they are birds, let them talk.'
> And further on the way other birds said:
> 'Isn't it unjust and strange and quite wrong,
> The living to be walking with the dead!'
> 'Constantine, did you hear what the birds say?
> How the living are walking with the dead?'
> 'It is April and they warble, it is May and they build nests.'
> 'I am afraid of you, little brother, you smell of incense.'
> 'Yesterday evening we went over to St John's,
> And the priest censed us with too much incense.'

Later the birds speak to them again; and Arete's heart cracks as she asks what it means.

> 'Leave the birds, Arete, to say what they will.'
> 'Tell me, where is your beauty, where is your manhood,
> Your fair hair and your fine moustache?'
> 'Long time I have been ill and my hair fell out.'

The Great Island

When they reach home he leaves her, for he must return to the grave.

> She sees the garden naked, the trees withered,
> She sees the balsam dried up, the costmary blackened,
> She sees grass growing in front of her door. . . .
> She knocks hard on the door, the windows creak.
> 'If you are friend, come in, if you are enemy, go.
> If you are Death the bitter, I have no other sons,
> And my poor Aretoula is far off in foreign lands.'
> 'Get up, mother, open, sweet mother, get up.'
> 'Who is that that knocks and calls me mother?'
> 'Open up, open up, I am your Arete.'
> She went in; they kissed; and together they died.

Thus the vampire need not be bad. But, even if it was bad luck which made him into a vampire, once he has become one he is peculiarly subject to the devil's influence. I mentioned the Cretan vampire who was banished to Santorin; this happened because Santorin was a notorious haunt of revenants, and was regarded almost as their natural home, where one more would make no difference. (The advantage of banishment was that vampires are incapable of crossing salt water of their own accord, and so could not come back. The formula of banishment was potent to convey them across the sea.) Much of our evidence for vampires comes, strangely, from a Jesuit priest, Father Richard, who was on Santorin at the height of the trouble.

Father Richard believed in vampires. At first he thought they were souls returning to ask help in escaping quickly from purgatory. But the excesses they committed convinced him that diabolic possession was the only explanation. This was, of course, orthodox belief. Leo Allatius quotes an Orthodox ordinance: 'It is impossible that a dead man should become a vampire, save it be that the devil maketh these portents; and men in their dreams see visions, and the dead man appears to have flesh and blood and nails and hair. . . . [These things exist only 'in fantasy'.] But when such remains be found, the which, as we have said, is a work of the Devil, ye must summon the priests to chant an invocation of the Mother of God and to perform memorial services with *kollyva*.'[2]

Leo also believed in vampires; he claimed actually to have seen one in his youth on Chios. 'It is great folly to deny altogether that such bodies are found in the graves incorrupt, and that by use of them the Devil, if God permits him, devises horrible plans to the hurt of the Greek race.' Now Leo and Father Richard and many other believers were not unsophisticated; and it is clear that the existence of vampires

Canea from a 17th century print by Boschini

Western Cretan wedding

The laouto (lute)

was accepted in the seventeenth and eighteenth centuries. One reason was that the belief accounted for several kinds of phenomena; for the Greeks had added to the more horrifying, Slavonic, bloodsucking activities of the vampire, which would account for anaemia and death after long decline, the down to earth function of the poltergeist. The vampire Tournefort found on Mykonos was no more than this. The belief was vastly helped by the vacillating attitude of the church. The ordinary village priest, being no different from his fellow villagers, and hardly trained under the Turkish régime, was just as superstitious as anyone else. But even the bishops were sometimes prepared to accept that there were vampires. (Not always. In about 1800 the Metropolitan of Larissa fined a priest for having exhumed two corpses and thrown them into the Haliacmon; and this put a stop to the current epidemic of vampire stories.)

There were two reasons for the attitude of the church. First, the Greek church has always chosen, partly because of the natural sympathies of her priests, to coexist with paganism rather than crush it. Second, the church was put in a difficult position by certain beliefs about excommunication; (and these beliefs themselves stemmed from the people's superstition). It could be held that the body of an excommunicate would remain undissolved. The phrase used by priests in the formula of excommunication – *kai meta ton thanaton alytos kai aparalytos* ('and after death unloosed and unresolved') – implies this. And although there was nothing to show that such corpses could do any harm, it was natural that the Slavonic belief in bloodsucking corpses should hook on to Orthodox doctrine. Lawson shows how this must have happened; and the manuscript from St Sophia of Salonika which he quotes displays several nice distinctions among the categories of vampire. 'Whoever has left a command undone, or is cursed, has the front parts of his body only preserved. Whoever is under an *anathema* looks yellow and has wrinkled fingers. Whoever looks white has been excommunicated by the divine laws. Whoever looks black has been excommunicated by a bishop.' In general an excommunicated corpse was inflated like a drum. But naturally these distinctions failed to appeal to the masses, among whom a simple confusion prevailed.

Not to be buried with due rights was one of the worst disasters which could befall a man in ancient Greece. Undoubtedly this belief has survived, and not only in vampire stories. There are folk songs of *xeniteia* in which the singer laments his exile not only because he is homesick but also because he will not get a proper burial abroad. One might assume therefore that the survival of vampires in western Crete was due to the violent history of the area; in a country where frequent revolts and sudden deaths by murder and blood feud supplied plenty of unburied corpses, it is not surprising that the superstition should be tenacious. Curiously, however, it is not so. For if *every* unburied corpse turned into a vampire there would be too many to 'save the phenomena' which vampires explain. Thus when Pashley asked why the war had not created more vampires he was told that no one turns vampire in time of war; a very neat example of the way superstitions adapt themselves to the phenomena.

So the strength of this belief and the frequency of vampires is not directly related to the number of unburied corpses and violent deaths. The belief waxes and wanes mysteriously according to the conditions of the society. Superstitions go in 'crazes'. There was a time when the Akrotiri, the headland just east of Canea, was said to be teeming with vampires, who roamed the peninsula at night and caused confusion in every house: to the benefit of the monastery of the Holy Trinity, where the priests were able to bury the dead with full rites. For as soon as this was known, corpses were brought in from all over the countryside. And the monks got their baksheesh: a field here, a vineyard there, a barrel of oil here.

After some time however – perhaps the monastery was as rich as it could decently be – a priest succeeded in banishing all the troublesome vampires to the neighbouring island of Kalathas, where they are condemned to shift sand from one mountain to the other, night and day, with only a shell.

The best Cretan vampire story comes from Kallikrati, a tiny mountain village between Asi Gonia and Sphakia. Pashley recorded it.

A vampire was haunting the village, and no one knew what was his history or where he came from. He destroyed children and even grown men, and created havoc throughout the village in his nocturnal rambles. It so happened that the vampire's *synteknos*,* who was looking after his sheep near the church of St George, went into the churchyard to shelter from a shower of rain, and stood just by the grave where the vampire lay. Since there was an arch over the grave and it was a dry place, he decided to have a nap there. He therefore unslung his weapons, and laid them crossways by the tombstone.

* *Synteknos* (translated correctly by Pashley 'gossip'), or *koumbaros*, is a relation in God. You are my gossip if I am godfather to your child, and *vice versa*. The relationship is an extremely close one in Crete, involving ties often as exacting as those of consanguinity. (Your son, for instance, cannot marry your goddaughter.) And it was without doubt the sanctity of these ties which led the shepherd to be lenient with the vampire. *Synteknos* is also used familiarly of any friend.

Sphakia – The Vampires

During the night the vampire was seized by the desire to emerge and pursue his grisly business, and called (in Pashley's translation), 'Gossip, get up hence, for I have some business that requires me to come out.'

The shepherd, instantly realizing that this man, his own *synteknos*, was the vampire whom everyone had been looking for, refused to answer. After the vampire's third demand, however, he said, 'I shall not get up hence, gossip, for I fear that you are no better than you should be, and may do me some mischief. But, if I must get up, swear to me by your winding-sheet that you will not hurt me, and on this I will get up.'

The vampire prevaricated until he saw that the shepherd meant what he had said. Finally he swore by his winding-sheet and the shepherd removed his crossed weapons. (It was the coincidence that he had laid them down in the form of a cross that kept the vampire immobile.) The corpse then came out of the tomb and told the shepherd to wait in the graveyard until he came back.

When he did return it was with a liver in his bloody hands. He had killed a newly married couple some ten miles away. The shepherd watched him blow into the liver, as a butcher does, to increase its size; he was then invited to share the meal, but wisely he merely pretended to do so. The vampire's parting instructions were that the shepherd must never tell, 'for if you do, my twenty nails will be fixed in your children and yourself'.

The shepherd told, however. The village priest, with a party of bold assistants, dug up the corpse and found it perfectly preserved, as on the day of burial. They made a fire and burnt the corpse; but the *synteknos*, who arrived late, was touched on the foot by a single droplet of the vampire's blood, which ate into his foot like fire. They therefore sifted the ashes, and found the vampire's little fingernail still intact. When this was burnt, the vampire's power was finally and for ever destroyed.

These supersitions have lost some, but not all, of their power. Most men are sceptical; the women less so. George Psychoundakis tells of an old woman who had the fear of vampires in her bones, and suffered in consequence. She kept a great jar of pork, from which she ate whenever she felt hungry, and a group of scoundrels, coveting the meat and knowing that she was nervous, came at night and crept into her house. One of them took up the lamp and began to dance. The woman covered herself in her heavy handwoven blankets and screamed prayers to all the saints, her teeth chattering with fear. She lost the pork of course.

But that could happen to anyone who disliked the dark. I myself

The Great Island

never saw a vampire, ghost, Nereid or phantom army. I wish I had; I should then have been better placed in arguments about their existence and explanation. The total sceptic tends to look smug in such circumstances.

This excursus round Sphakia would not be complete without a side trip to Frangokastello, a few miles eastward down the coast.

Frangokastello stands like a lonely sentinel a few yards from the sea, where the twisting cliffs have receded and left a few miles of scrubby plain along the shore. From the hills above Sphakia you look eastwards and see a pinpoint of light gleaming in the distance – a gold sovereign dropped by some passing Frankish millionaire. The Franks, all of them rich in the eyes of the Cretans, left treasures buried all over Crete, we are told. Of these Castel Franco is the unique golden survivor. This is not to say that there are not other Genoese or Venetian remains and buildings – the monastery of Arcadi is a splendid example of sixteenth-century baroque, with its scrolls and flowery garlands, its light Corinthian columns splitting the façade; only that Frangokastello in its lonely eminence seems untouched by subsequent history, totally foreign. From a distance the castle seems perfect, unscarred. The golden, honey-coloured stone glows and traps the light. Only when you approach can you see that the weather-beaten, battered lion of St Mark, who stands guard over the southern door, is protector of a ruin. The roof has gone. Lizards bask on the sun-baked stone. Coarse grasses and pungent herbs have wedged themselves into the fissures and taken possession of the Franks' preserve.

I thought of Pashley, whom ruins inspired to almost Gibbonian aphorisms. In Gaidouropolis, over the gateway of a palatial Venetian building, he saw the motto OMNIA MUNDI FUMUS ET UMBRA:

a moral aphorism of the truth of which Venice has certainly afforded a memorable example. What a contrast between her state at the time to which these few words carry us back, and at the present day! Then, the shade of her power was spread over several of the fairest countries of the world; now, her very name is blotted out from the list of nations. And yet how little can anyone, who loves his kind, regret her fall?

Smoke and shade. From Castel Temene, erected in 961, the year when Nicephoras Phocas reclaimed Crete from the Arabs, to Castel Sfacchia (1526), all the great castles are more or less gone, and Frangokastello is the best preserved. Of the others, Boschini's drawings are the memorial.

Sphakia – The Vampires

Frangokastello was built in the fourteenth century, after the feudarchs had demanded protection from the corsairs. It was called at first Castel St Niketas after the patron saint whose chapel stands close by, but quite soon the local nickname 'the Frankish Castle' caught on. Such a stronghold in this turbulent area must have served also to control the inhabitants of Sphakia, who until the sixteenth century were as much of a threat to Venice as the corsairs. Crete was the target of the Barbary pirates in 1537, when Khaireddin Barbarossa attacked, having already harassed the western Mediterranean, the Peloponnese and the Ionian islands.

The scourge fell on Canea, Rethymnon and Sitea, but also generally on the south-west coast. It is round Frangokastello that stories and memories of the pirates remain:

> Sun, you rise in a flash, you give yourself to all the world;
> Rise over all the earth, over all the inhabited globe!
> Over Barbarossa's roofs, sun, do not rise –
> And if you do rise, my Sun, set swiftly –
> For they have slaves, beautiful, in pain,
> And your rays will be damp with the tears of slaves.

In the memory of the Cretans, the corsairs are a scourge of supernatural power, descending on the coast like the irresistible storm wind. It was not only that the pirates took fine young men away into slavery, it was also that the Venetians, in their necessity to defend Crete, became themselves more exacting. If it was not the swift ships of Barbarossa it was galley service for the colonialist. Caught between these two oppressive masters, the Cretans could only go to their saints and their God for help. And most of the churches along the south coast have their stories of miraculous intervention.

St Niketas near Frangokastello, for instance. One day some girls were washing their clothes by the sea when a ship appeared and put down a boatload of ruffians to seize the girls. A Christian who was on board ship had the presence of mind to sing an apparently harmless verse which contained a concealed warning, but the girls failed to catch on, and one of them was abducted. Years later, on St Niketas' day, her master saw her weeping as she dutifully served him his glass of water, and asked why. She told him; and prayed to the saint; and the miracle happened – she woke up to find herself back by the saint's chapel, safe and sound.

Spratt heard a similar story, which explained why the 'credulous and benighted' community round St Niketas on the Messara plain hold the saint in such respect. The villagers had collected on the eve of the saint's day to prepare for the celebration, and a shipload of Barbary pirates, seeing the lights twinkling, landed and shut them all up in the church, intending to round them up in the morning. All, however, escaped through a secret passage, except one small girl who had fallen asleep in a corner. She was made personal slave of the captain in consequence of her remarkable beauty; and was subsequently restored miraculously by Niketas, who flew her home on a white-winged horse. St George is credited with a similar miracle; he is sometimes pictured on a flying horse, with the rescued girl sitting behind him, still holding the pitcher from which she was pouring her master's glass of water.

In later years the area has been haunted by other supernatural beings. It was here that Hadzimichalis Daliannis, not to be confused with Hadzimichalis Iannaris of the Omalos, led the last stand against the Turks in 1828. Hadzimichalis, a typical *palikari* who had led his private army around Greece and even as far as Beirut, in the course of the war of independence, ended up in command of an Epirot garrison (and thus of the local Cretans) at Frangokastello, when the Turks controlled all Crete except this coastal plain. He unwisely defended the castle against Mustapha Pasha's vastly greater army, instead of resorting to appropriate guerrilla tactics from the neighbouring foothills. Hadzimichalis's garrison was cut to pieces; their commander decapitated, and mourned, it is said, by Mustapha Pasha himself, who came from the same part of the Morea as Hadzimichalis.

Folk poetry has surrounded Hadzimichalis himself with a supernatural aura; for instance:

> When he rode, his horse wept
> And then he knew how it was to be his death.

And like the shades which haunted the field of Marathon in Pausanias's time, Hadzimichalis's 385 men still ride across the plain.

> But still on 17 May the phantom army appears,
> Hadzimichalis and his men; and in the mists
> They fight again; and still is heard below the castle
> The shouts of wicked Turks, the hoofs of horses.
> Those with the gift of sight see them and are afraid,
> But, may God rest them, they can harm no man.

The shades, some on foot, some mounted, with Hadzimichalis himself prominent, appear on 17 May or soon after, in the dewy hour before sunrise. Hence their name *drossoulites*, 'dew-shades'. Fielding, who spent these days waiting for them to materialize, and was disappointed, concluded that they were probably an optical illusion, the projected shadows of some distant caravanserai. Or simply mist-formations; for they only come in the misty morning, and the concrete descriptions of the villagers could as well be based on the known story of Hadzimichalis as on the physical appearance of the wraiths.

In the blazing midday hours of July it was impossible to imagine the scene. We sat under a mulberry tree idly eating the fruit and questioning an old man who claimed to have seen them. But his description made no sense. Instead of pursuing the matter, we spent the afternoon bathing in the lagoon below the castle. Which, if you are in the area, do not miss, for it is the most beautiful place to bathe in Crete, probably in all the world. The sand shelves suddenly away where the sea begins; so suddenly, so sheer, that you can dive off firm gold sand into ten feet of sparkling water.

14

Return to Asi Gonia

I went up to Asi Gonia for the last time as summer was Septembering to a close; the days still hot, but filled with the dusty tatters thrown up by four months of sun and crumbling earth; the nights longer and colder.

Leaving Athens was a deliverance, from the endless sweating summer, the nervous pettiness of overheated people, and my own life, which was in a mess. Leaning over the ship's rail in Piraeus I watched the sun wheel its way down through flaming rings of orange and red, and die in pale green. Scabby rinds of water melon floated in the oily water. The sailor kissed his girl goodbye, then passed through the ticket-barrier and talked to her through the enclosure rails. One of the sad, trivial conversations it must have been – 'You will write?', 'Don't forget to feed the cat', and so on. The great neon lights of the capitalists began to wink; METAXAS, the genuine brandy, PAPASTRATOS cigarettes, TYPALDOS. There was a satisfaction in being alone, leaning on the rail and dropping dead matches into the narrow gap between ship and quay, watching the others saying goodbye and the Athenian night closing in. Because for me it was not a case of leaving a dear place; rather I was leaving an encampment which held me and my friends inexplicably, like a drug, and I was breaking the habit and going home. Yet stirred by memories of other departures I waited idly for someone to come down to the quayside and say goodbye, to appear suddenly, at the last minute, behind the crowds of friends and relatives, waving a silk square in the last of the light.

The boat pulled out.

Everyone, I think, has to some extent these ambivalent feelings about Athens. The colony of writers, artists and teachers which it has collected is divided between those who hate it and those who like it but feel they should be elsewhere. There are exceptions of course. But the trouble is that the Athens colony is not a satisfactory one for writers – for artists I would not know – because the ingredients of life are too few.

I mean this. The English in Athens fall into several categories. There

Return to Asi Gonia

are the Embassy crowd, with whom one might associate those who have, say, steady salaried jobs in companies like B.P. There are the teachers, verging from the respectable and settled who have jobs with the British Council or run their own institutes, to those who teach privately and illegally (very often teaching in an institute at the same time). There is the 'artistic' set, many of whom coincide with this last group of unofficial teachers. There are the students; mostly archaeologists at the British School. And there are the *au pair* girls.

Between the first class, the steadies, and the floating population of writers and teachers, there is not much contact. In fact, the contact the artists have is mostly with each other, and with a few pretty unrepresentative Greeks. The results of this are unfortunate, and can be seen by anyone who cares to go up to the 'Nine Muses' in the Plaka for a few nights and listen to the conversation. Any colony of expatriates has its phonies; but the difference between Athens and, say, Paris in the Twenties is that in Paris, concealed behind all the nonsense and show-off, there was a ferment of ideas and a handful of terrific talents. In a sense the talented could feed on each other. In Greece the talented are lucky if they find each other; they are far more likely – Durrell is the obvious example – to feed off the land. But this is precisely why the Athenian colony is hollow, because its members do not know the land. The land is strange, not entirely European; the people behave differently, they talk a language that cannot be picked up, like a Romance language, in a few weeks from remembered scraps of school-lessons. All this drives the floaters, who came to Greece not for the sake of the country but for their own sakes, back on to themselves.

If there is one thing an artist needs it is roots. The philosopher Moore once said that his inspiration came not from philosophic puzzlement presented by problems in real life but from the puzzles set up and argued over by other philosophers. Many writers could say the same thing. ('Real' problems often seem too difficult, complicated and even trivial to be written about.) Nevertheless such a writer, feeding on other books, on technical problems, must be able to relate what he finds to the life, the culture in which he is rooted. Distant memory is an insufficient prop. The expatriates have uprooted themselves from their own ground, and fail too often to push out new roots in Greece.

An extreme example of this is provided by an American acquaintance of mine, who taught at an American school and lived near me on Mt. Lycabettus. When I got to know him he had been in Greece a year, and spoke a few words only of the language. Thus his circle of friends was confined to those who spoke English. He made little effort to learn

The Great Island

Greek, on the assumption I suppose that enough Greeks knew English. From time to time he would drop in and ask me to make telephone calls for him in Greek.

The sad thing was that, despite his circumscribed access to Greeks and their history and language, he became violently anti-Greek. His attitudes to American domestic issues were those of a liberal and nuclear disarmer. Yet his attitude to the Greeks shared some of the characteristics of racial prejudice, and was based on the same cause – fear of difference. I remember one occasion at a party when he attempted to demolish the myth that the Greeks were courageous – in front of Greeks – by pointing out that it took the Germans only three days to sweep through mainland Greece. One could hardly find a clearer example of prejudice.

He was exceptional, of course. But the cause of his prejudice – failure to latch on to any kind of reality, political, cultural or linguistic, in Greece; failure even to try – works also in others. This is partly why Athens is in some ways an unsatisfactory city. But there is another reason; Athens lacks solidity, it lacks a heart. There is not the presence of that tradition embodied in palaces, cathedrals and ruined monuments which makes Rome a capital city, where you can walk the streets and feel the past stretching back in an unbroken chain whose links are these memorials of unforgotten craftsmen. Always in Athens you are conscious of the long gap, the void which opens up after Hadrian's magnificent adornment and yawns until the neo-classical libraries and university buildings begin to sprout in the last century. Constantinople is the City. Athens is a construction in concrete in which the shambling Plaka twines itself into the roots of the Acropolis like a tough and lovely creeper at the foot of some marvellous tree.

And still it draws like a magnet, it fascinates. Like Cavafy's Alexandria:

> The city will follow you. You will walk the same streets.
> And in the same neighbourhoods you will grow old.
> And it is in these same houses you will turn grey.
> Always it is at this city you will arrive. Elsewhere – hold out no hopes –
> There is no ship for you, there is no road.
> Just as you have destroyed your life here
> In this little corner, so you have ruined it in all the world.

In this way Athens, and Crete, and Greece herself all infiltrate our bodies, so that we carry them in us for ever. Those who have lived there know this well. And I knew too that when I went to Crete I was

Return to Asi Gonia

carrying within me ruins that could not be expelled for long even by the calm and balanced life of the sixth continent.

But for a time.

On the way up to Asi Gonia I met the grocer Daskalomarkakis and an old white-haired man whose name I could not remember.

'You were here last year with Ruth and Katerina.'

These were the two girls from Cambridge with whom we had visited Asi Gonia three years before. Everyone in the village except Psychoundakis had forgotten how long ago it was; some said two years, most one. But there is a refreshing vagueness about expressions of time; *procthes*, for instance, 'the day before yesterday', can cover anything up to three or four months back.

'How are they?' they asked. 'What are they doing?'

'They are very well. Ruth is in Israel. Katerina is married.'

'*Po po po!* Married! We thought you were going to marry her.'

'No,' I said. 'I was never going to marry her. Anyway, it was Ruth I was going around with. But that was after we got back to England.'

'Who did Katerina marry then? Do you know him? Was it Brian?'

'No. I haven't met her husband. She got married while I was here in Greece.'

'Well well,' he said. 'We all thought you two boys were going to marry them.'

He turned to his friend, the old white-haired man, and explained the whole affair again; his folklorist curiosity was aroused. 'D'you hear that?' he said. 'They were living up there by the spring with the two girls and they weren't even engaged.' They both laughed.

'We only met them in Athens three weeks before,' I said.

They laughed again. 'We thought you'd known them all your lives.' The affair became more and more curious.

'No. But that's the way it goes in England. Different customs.'

They whispered together for a few seconds.

'And then Katerina married someone else?'

'Yes,' I said patiently.

More whispering.

'Excuse me, but tell me – it's pure curiosity, just interest you understand – did you sleep together?'

'No.'

'*Po po po!*' They talked to each other rapidly. I distinguished the words 'No, he's not lying,' uttered by Daskalomarkakis; but the old man appeared to be doubtful about this.

'I'm not lying,' I said, and explained pompously, 'There's no reason to. People do sleep together without being married in England more than in Greece. It happens that we didn't. It's just that our customs allow us to go on holidays together without even being engaged.'

They found this extraordinarily interesting and later repeated it all to those who cared to hear throughout the village.

The mountains were closing in now, and the air became filled with the scents of herb and scrub from the encroaching hillsides. Below us wound the dry river bed, the straggling plane trees. As we passed the church on the outskirts of Asi Gonia, Daskalomarkakis, encouraged by his new insight into different social and cultural norms, suddenly asked:

'Do you believe in a life after death?'

'What?'

'Because they say the soul goes on living for ever.'

'That's right,' said the old man. 'The soul is immortal, so how can it die?'

This sounded like a variant of the ontological argument; I was not prepared to go into defining properties and like abstractions.

'But do you believe all that?' said Daskalomarkakis.

'I'm an agnostic,' I said.

He saw I was trying to get out of it.

'But look, if you're under pressure, if you have to say yes or no, what do you say?'

'What do you say?'

'Well,' he said. 'You know what the priests say, everyone says it in fact, but – ' and his face crinkled as if he had been let in on a secret denied to the rest of us – 'I'd say no.'

'And so would I,' I admitted.

The conversation interested me, not least because I had felt creeping up on me that pseudo-respect for other sets of cultural values that is difficult to repress. Why should one arrogantly try to protect those who belong to a different society (which one respects) from one's own different views? Because this is a form of arrogance. It happened this time that Daskalomarkakis and I agreed to **differ** from the norm. But on other occasions I have often found myself trying to fit into Cretan society by suppressing my own views. This **can** lead to absurdities – it led, for instance, to my agreeing with Julie du Boulay, in a fit of weak-mindedness, that we should agree to be cousins, so as not to offend Cretan susceptibilities with what must appear to them to be our immoral proximity to each other. We had not reckoned on Cretan curiosity, and so had not rehearsed our story well enough. Someone asked me exactly what the relationship was. Well, I said, our fathers are brothers

Return to Asi Gonia

actually. Ah, so you have the same name. Well, yes, I suppose we do. Smith. But Julie had already claimed the opposite in another village. We went in constant fear of exposure.

This sort of subterfuge does no good. Apart from landing you in these genealogical complexities, it is in a way an insult to Cretan tolerance, as illustrated by Daskalomarkakis. It is true that the foreigner is very well placed; he gets more than his fair share of tolerance. And I have often wished that my Cretan friends would be tougher and more argumentative with *xenoi*, instead of letting politeness and respect for those 'with letters' stifle disagreement; for this politeness sets up another barrier, perhaps more formidable than the substantial cultural differences. Frankness does no harm, given goodwill.

I wandered slowly up through the village to the ilex grove and the spring. Pigs wallowed in the road, grunting evilly. The priest called to me to come and drink a coffee; he had just returned from Athens and was telling everyone about the Corinth canal, a marvel which he had just seen for the first time. Stelios, his son, our old interpreter of three years back, was on Chios now doing his military service, and married. Up by the spring, a tall, dark man began to talk to me while the women washed clothes. He was wrapped in melancholy.

'Temptation has not left the world,' he said, and pointed to St George's chapel where Brian and I had sheltered one rainy night: 'Do you have churches like that?'

'In England? Our churches are bigger, they have no icons.'

'Why? What do you believe in?'

'Much the same as you, many of us.'

'In Jesus Christ? Everyone, all the world, should believe in Jesus Christ, even more than in God, because Christ died to save us. What man would do that?'

My world is full of evangelists. The preacher at Sphakia, a Methodist who gave me a lift from Bedford to Bicester and told me the sin-laden story of his life, inviting me to repent, and now Markos. He began to tell me of St George's local miracles, all of which I had heard before. Finally he narrated an involved and marvellous tale about George himself, which I compress.

'George was chief general of the King of Cappadocia. Now the King had ordered that all the Christians were to be killed. "Everyone is to worship idols." So the King arrested George; he didn't want to kill him, you see, he was such a valuable soldier. So George was tortured to give up his faith.'

There followed an incredible series of tortures – fire, nails, the rack, the wheel, iron shoes studded with red-hot nails, and poison ('But George, he drinks it down like water!'). After any one of these tests a rational man would have concluded that George was under divine protection, and given up. But the King just got madder and madder. The tortures hurt abominably, but George never gave up. Finally in his exasperation the King tried to kill the saint – but even this he found impossible.

The King therefore organized a test to discover whether George's God is the only true God. 'They take four men, a lame man, a paralytic, a blind man and a dead man. And first the priests of the idols try to cure these men, but they can't manage it.

'So George says, "King," he says, "no wonder they fail, because the idols are artificial," he says, "they are gold, bits of metal, ordinary human products."

'And then he calls on God and God helps him to cure the lame man, so he walks, and the paralytic, so he gets up and moves, and the blind man, so he sees, and the dead man, so he comes to life again and sings! And the King is amazed and says, "George," he says, "George, how do you do it?"'

And the story ends in wholesale conversion and light.

I went up to visit Pavlos Gyparakis, the best singer I heard in Crete, and one of our supper-guests of three years back; intending to work with him on the origin and transmission of these old songs. But conversation turned to war, and he put into my hands the record he had written after it was all over – a document of classic simplicity, and worth more, every page of it, than notes on his repertoire of songs. He had written:

The Germans occupied Crete in May 1941.

At that time there was in Crete, unfortunately, a party of men who said that the Germans were a kind and civilized people. It was not long, however, before we saw the opposite. They made mass arrests of Greek patriots and executed them, they burnt whole villages on any pretext. By all this they gave us to understand that they had come not merely to enslave us but to exterminate us.

The situation was desperate because it was not only the Germans but also the misfortune of hunger and lack of clothes.

People began to give up hope, but not all. Those who believed in their faith and their country were mastered neither by fear of the Germans nor by hardship and hunger; these gave them strength and courage, and they had a secret hope, that one day our country would be free, however few of us were still alive.

As for those who gave up hope or wished to avoid hardship, I do not know what roads they followed. The few however who kept their morale unshaken, inflicted great wounds on the Germans, saved many of our men, and did not follow the way of corruption. In March 1942 the clouds of occupation were blacker than ever before.

At that time it was no small thing to work with the Allied command, because you took on yourself great responsibilities and you had to have the necessary qualifications; with one frivolity or carelessness you could cause a catastrophe in the area of your action or in your village. Thus not everyone was able to work with our allies the English . . . for they were in a position to inflict wounds on the occupier without giving him the right to take reprisals. If someone killed Germans in a village, that neighbourhood would be destroyed, but if the English signalled by radio the movements of the German army, and the Allied planes bombarded, the Germans took no reprisals on us.

There follows an account of how Pavlos's superior Petrakas, when he had to go to the Middle East, left Pavlos as his substitute ('You must represent me until I come back. I leave to God and to you my sacred struggle'); and a narrative of Pavlos's part in the resistance movement. Then:

Those days were hell in Kallikrates.

Most houses they burnt. The barbarians were not satisfied merely to burn houses, they burnt four women inside their houses.

Whatever valuable they fancied they took. They collected all the men they had taken – about 300 – and executed them in an old deserted house. They took the women and little children as hostages.

Also they burnt the village of Kali Sykia and burnt a pregnant woman, in her house too. They plundered Alones completely. Asi Gonia they did not burn but they plundered it and left nothing but the walls. The area remained without hope, like a corpse. . . .

At the end of September 1944 one night I dreamed a dream, as if someone were saying to me that 'the Germans are leaving, the Germans will leave', and when dawn came someone comes and tells me that squads of German cars are moving from Rethymnon to Canea. . . .

And that was, one might have expected, the beginning of the end. But in a way the worst time was still to come, for when the Germans had left Rethymnon, the internal struggle with the communists came to a head over the establishment of *ethnophroures* ('national guards'), which the communists resisted. Pavlos and his uncle, Pavlos Gyparis the elder, a distinguished old soldier who had fought in Macedonia in the early years of the century, were in Rethymnon during the struggle. Pavlos the elder, standing on an elevated piece of ground, was wounded in the left hand by a communist bullet.

The Great Island

Now Gyparkis Emmanuel [a cousin] was not with us, but as soon as he heard the shots he came to the house where he expected us to be and asked 'What of my uncle?', and they pointed out where we were and he came to meet us.

As Emmanuel was walking, he had his gun slung on his shoulder, because as I wrote earlier gunshot could not dazzle his eyes; and when he reached a certain point in the central street the Bulgarians saw him and saw well that he was a Greek; and since German bullets had been ashamed to kill him in the battle at Tsilivdika, it had to be the Bulgarians that killed him.

They shot him, and he took his gun in his hands and without wasting time or protecting himself, he stood upright and shot at the place where the Communists were and at the same time he moved towards them.

He fell to about thirty armed men under cover; he fell to thirty guns, and he alone and upright and exposed, he was killed in the central street without succeeding in meeting us.

Pavlos writes with difficulty. This account, from which I have omitted most of the narrative details, since a fuller, richer story is in George Psychoundakis's book, must have cost him great labour. It is one of many similar records kept by Cretan patriots to remind them of those momentous days; and it sums up the philosophy which I have traced through a thousand years of history. Throughout these years there have stalked two enemies; the invader, Venetian, Turk or German; and the traitor Ephialtes, the betrayer of Candia, the man who sold the Aradaina gorge to the Turks in 1770, the treacherous Thymakis whose information caused the death of Marko, another of Pavlos's cousins. Thymakis, says Pavlos, was 'no Greek'. The communists were 'Bulgarians'. Pavlos's account, in theme and attitude, is rooted in the Cretan heroic tradition.

But perhaps it is the last of a long line, for even the short taste of liberty which Crete enjoyed between 1913 and 1941 was enough to weaken this tradition. Proof of this is to be found in the folksongs which date from the war. In formula and even sentiment they are like the older *rizitika*, but the inspiration has gone. This, for instance, is one of the better examples:

> A bird from the plains flies to Epanomeri,
> Bringing fearful news, bringing bitter news.
> The Germans have borne down with a thousand aeroplanes.
> They throw down cannons, soldiers with parachutes
> To take Crete and to enslave her.'
> 'Fly away, bird, to your plain and tell your people
> To endure the war until we come down,
> And show the corsair Germans how Crete makes war,
> How she fights and how she strikes for her Freedom.'

George Psychoundakis and family

Pavlos Gyparakis

The author with Aleko above the gorge of Samaria

Goat-skinning at Anopolis

Return to Asi Gonia

Corsairs have become an irrelevancy, next to parachutes. The old metaphors are ceasing to speak clearly, and it is left to men like Psychoundakis and Gyparakis, with their unsophisticated prose, to express the agony of the war.

Even so, although nearly fifty years of freedom, only briefly interrupted, have sapped the force and inspiration of folk expression, the formulae and the philosophy survive. It would not occur to Cretans of the mountains to express themselves in terms other than those taught by a thousand years of subservience to foreigners, and handed down by so long a line of poets. The personification of Crete as a hard, beautiful, demanding mother, the heroic attitudes, the insistence on Freedom, have been built into the philosophy. And when freedom came, bringing with it the need for new attitudes, there was no room for them. As it became apparent that there was no longer any foreigner to blame for the difficult life, the poverty, the unproductive land, it began to appear too that all the time there had been another enemy – the land. So each barbarian invader begins to look like a 'kind of solution'.

> What are we waiting for, assembled in the market-place?
>
> The barbarians are to arrive today.
>
> Why such inaction in the senate house?
> Why are the senators sitting without legislating?
>
> Because the barbarians will arrive today.
> What laws will the senators make from now on?
> The barbarians when they come will legislate.

The barbarians engaged most of the activities and energy of Crete for a thousand years; what was left went into the land, but it was recognized that until the barbarians were expelled, other problems were secondary. Cavafy's poem expresses exactly the dilemma of a society in a state of transition, loaded down with a set of attitudes which will no longer completely serve. The questioner asks why the streets are emptying, the people returning to their houses deep in thought.

> Because night has fallen and the barbarians have not come.
> And some men have arrived from the frontiers,
> And said that there are no barbarians any more...
>
> And now what will become of us without barbarians?
> These people were a kind of solution.

It is possible that the barbarians might one day return, and the old attitudes flicker into life again. But so far as one can foresee, Crete is free of them and must fend for herself. The demands now are clear; better communications, better education, not only in the schools but throughout the country so that the smallholder may understand what sort of damage his goat is doing; increased productivity. If the Cretan's energy could be harnessed to these tasks the island would gradually turn into the kind of paradise it might have been under the Venetians. What would be lost would be not the valuable qualities which sustained Crete through successive occupations, but the trappings of a dated philosophy which was nourished by the very forces it sought to combat. It is pathetic sometimes to hear Cretans talking about the last war, and to realize that, hellish as it was, they do not know what to do now that it is over. Those who go to Germany to find work do not go because they expect to like it abroad, but because the life at home is a poor one, lacking in comfort and purpose. There is still no substitute for the purpose that is now dead – 'Freedom or Death'. Other societies, like our own, having grown used to materialism and tired of abstractions, have no need for a substitute. But a heroic society like the Cretan does need one.

George Psychoundakis has not changed. His son Nikos, who gave such trouble when he was born three years ago that I had to take George's wife and her mother on that alarming emergency ride down to Rethymnon hospital, is growing up. He has one of those deliberate, husky, serious voices in which you can hear the intelligence growing. Suddenly his face goes puzzled, widens and breaks into laughter – a short intense burst. Whereas Angelica, the baby, is just *amazed* by the world.

George has started keeping bees. His front parlour has a honey extractor alongside the divan, under the family photographs. This year he got forty kilos of honey, dark and ambrosial. Next year he will expand the business, if he has not emigrated to Germany by then. I think even George hopes that he will decide not to emigrate. We went down to inspect the beehives, and while I sat on a rock and watched, George slaughtered bumblebees with a stiff besom, giving a running commentary:

'They're the greatest enemy – got you! – of the bee. It's all – got you, you cuckold! – all in my book up at the house – CUCKOLDS!'

Later we sat in the café with Pavlos, who says he wishes he had a record of his songs. He can remember recording 'And what became of them, the brave ones of the world?' for us. 'I sang you that song for its meaning, not for the tune. It is an allegory'; and he explains to the others who are with us. 'In war it *is* the best who are killed, "the brave ones of the world" . . . .'

George says, 'When I was in London I heard a piece of Byzantine folk music from Mt Athos; the oldest they've ever found.'

George went to London three years ago as one of the two Greeks invited to a grand Reunion of Resistance heroes who had helped the allies.

'How many days were you there, George?'

'Four.'

'And of those four, how many did it rain?'

'Po po po! All four.'

'Did you like the English food?'

'Wherever I am, I *always* like the food.' His eyes go watery. The abstracted look comes over his face. 'But our food was special. We were official guests. We went to a dinner at a big hotel – what's it called? – Claridges? – and do you know?' (for the benefit of the others) 'They start the meal with melon and you eat it with a *spoon*.'

'We don't often get melon in England,' I said.

'We had it *every day*,' he says firmly. 'They'd invited all the ambassadors from all the countries represented at the Reunion, and there were flags for each country put out on the table. I thought the Greek flag was to show us where to sit and I was just going over there to sit down with my Greek friend when,' he begins to laugh, 'the Greek ambassador, Mr Sepheris the poet, sits down there. And there was a man all dressed up, with a big hammer, and BAM BAM BAM he bangs this hammer and someone gets up and makes a speech. It was happening all the time, speeches, speeches. We just ate.'

George has become the village story teller.

'What about the rain?' says Pavlos. 'It was summer, wasn't it?'

'Yes. The next day we went to a "Garden Party" at Buckingham Palace to meet the Queen. There was I looking round me, expecting a being different from other beings, and then in she comes followed by a lot of ladies and everyone is looking at them and I have to ask, "Which is the Queen?" because they're all the same to me. Then a cloud comes up and brrr! – it rains. The Queen is all right, someone holds an umbrella over her. So I run up to some lady and say "Excuzz me, can I stand under your umbrella please?" Then of course the rain stops.'

Darkness falls. Click click of worry beads. The women still plod down the street carrying their water jars. The clocks have stopped here.

Epilogue

At this point one thinks of all the things one has left out, and they are legion. No word about costumes and embroideries, very little about the life of the three big towns, nothing of the architecture, very little about the way Crete is run today. There is one omission that I must correct, by emphasizing that travel in Crete can be very boring. Since it is almost part of the writer's job to improve on his subject, the impression is often given that foreign parts are some sort of paradise. This is inevitable. If I had a nightmare about Crete it would be peopled by young men who stare and stare, and when they do ask a question it is 'Deutsch?' I should be sitting in a flyblown café surrounded by these men, who sit astride the wooden chairs and lean their forearms on the back of the chair. One or two of them are clicking worry beads. Then the gramophone comes to life, grotesquely loud and distorted, broadcasting monotonous dance music throughout the whole village. No one tries to turn it down. No one seems to be listening. Sitting engulfed in this noise, you can still just hear against it the click of the beads and the slap of dirty playing cards on the table. Someone starts a conversation.

'Deutsch?'

'No, English.'

'Ah, English. Good. What do you think of our place? It's a nice place, isn't it?'

'A very nice place, yes.'

And in a few moments one is comparing Crete with England, saying for the thousandth time that we have no olives, no grapes, precious little sun, and drawing for the thousandth time the same expressions of surprise or of tolerant superior knowledge. All such conversations repeat themselves to the very words used. Certain phrases imprint themselves on the memory: ('You look alike, are you brother and sister?' or 'You must marry a Cretan girl') and one finds oneself answering in formulae too.

If it were an extravagant nightmare it might contain the dignified white-haired Greek-American who buttonholed me once in St Nicholas and would not let me go.

'Listen to me, boy. How old do I look, eh?'

'Sixty?'

Epilogue

'Seventy years old, seventy goddam years, and you know why? Listen to me, son, you know what my father says to me? He says to me, don't go with whores, and he was goddam right, the sonovabitch. That's why I look fifty today, because I don't go with bad women. You listen to me, son, you find a clean woman and settle down. . . .'

And so on and on. It would be unfair to write about Crete without mentioning such things. And it is not surprising that there are times of boredom on an island whose people are content to sit around all day. Of course, these times can be minimized.

If one must 'sum up' Crete, then one must find out what she has meant to the Cretans and the Greeks. That is what this book has been about. I wrote in 1960 of the village Asi Gonia: 'Her simple message rang in my ears as we came down to Canea and civilization:

> The courage of man is great wealth;
> Eat, drink and enjoy this deceitful world.'

It is time to see what this message has meant to modern Cretan writers and how they have treated of it in their work.

There have been three distinguished Cretan novelists: John Kondylakis, Nikos Kazantzakis and Pendelis Prevelakis. All were preoccupied by Crete. Kondylakis was born in 1861, and therefore grew up in Turkish Crete, in the village of Viannos in the east. At the age of sixteen he broke off his studies at the Gymnasium in Athens in order to return to Crete and fight the Turks. After the revolt he worked as a clerk in Canea and read prodigiously, then went back to Athens to try journalism. Apart from a period spent teaching in Crete – which inspired one of his best works, *When I was a Teacher* – he lived and wrote in Athens. He returned to Crete only at the very end of his life. The trip was a bitter disappointment. The island was changed. The excitement and colour which was associated with his youth, was gone. He died in hospital in Heraklion in 1920.

Kondylakis lived in exciting times for Greece and Crete, and was fortunate in the time of his death, for the Smyrna disaster two years later was a horrific shock to men of his generation. His work was a perpetual dialogue with Crete. In his journalism he wrote directly of the Cretan issue, and his stories are set in Crete. *Patouchas*, the most famous, is about an awkward Cretan lad growing up and falling in love and finding himself (Patouchas means Big-Feet); and apart from all else, it is a wonderful picture of life in a Cretan village in the last century, far more accurate than Kazantzakis's picture, not only because Kondylakis knew Turkish Crete at first hand better than Kazantzakis did, but also because he wrote about ordinary people, not heroes and freaks.

Kazantzakis is as different from Kondylakis as chalk from cheese, for he lacks the relaxation, the easy-going accuracy and the deliberately confined scale of Kondylakis. Kazantzakis was always trying to escape from confines. He is one of those figures who, annoyingly but hardly through their own fault, turn readers into aggressive partisans. Some (very often foreigners) will hear no ill of him. Others condemn him out of hand. I find this particularly irritating because it seems so clear that both sides are wrong, and that Kazantzakis was a successful, even a great, novelist, but a rotten philosopher. The rotten philosophy unfortunately pervades his epic *Odyssey*. When Odysseus asks the world-famous prostitute Margaro for the highest fruit of her experience and wisdom, she tells him,

> 'When on my knees I hold the man I love, I cry:
> "Beloved, I feel at length that we two are but one!"'

And Odysseus replies, 'Even this One, O Margaro, this One is empty air!' a conclusion which shatters her, and which is in fact drawn from Kazantzakis's *Spiritual Exercises*. It is lucky that Kazantzakis kept this sort of stuff out of the novels. The truth is that he was an intellectual magpie, who went through life picking up authors and theories in turn and taking from each what he could, so that his thought is a hash-up of Nietzsche, Bergson and many others. The story of his struggle for enlightenment is more interesting than the resulting philosophy.

Kazantzakis was born in Heraklion in 1883. He travelled enthusiastically all over the world and wrote many travel books including one about England. His life was a battle, and he saw everything in terms of struggle; hence it was natural that he thought also in terms of heroes and great men pitted against odds, and identified himself now with one, now with the other. In 1929 he wrote that his own leader was not one of the three archetypal leaders of the human spirit, Faust, Hamlet and Don Quixote, but the mariner Odysseus – and not the nostalgic, home-loving Odysseus, but the Odysseus who set out from Ithaca on new travels. Thus the Odysseus who is hero of Kazantzakis's epic poem is the traveller and seeker after knowledge and experience, whose prototype is found in Dante and Tennyson.

> I am a part of all that I have met;
> Yet all experience is an arch wherethro'
> Gleams that untravelled world, whose margin fades
> For ever and for ever when I move.

Kazantzakis and Tennyson make strange bedfellows, yet the urge of

Epilogue

Tennyson's Ulysses – 'to follow knowledge like a sinking star, beyond the utmost bounds of human thought' – is exactly that of Odysseus: to go beyond bounds, to merge with what one meets.

Kazantzakis wrote in his introduction to *Zorba the Greek*:

The greatest benefactors in my life have been travels and dreams. Of men, living and dead, very few have helped my struggle. If however I wished to distinguish those men who have imprinted themselves most deeply on my soul, perhaps there would be three or four – Homer, Bergson, Nietzsche and Zorba.

The first has been for me the calm light-filled eye – like the sun – which illumines everything with redeeming light. Bergson delivered me from the unresolved philosophical torments which tyrannized over me in early youth. Nietzsche enriched me with new torments and taught me to turn misfortune, unhappiness and uncertainty into pride. And Zorba taught me to love life and not to fear death.

Zorba also inspired Kazantzakis's most delightful book. Anyone who loves Crete must read *Zorba the Greek*, for it is a poem fashioned out of nostalgia for the island and for Zorba himself, both lost to Kazantzakis. 'This Cretan landscape seemed like good prose,' he wrote. 'Well fashioned, economical, shorn of excessive riches, powerful and controlled ... it said what it wished to say with manly austerity. But between its austere lines you could discern in this Cretan landscape unexpected sensitivity and tenderness – the lemons and oranges smelled sweet in sheltered hollows, and beyond, from the boundless sea, came an endless stream of poetry.' In this landscape Kazantzakis fell under Zorba's spell. It could easily have been a bore, this story of the penpushing intellectual's admiration for a 'natural' man. But it succeeds just because Kazantzakis is not out to convince anybody – he loves Zorba too much for that. He is one of the few authors who seem genuinely, physically to love their characters, whether they be real or imagined. And he loved the memory of Zorba especially, it seems to me, because Zorba remained, even after they had parted, the antithesis of Kazantzakis.

One day in Berlin Kazantzakis received a telegram. 'Have found most beautiful green stone, come at once. Zorba.' It was winter, bitter cold, the snow was falling, there was famine in Berlin. At first Kazantzakis was angry at this message which arrived when people were dying all around him. Curses on beauty: it is heartless, and human pain is of no concern to it. Then, suddenly, he realized that the inhuman message answered to an inhuman urge in himself. He *wanted* to go. But Kanzatzakis stayed. He failed to make the noble, unreasonable gesture, and followed the cold voice of logic. He wrote to Zorba, who replied,

The Great Island

'Excuse me for saying so, boss, but you're a penpusher. You had the chance, you poor thing, once in your life to see a beautiful green stone and you didn't see it. By God, I used to sit down sometimes when I had no work, and say to myself: "Does hell exist or not?" But yesterday when I got your letter I said, "There must be a hell for certain penpushers!"' It was typical of Kanzantzakis that he should have tormented himself for not making the quixotic Zorba-like gesture, and regarded his failure to follow the green stone as a failure of courage. His life was a succession of such mental struggles.

Zorba the Greek is nostalgic for Crete. It gains in tension in that Kazantzakis, the Cretan, is throughout the book divorced from the land, isolated in a sort of mental prison of the intellectual; whereas Zorba, the Macedonian, is a man at harmony with the land, and himself reflects the qualities of Crete which Kazantzakis lacked. But *Zorba the Greek* is almost an entr'acte in his life work. The other Cretan novel, *Freedom and Death*, which tells the story of the last days of one Captain Michalis in the 1889 revolt, is Kazantzakis's greatest novel. He found in the Cretans' attitude to life and death – their *levendia* – an example of the stance a man should take up. It was only elsewhere that he felt bound to interpret the Cretan attitude, to fit it into his scheme of thought. 'Crete, for me (and not, naturally, for all Cretans), is the synthesis which I always pursue, the synthesis of Greece and the Orient. . . . I feel a synthesis, a being that not only gazes on the abyss without disintegrating, but which, on the contrary, is filled with coherence, pride, and manliness by such a vision. This glance which confronts life and death so bravely, I call Cretan.'[1] This Cretan attitude, says Kazantzakis, goes back to Minoan Crete with her bull dance, which is the supreme example of it; for man confronts the bull (the abyss) and plays with him joyfully. So Kazantzakis thought, and if he imposed his own ideas too rigidly on to history, if he got too much out of the *levendia* of the unassuming Cretans, no harm was done. All theorizing is kept out of the novel. And if perhaps the novel is in some ways unrealistic, the characters too elemental, that was the price paid for the power and range of *Freedom and Death*. The book was Kazantzakis's debt to his country, with which he was in love. In *Freedom and Death* Crete is the Mother. In the Odyssey she is a mistress:

> For, many-breasted, shameless, nude, Crete's body spread
> Her practised thighs amid the waves, swarming with merchants.

Kazantzakis died in 1957 in Germany. He is buried in the Martinengo bastion of the Venetian walls which surround Heraklion. Crete is very

Epilogue

proud of him. His burial was a big affair, and a room in the Historical Museum has been made into a replica of his study. On the stone over his grave there was inscribed 'I hope for nothing. I fear nothing. I am free.' – a quotation from his own works. But the inscription was not allowed to survive. It was deleted, as being hubristic and atheistic, through the pressure of the church, which waged intermittent war on Kazantzakis all his life. He was an unorthodox sort of Christian. It is a pity that after his death he was still shown no charity.

The last of this Cretan triumvirate of novelists is Pandelis Prevelakis, born at Rethymnon in 1909, and as one might expect of a Rethymniot, a man of letters. (The proverb goes, 'Canea for weapons, Rethymnon for letters, Heraklion for wine.') Prevelakis was a close friend of Kazantzakis, and wrote a study of him. He has also written a biography of El Greco. Also *The Chronicle of a City*, an account of his home town Rethymnon; *Desolate Crete*, an account of the 1866 insurrection; and a large three-volumed novel *The Cretan*, which covers the fifty years before independence. Personally I would much rather hear Prevelakis quietly and reflectively musing on Rethymnon than narrating the revolts of Crete. *The Chronicle* is a beautiful book – it is available in French – and tells of an unfamiliar side of Crete; whereas the revolts are staple diet. But the important thing to note is that although Prevelakis has studied and worked and lived in Paris and Salonika and Athens, almost all his works are devoted to things Cretan. He carried Crete around within him as his City; and, as he wrote himself, it was a consolation to him in his exile.

All three of our novelists, then, were animated by an extraordinary love for Crete and her history, her 'myth' – the sort of love which in England has been unfashionable since about the middle of the First World War. And these three are not exceptions. Cretans, I am sure from meeting them in all sorts of places, love their island even more than other Greeks love their own particular place. The pages of the Cretan periodical *Cretan New Year* are always full of articles ranging from intense patriotism to a fairly crude nationalism. The three novelists not only draw on myth, they help create and preserve it. And this being so, it is a pity that Kazantzakis's work is read while the other two are neglected, for they complete the picture. Between them they provide a rich and comprehensive panorama of a hundred years of Cretan history. But this vein has now been worked enough. No Cretan, I guess, will write importantly about that heroic age again. For the writers as well as the ordinary Cretans there must be a revolution of **attitudes**.

The Great Island

When all is said and done, as Kondylakis, Kazantzakis and Prevelakis would be first to admit, the voice of Crete is not that of any one writer, but that of an 'unknown poet'; and his work is the songs which the people have chosen as worthwhile, to preserve and pass down to their children. It is on his cenotaph that we should lay the garlands of honour. For his work – an anthology created through the tension which holds between the singer and his audience – has moulded Kornaros, Barba Pantzelios, Kondylakis, Kazantzakis, Prevelakis, Psychoundakis, and all forgotten and unforgotten Cretans. All have a share in this work since all constitute the audience. The Cretan culture is single.

Our share as Englishmen is of a different kind – inevitably self-conscious. Travelling the road northwards from Kandanos one evening, the donkey shambling in our wake, we came through a cleft in the hills where the way winds up the right-hand side of a fertile valley. The sun was going down, and below us in the fields an unknown labourer was singing a *mantinada*:

> Friendships are forgotten, loves are forgotten;
> You meet in the road like strangers, like passers-by.

And I thought, one is unlikely to forget these friendships, this land; but perhaps all the time we were strangers, passers-by.

References

Chapter One – INTRODUCTION, pp. 1-11.
 1. Claude Lévi-Strauss, *A World on the Wane* (Hutchinson, 1961), pp. 38ff.

Chapter Two – ROMAN, BYZANTINE AND ARAB CRETE, pp. 12-23.
 1. cf. Professor Dawkins's article in the *Journal of the Hellenic Society*, 1906.

Chapter Four – ART UNDER THE VENETIANS, pp. 34-49.
 1. cf. the article on this church (in Greek) by C. Kalokyris, *Cretica Chronica*, 1950.
 2. Translated by Timothy Ware in *The Orthodox Church* (Pelican, 1963), p. 260.

Chapter Five – THE CRETAN RENAISSANCE, pp. 50-62.
 1. For material in this section I am indebted to articles in *Cretica Chronica*, and especially to *Greek Scholars in Venice*, by Deno Geanakoplos (Harvard, 1962).
 2. Translated by Geanakoplos, op. cit., p. 95.
 3. Translated by Geanakoplos, op. cit., p. 125.

Chapter Eight – THE REVOLT OF DASKALOYIANNIS, pp. 81-88.
 1. For 'The Song of Daskaloyiannis', cf. 'Homer and Cretan Heroic Poetry', by J. A. Notopoulos (*American Journal of Philosophy*, 1952). Most of the extracts in this chapter are translated from B. Laourdas's Greek edition (Heraklion, 1947); but the invocation ('God give me thought etc.') is from a version recorded by Professor Notopoulos at Askyphou in 1952-3. A thirty-line fragment of this version can be found in *Modern Greek Heroic Oral Poetry*, the booklet which accompanies a 12-inch LP of Professor Notopoulos's recordings (Ethnic Folkways Library album FE 4468).

Chapter Ten – THE DEATH OF PAN, pp. 103-12.
 1. The story of Alexander and the water of immortality is common. This version is from the great collection of traditions (*Paradoseis*) compiled by N. Polites, Greece's first and most distinguished folklorist.
 2. This version, recorded by Professor Notopoulos, is in his *Modern Greek Heroic Oral Poetry* (accompanying Ethnic Folkways Library album FE 4468).

Chapter Eleven – THE SONG, pp. 113-25.
 1. J. A. Notopoulos, op. cit., pp. 11-12.
 2. I. E. Mathioudakis, quoted and translated by Gareth Morgan in 'Cretan Poetry: Sources and Inspiration' (*Cretica Chronica*, vol. XIV, 1960).
 3. cf. principally *Modern Greek Folklore and Ancient Greek Religion*, by J. C. Lawson. There is a stimulating introduction to the subject in Chapter 13 of

Mani, by Patrick Leigh-Fermor. Cf. also 'Soul and Body in Greek Folklore', an excellent study by Professor R. M. Dawkins (*Folklore*, vol. LIII, 1942).
    4. N. Polites, *Paradoseis*.

Chapter Twelve – SPHAKIA – IMPRESSIONS, pp. 126-41.
    1. For the *kollyva*, see Dawkins's 'Soul and Body' (*Folklore*, vol. LIII, 1942).
    2. For the *anaskelades*, see Polites's *Paradoseis* (*passim*).

Chapter Thirteen – SPHAKIA – THE VAMPIRES, pp. 142-55.
    1. Versions of this, and of the vampire story above, are in Polites's *Paradoseis*.
    2. Translated by Lawson, whose chapter on vampires is seminal.

Epilogue, pp. 168-74.
    1. Translated by Kimon Friar in his introduction to *The Odyssey, a Modern Sequel*, by N. Kazantzakis. The quotations from *The Odyssey* above are also in Kimon Friar's translation.

Select Bibliography

I have not listed works in Greek. Those who require an extensive bibliography, which includes Greek works, will find one in Raymond Matton's book. For serious students of Crete, the periodical *Cretica Chronica* (Heraklion) is essential; it contains articles on every aspect of Cretan history and culture in Greek, English, French and Italian.

General
BOWMAN, JOHN, *Crete*, Secker and Warburg, London, 1962: a practical guide-book, but short on background material, expensive, and not always accurate.
ELLIADI, M. N., *Crete Past and Present*, Heath, Cranton, London, 1933.
MATTON, RAYMOND, *La Crète au Cours des Siècles*, Athens, 1957: an excellent and reliable potted survey of Cretan history and culture from Minoan times to the present day.
RAULIN, VICTOR, *Description Physique de l'Ile de Crète*, Paris, 1869.

History
GERLAND, E., *Histoire de la Noblesse Crétoise au Moyen-Age*, in *Revue de l'Orient Latin*, 1907.
GEANAKOPLOS, DENO JOHN, *Greek Scholars in Venice*, Harvard, 1962: an account of the dissemination of Greek learning from Byzantium, via Crete, to western Europe.
MILLER, WILLIAM, *Essays in the Latin Orient*, Cambridge, 1921: contains an essay on the Venetian period.
—— *The Ottoman Empire and its Successors*, Cambridge, 1927: contains an incidental account of Cretan history from the Greek war of independence until the union of Crete with Greece.
PSYCHOUNDAKIS, GEORGE, *The Cretan Runner*, John Murray, London, 1955: the only account of the resistance movement in Crete written from the Cretan point of view.
ALLBAUGH, LELAND, *Crete: a Case Study of an Underdeveloped Area*, Princeton, 1953: the report on a study carried out in 1948 under the auspices of the Rockefeller Foundation.

Travel
BELON, PIERRE, *Les Observations de Plusieurs Singularitez et Choses Memorables Trouvées en Grèce*, Paris, 1554.
DAPPER, D. O., *Description Exacte des Iles de l'Archipel*, Amsterdam, 1703.
FIELDING, XAN, *The Stronghold*, Secker and Warburg, London, 1953.

The Great Island

PASHLEY, ROBERT, *Travels in Crete*, Cambridge, 1837.
POCOCKE, RICHARD, *A Description of the East*, London, 1745.
SPRATT, T. A. B., *Travels and Researches in Crete*, 2 vols, Van Woorst, London, 1867.
TOURNEFORT, J. P. DE, *Relation d'un Voyage au Levant*, Paris, 1717. (English translation by John Ozell, London, 1718.)

Art and Literature
GEROLA, G., *Monumenti Veneti nell' Isola di Creta*, Venice, 1905-32.
KALOKYRIS, C., *La Peinture Murale Byzantine de l'Ile de Crète*, *Cretica Chronica*, 1954.
MARSHALL, F. H., and MAVROGORDATO, J., *Three Cretan Plays*, Oxford, 1929: translations of *The Sacrifice of Abraham*, *Erophile*, and *Gyparis*.

Folklore and Music
BAUD-BOVY, S., *La Chanson Populaire Grecque du Dodecanèse*, Paris, 1936.
DAWKINS, R. M., 'Folk Memory in Crete', *Folklore*, 1930.
—— 'Soul and Body in Greek Folk Lore', *Folklore*, 1942.
LAWSON, J. C., *Modern Greek Folklore and Ancient Greek Religion*, Cambridge, 1910.
NOTOPOULOS, J. A., 'Homer and Cretan Heroic Poetry', *American Journal of Philosophy*, vol. LXXIII, 1952.
—— *Modern Greek Heroic Oral Poetry* (booklet accompanying Ethnic Folklore Library album FE 4468, a 12-inch LP record).

Modern Cretan Literature
KAZANTZAKIS, N., *The Odyssey: a Modern Sequel*, translated by Kimon Friar, Secker and Warburg, London, 1958.
—— *Freedom and Death*, Bruno Cassirer, Oxford, 1956.
—— *Zorba the Greek*, Bruno Cassirer, Oxford, 1959.
PREVELAKIS, P., *Chronique d'une Cité*, Gallimard, Paris, 1960.
—— *Le Crétois*, Gallimard, Paris, 1962.

Index

Aberdeen, Lord 91
Abu Hafs Omar, 22
Agia Eirene, 137
Agia Roumeli, 135
Agii Deka (The Ten Saints), 17-18
Agrimi, *see* Ibex
Akritic ballad cycle, 108, 110
Akratos, Michael, 135
Albanians in Crete, 93
Aldine Press, 52
Aldus Manutius, 52
Alexander the Great, 59, 88, 105-6
Alexandros, Capt., 65
Alikambos, Church of the Dormition, 39
Alikianos, 28-9
Ali Pasha, 75
Allatius, Leo, 148
Ambelouzou, 18
Anand, Col. Thomas, 73
Anaskelades, 130-1
Anastenaria, 19
Andreyev, Admiral, 100
Anopolis, 142-3
Aphendoulief, Michael Comnenus, 91
Apodoulo, 65
Apostolis, Arsenios, 52
Apostolis, Michael, 51-3
Arab occupation of Crete, 22
Archanes, Church of the Asomatos, 39, 43
Archontes, 27, 30
Archontopouli, 23, 27, 28, 32, 35, 67
Arethas of Caesarea, 108
Aristotle, 136
Arkadi Monastery, 35, 95-6, 152
Art, Byzantine, 35ff.
Arta, Bridge of, 109
Asi Gonia, 4ff., 159ff.

Baldwin, Count of Flanders, 25
Ballot, Jules, 95
Barbarossa, Khaireddin, 63-4, 153
Baud-Bovy, S., 123
Beaufort, Duke of, 71-2
Belon, Pierre, 13, 26
Bessarion, Cardinal, 51
Boniface, Prince of Montferrat, 25
Bounialis, Marinos, 60
Byron, Robert, 47

Callimachus, 20

Candia, etymology of, 22; as centre of learning, 52; fall of, 71-3
Canea, fall of, 71
Canevaro, Admiral, 99
Capuchins, 94-5
Catherine the Great, 82
Catholic Church, Roman: her relations with Orthodoxy, 34-5, 94-5
Cavafy, Constantine, 158, 165
Cavalli, Marino de, 30-1, 67
Charles IV, Emperor, 27
Charos in Cretan poetry, 55, 111-12, 118-20
Chernside, Col., 99
Churches, painted, 35ff.
Comnenus I, Alexius, 23, 25
Constantine, 20, 21
Constantine XI, 50
Constantinople, as centre of Greek world, 24, 100; fall of, 50
Conversion to Islam, 22, 76-8; to Roman Catholicism, 94-5
Corner, Andrea, 70
Corner, Hieronymus, 32
Corsairs, *see* Piracy
Craterus, 22-3
Cretan Question, 91, 98-9
Cretan Revolts: against Venice, 27-33; against the Turks, 80, 81ff., 90ff.
Crete, as Mother, 13; as refuge of Hellenism, 50ff.
Cronus, 19
Crusade, Fourth, 24-5
Crypto-Christians, 78-9

Damaskinos, Michael, 44-6
Dandolo, Duke, 27
Dapper, D. O., 23, 72
Daskaloyiannis, 80, 81-8, 144
Dawkins, R. M., 19, 127, 175-6
Decius, Emperor, 17-18
Decius, Proconsul of Crete, 17-18
Dellaporta, Linardos, 54
Dermitzakis, John, 123-4
Dicte, Mt, birthplace of Zeus, 19
Digenes Akritas, 57, 59, 88, 108-11
Dionysus, 18-19
Disney, Walt, 39
Dittany, 136
Doukas, Demetrios, 53
Drakoulakis, Aphrodite, 132

Du Boulay, Julie, 126, 128-30, 134, 137-9
Dunbabin, Professor Tom, 4
Du Tour, French Consul, 94-5

El Greco, *see* Theotokopoulos
Elliadi, M. N., 99, 101
Epimenides, 15, 20, 56
Erasmus, 52
Erophile, 54, 56
Erotokritos, 24, 54, 56-62, 88
Evans, Sir Arthur, 13

Farmer, Angelika, 123
Fatma, Hatoum, 86
Fielding, Xan, 6, 11, 15, 32, 90, 154
Fodhele, 46
Foscarini, Giacomo, 63, 66-70
Frangokastello, 152-4
Frescoes, 35ff.
Friar, Kimon, 176

Garibaldi, 96
Garzoni, 69-70
Gavdos, 14, 15, 138
Geanakoplos, Deno, 175
Gennadius, 11, 75
Genoa, 25-6
Genoese occupation of Crete, 25
George I, 96
George, Prince, 98
Germanos, Bishop, 89
Gerola, Giuseppe, 35
Giants in Cretan folklore, 110
Gibbon, Edward, 78
Gonia Monastery, 35
Gortyn, 14, 17, 36
Gradenigo, Marco, 27
Gradenigo, Tito, 27
Great Idea (Greater Greece), 100
Grivas, General, 109
Gyparakis, Emmanuel, 164
Gyparakis, Pavlos, 4, 6, 162-5
Gyparis, Pavlos, 163

Hades in Cretan poetry, 54-5, 118-20
Halepa, Pact of, 97
Halliday, W. R., 143
Haratch, 76
Hartley, the Rev. John, 77
Hadzidakis, Manolis, 35, 44n., 45
Hadzimichalis, Daliannis, 91, 154-5
Hadzimichalis, Iannaris, 132-3
Hellenism, 62
Heraklion, foundation of, 22 (*see also* Candia); Church of St Menas, 44-5
Hercules, 15, 16
Heroic in Cretan folklore, 85, 87-8, 111-12, 117-18
Hesiod, 20
Hierapetra, 74

Homer, 20, 85
Hortense, Madame, 99-101
Hugo, Victor, 96
Humbert, Papal Legate, 34

Ibex, Cretan, 135-7
Ibrahim I, Sultan, 65, 70
Iconography, 37ff.
Icons, 44ff.
Ida, Mt, *see* Psiloreiti
Iouktas, Mt, 20
Ioussuf Pasha, 71
Islam, conversions to, 22, 76-8

Janissaries, 80, 89
Jews in Candia, 68-9
Julian the Apostate, 127

Kali Limenes (The Fair Havens), 14, 15
Kallergis, Alexios, 27
Kallergis, Leon, 27
Kallergis, Zacharias, 52-3
Kallikrati, 150
Kalokyris, Constantine, 35, 175
Kandanoleon, George, 28-32, 128
Kandanoleon, Petros, 28-30
Katsamerakis, Georgia, 133
Kazantzakis, Nikos, 1, 13, 39, 80, 99-100, 123, 169-74, 176
Khussein Bey, 90
Kollyva, 127-8
Komitades, Church of St George, 43
Kondylakis, John, 110, 169-70, 174
Koprili, Ahmed, 71, 73
Koraes, A., 54
Kornaros, John, 48-9
Kornaros, Vincenzos, 57, 59, 62
Koundouros, Nikos, 54
Koustoyerako, 28, 30
Kritsa, 9; Church of the Panagia Kera, 18, 39-42; Church of St George Kavousiotis, 39
Kroustallenia Monastery, 38
Kurmulidhes family, 78
Kyprios, John, 44n.

Lakki, 126-7, 128
Lambrakis, Gregory, 124, 127
Lassithi, 14, 19, 27, 38, 131
Lawson, J. C., 149, 175-6
Leigh-Fermor, Patrick, 176
Leo Allatius, 148
Leopold, Prince of Saxe-Coburg, 91
Lévi-Strauss, Claude, 2-3, 175
Liakoni, 16
Lissogeorges, 32 (*see also* Kandanoleon, George)
Llewellyn Smith, Elizabeth, 138, 140-1
Louis XIV, 71
Loukaris, Cyril, 53
Loutro, 14, 15

Index

Lucian, 105
Lyraris (Lyre-player), 122-3

Malta, 15, 16
Mantinades, 120-2
Manuscripts, transmission of, 51ff.
Markezinis, Spyros, 123
Mathioudakis, I. E., 175
Mehmet, Ali, 90, 92-3
Melidhoni, 90
Mertzios, C., 46
Meskla, 28-30, 126, 128, 129
Metellus Creticus, Quintus Caecilius, 14
Michael the Stammerer, 22
Michiel, Luca, 35
Mills, Hayley, 39
Milton, John, 104
Minoan religion, 13-14
Mocenigo, Domenico, 92
Mohammed, 11, 75
Molino, Francesco, 28-9
Moore, G. E., 157
Morgan, Gareth, 175
Morosini, Francesco, 71-3
Mother-Goddess, 13
Motraye, La, 78
Mousouros, Markos, 52-3
Moustier, Marquis de, 96
Mournies, 92-3
Mustapha Bey, 79
Mustapha Pasha, 92-3, 95-6, 132, 154
Mykonos, vampires on, 144-6

Navailles, Duke of, 71-2
Nereids, 14, 122-3
Nicon the Armenian, 22
Nikouses, Panagiotes, 73
Notopoulos, J. A., 111, 175

Omalos, 131-4
Orloff, Count, 82-3
Otho, King, 92

Paganism, incorporated in Christianity, 18-19; survival of, 104, 107
Palamas, Kostis, 61, 103
Palaia Roumata, 9-10
Palladas, Gerasimus, 17-18
Palladas, Theodore, 18
Pan, death and survival of, 103-7
Pantzelios, Barba, 81-3, 85-8, 122
Papagregorakis, Idomeneus, 9-10, 114-15
Pashley, Robert, 21, 26, 35, 65, 77, 78, 89-91, 93-4, 150-1, 152
Pasqualigo, Filippo, 32, 70
Patelaros, Dr, 65
Patelaros, Neophytus, 76
Pausanias, 107
Pendozali dance, 8
Pescatore, Enrico, Count of Malta, 25
Petrakis, Andreas, 4-5

Phalangium, 16
Pheidippides, 106
Philarges, Peter (Pope Alexander V), 53
Phocas, Nicephorus, 22-3, 77, 152
Phoenix, 15, 74
Photinus, Dionysius, 61
Piracy, 63ff., 153-4
Pitakoros, John, 54
Plato, 13
Pliny, 136
Plutarch, 103
Pococke, Richard, 16
Polites, N., 175-6
Potamies, Church of the Virgin, 39
Pound, Ezra, 104
Prevelakis, Pantelis, 38, 42, 80, 100-1, 169, 173-5
Psiloreiti, Mt, 20, 110
Psychoundakis, George, 4, 6, 8, 10, 11, 32, 60, 143, 151, 159, 164-7
Pythagoras, 105

Raimondi, Marcantonio, 45
Raphael, 45
Reinach, Theodore, 106
Religion under the Venetians, 34-5; under the Turks, 75-9
Renaissance, Cretan, 53ff.
Renegades, 77-8
Rethymnon, Church of St Barbara, 38; Veneration of the Virgin in, 42
Rhymadori, 85, 123
Richard, Father, 148
Ritsos, Andreas, 44, 46
Rizitika songs, 4, 113ff.
Romaiosyne, 62, 81
Roman occupation of Crete, 14ff.
Romanus, 11, 77

Sachlikis, Stephanos, 54-6
Sacrifice of Abraham, 54, 56-7
St Constantine, 19
St Elene, 19
St Elias, 14, 20
St George, 154, 161-2
St John the Stranger, 34
St Mark, 17
St Michael, 119
St Nektarios, 128-9
St Niketas, 153-4
St Panteleimon, 132
St Paul, 14-17, 56
St Titus, 15-17, 73
Samaria Gorge, 133-6
Santorin, as haunt of vampires, 148
Saperia, Brian, 2
Saracens, 22-3
Sarpi, Fra Paolo, 70
Sepheris, George, 59-62, 109, 118, 167
Sitea, 47
Skaloti, Church of the Prophet Elias, 43

181

Skordylis, Syphis, 81
Smyrna disaster, 100-1
Solomos, Dionysios, 61, 73
Sophroniou, Patriarch, 48
Spenser, Edmund, 103
Sphakia, 14, 86, 126, 137-9, 141, 142-4
Spinalonga, 35
Spratt, the Rev. Devereux, 64
Spratt, Capt. T. A. B., 97, 153
Squill, wild, 24, 105-6
Stanley, Lord, 97
Struys, Jean, 26
Stuart-Glennie, John, 104
Suleiman the Magnificent, 63
Survivals, 13, 18-19, 104-5, 107
Swinburne, A. C., 104
Syrtos dance, 8

Talbot Rice, D., 47
Taxation under the Turks, 76, 86
Tennyson, Alfred Lord, 170-1
Theocritus, 121-2
Theodosius, 21
Theodosius the Deacon, 77
Theophanes the Cretan, 44-5
Theotokopoulos, Domenicos (El Greco), 24, 43, 46-7
Thrace, Dionysian rituals of, 18-19
Tiberius, 103
Tiepolo, Duke, 27
Tintoretto, 45

Toplou Monastery, 47-8, 64
Tournefort, J. P. de, 36, 65, 74-5, 77, 135, 144-6, 149
Tradition in the Orthodox Church, 37-8
Trivan, Antonios, 28, 31, 33

Vai, 74
Valsamonero, Church of St Fanourios, 36, 39, 43
Vampires, 143-6, 148-52
Vaphes, 90
Vathi, Church of St Michael, 39
Veli Pasha, 97
Venetian occupation of Crete, 24ff.
Venier, Dolphin, 70
Venizelos, Eleutherios, 98
Vergil, 121-2, 135-6
Virgin Mary, Veneration of, 41-2
Vrondisi Monastery, 39, 44

Ware, Timothy, 175
White, T. H., 136
Woodhouse, the Hon. C. M., 32

Xeniteia, 54, 64, 115
Ximenes, Cardinal, 53

Zambeliou, Z., 28, 32
Zeus, birth and death of, 19-21
Zoudianos, N. D., 32